LIGHT AND COLOR
IN THE ITALIAN RENAISSANCE
THEORY OF ART

MOSHE BARASCH

LIGHT AND COLOR
IN THE ITALIAN
RENAISSANCE THEORY
OF ART

New York · New York University Press · 1978

Copyright © 1978 by New York University

Library of Congress Cataloging in Publication Data

Barasch, Moshe.
    Light and color in the Italian Renaissance theory of
art.

    Bibliography: p.
    Includes index.
    1. Painting, Italian.   2.   Painting, Renaissance–
Italy.   3.   Light in art.   4.   Color in art.   I.   Title
ND615.B29   759.5   77-92324
ISBN 0-8147-0995-8

MANUFACTURED IN THE UNITED STATES OF AMERICA

PREFACE

I STARTED MY studies, from which the present book emerged, many years ago, and in these years I have received encouragement and help from many scholars. With gratitude I remember the talks with the late Erwin Panofsky on my first attempts to understand the meaning of light and color in Renaissance culture. Later I was greatly helped by the stimulating discussions with Professors Meyer Schapiro, E.H. Gombrich, A. Blunt, and H.W. Janson. In the preparation of the manuscript I received help from Mrs. M. Reich. Professor Philip P. Wiener carefully read the manuscript, and made valuable suggestions which improved the formulation. I am grateful to Miss Mary Davis for her interest in this book, and for performing the thankless task of reading the proofs. Professor H.W. Janson again proved his unfailing friendship by carefully reading the manuscript, making constructive suggestions, and helping to give the book its present shape.

M. B.

October 1977

CONTENTS

Introduction   ix
  I. Functions of Light and Color   ix
  II. Renaissance Theory of Art   xiv

1. *Cennini and Alberti*   1
  I. Cennini   1
  II. Alberti   11

2. *Leonardo*   44

3. *The School of Venice*   90
  I. Introduction   90
  II. Characteristics of Venetian Art Theory   92
  III. Pino's System   95
  IV. "Tone" and "Value"   102
  V. Texture   111
  VI. Oil Colors   117
  VII. The Expression of Colors   119

4. *Lomazzo: The Milanese Theory of Art*   135
    I. Background   135
    II. Light   140
    III. Color   159
    IV. The Color Scale   171
    V. Styles of Light and Color   184

5. *Conclusion*   210

    Bibliography   213
    I. Sources   213
    II. Studies   219

    Index   227

INTRODUCTION

I. Functions of Light and Color

IN THE FOLLOWING chapters I shall try to describe the history of light and color concepts in Renaissance theory of art. The subject has received less attention than it deserves for it is significant both in what it may contribute to a further understanding of Renaissance painting and in the insights it may provide into some trends of the culture of that period. In the following investigations, however, I shall limit myself to the theory of art, and shall venture into neighboring fields only so far as seems to be required by my effort to understand the treatises themselves and the spiritual world of their authors.[1]

Since light and color are the subjects of this book, a brief and general definition may serve as a point of reference for the following study. We must obviously limit ourselves to such aspects of light and color as were significant for the work of the Renaissance painter, and were discussed in the art theory of that period. But even within these narrow confines widely different meanings present themselves.

Primarily, light and color are, of course, elements of our visual experience; in fact, they are the most pervasive elements of the physical world reflected in our eyes. The painter intending to produce a recognizable image of the external world, or of "nature"—as the Renaissance artist did—finds light and color to be ever present properties; whatever the object of his representation, it is illumined and it has color. I do not have to point out that "nature" does not have as simple and clear-cut a meaning as many Renaissance artists and writers believed. What we call "visual experience" is an intricate process, and we do not have to go into a long scientific discussion to know that the light stimuli reaching us from the external world of "nature" pass through the mind's filter of interpretation. Modern psychology, as well as everyday experience, has taught us that what we perceive in nature is conditioned by cultural traditions and inherited images, and that it is within this context that visual sensations acquire their specific character and meaning.[2]

The part played by "interpretation" is most manifest in an art which attempts to represent nature, since such an art is a translation of what we perceive in the external world into another medium, the medium of art. This process has frequently been recognized in respect to outline, but it is more particularly true for light and color. While the pictorial representation of a color impression is not less of a translation than (to use an old example) the portraying of a Negro in white chalk,[3] for the painter, as for any ordinary spectator, it is more difficult to establish exactly the brightness of a shade, the saturation of a hue, or the expressive quality of a color than, say, the size of a limb. Light and color are, therefore, less strictly determined than outline, and leave more room for interpretation, that is, for reshaping what we perceive in different cultural and artistic contexts. In the following chapters we shall see that light and color did, in fact, have different meanings not only in art but also in art theory, different aspects of them being selected and emphasized. We may, then, say that as elements of visual experience light and color are both universal and extremely vague.

In the painter's actual work light and color acquire additional, and more concrete, meanings. Colors are composed of pigments which have certain properties; they can be blended only with some other pigments, and they can be applied only in certain ways. Moreover, besides referring to the reality portrayed, or even to the material nature of pigments, colors are also capable of inducing an aesthetic effect *sui generis* and *sui iuris*. We can enjoy colors singly and in relation to each other just as we may similarly enjoy precious stones; yet we do not think of them as material substances applied to an equally material surface.[4] Light is an intricate system of certain proportions of bright and dark areas produced by the artist himself. Here, then, light and color are either concrete materials or the result of the artist's creative activity.

In nature, and even more in art, light and color express still another meaning which, although difficult to define exactly, is often distinctly grasped, and constitutes an important aspect of the work of art; the meaning may be that of a "mood" or "expression." Color and degrees of luminosity frequently seem to be imbued with a specific mood; they are capable of transmitting feelings and of evoking emotional responses. While the power of evoking emotion that is possessed by color and light is probably one of the roots of color symbolism (a subject which stimulated great interest in the sixteenth century and was extensively treated),[5] in art it probably has greater significance when it is manifested in the less conventional form of (to use a phrase favored by late Renaissance authors) "moving the beholder" by a combination of colors, and by the types of light in the painting. Even where it can be shown that the attribution of a particular emotion to a specific color is based on stereotyped color symbolism, the authors of the sixteenth century emphasized the immediately experienced quality of the mood.

Oversimplifying the complex character of these phenomena, we may, then, say that light and color in painting are mainly sensations produced by material pigments, aesthetic effects, and emotional moods. Needless to say, in Renaissance literature these aspects were rarely, if ever, formulated with sufficient distinctness. Yet in spite of blurred conceptual outlines, these meanings constituted the main foci of Renaissance discussions of light and color in painting.

So far we have outlined some of the basic meanings of light and color for the painter. Renaissance theory of art, however, intending to instruct the painter in his work, or attempting to build up a systematic *scienza della pittura,* could not be content with the dim perception of general aspects; it necessarily ascribed more specific functions to light and color in painting and analyzed them in greater detail.

What are these more specific functions? They are diversified, changing from one period to another, from one school to another, and sometimes even from one picture to another. Obviously they are, to a large extent, determined by the general conception of art prevailing in a given century, or by the scale of pictorial values accepted by a given school; often they are also influenced by the cultural background of an individual author. Yet in reviewing this bewildering variety, two basic, and opposite, functions of light and color seem to emerge, all the other approaches falling between the two extremes. By way of introduction I may perhaps best deal with the variety of approaches by briefly outlining the characteristics of the two extreme types.

In the first type, light and color are considered mainly as instrumental means. Although their aesthetic value is never disregarded altogether, it is more marginal than it is in that of the other types of painting, as, for instance, in drawing. The major function of light is to illumine bodies and thus to render them visible and representable; the function of shadows in the painting is to produce a convincing illusion of relief, that is, of corporeality. Color is considered to be a quality of the surface of the represented objects and, like light, helps to make manifest the form and structure of the object or figure. Authors accepting this function of light and color often criticize the representation of dazzling light and iridescent color as detracting from the principal function of art.

From this general attitude some more detailed views have arisen. Authors of this type usually demand that the illumination in the picture be uniform so that the forms of the figures may emerge free from the local accidents of appearances. A subdued or "shaded" light is preferred to a glaring one because it is better suited to creating the illusion of relief, and of showing the *minutezze* of the represented body. Usually it is thought desirable that the represented scene be illumined by a single and well-placed light (the source of which is not seen), since illuminations emerging from many, or wrongly placed, lights "confuse the forms." Colors, too, should be subdued. The strict adherence to the principle of *Lokalfarbe*, according to which each object and figure has its own color which can be made brighter or darker but never loses its chromatic character and is never merged with the color of other objects, also makes of color a means of the clear representation of material, solid objects.

It is interesting to notice what authors of this type omit in their discussions. The fascination which light and color may exert on the beholder are not mentioned; and the aesthetic values embodied in their representation are rarely discussed and occupy a marginal position. The expressive, and even the iconographic, meaning of light and color is almost completely disregarded. Illumination and coloring are considered of no major importance for subject matter, and in discussing them no theme is mentioned as being intrinsically related to a specific scale of light or to a particular mood or combination of colors.

The rational attitude underlying all these views crystallizes into what may be termed a "functional" conception of light and color. In contradistinction to the functional approach is the conception of light and color in painting as having inherent values of their own, regardless of–and often in contradistinction to–the function of revealing the form and structure of bodies. We shall have occasion to see that, particularly in the sixteenth century, light itself, apart from reference to anything illumined by it, was discussed as a subject matter of painting. Dazzling brightness or mystical dimness, both obscuring the shape of figures, were considered to be imbued with meaning, and pictures or themes were discussed in which such types of light play a significant part. The second approach, then, contradicts the first, not only by not placing enough emphasis on light's functions of revealing the form of bodies, but also by relating it to contents and themes.

The authors belonging to the second type often evince an extreme sensitivity to slight nuances; they notice the softness or dynamic force of coloring and are sometimes deeply attracted by unstable, flickering lights which have a magic power on the beholder or by atmospheric effects that dissolve "nature" into a series of *macole.* To them, the distribution of shades and lights on the surface of the picture is an artistic value in its own right; and they sometimes suggest, though they never explicitly formulate, the idea of "picture color" as opposed to "object color." They also observe the differences in individual artists' coloring, an observation that culminated in the late sixteenth century in the concepts of "styles of light" and "styles of color."

It should also be noticed that the authors belonging to the second type were aware of the expressive character of light and color. Needless to say, almost any discussion of painting refers, however vaguely, to the emotional overtones of light and color. But it was only in the art theory of the sixteenth century that such vague allusions were transformed into detailed descriptions, or into explicitly formulated theoretical statements. In the treatises of this period we read about the power of colors to stir emotions, and we frequently find the attribution of specific feelings to individual hues. Elements from literary and symbolic heritages are transformed into artistic devices as the authors investigate the problems of light and color in painting.

II. Renaissance Theory of Art

Since the following study deals with the meaning and history of light and color in Renaissance theory of art, it may be useful briefly to recall some of the basic problems of art theory insofar as they may have influenced the subject of our discussion.

In modern scholarship several well-known studies have been devoted to Italian theory of art. Although many specific problems raised by the art literature of the fifteenth and sixteenth centuries still await careful investigation, the main characteristics and major lines of development of Renaissance theory of art are now clear [6] and need not be restated here. But we must mention some of the difficulties which are encountered when studying a specific, limited problem, such as ours, in that literature. In referring to these difficulties I want to emphasize that no simple and elegant solutions can be expected to problems which, because of the nature of the material, sometimes cannot be treated simply.

We shall start by outlining the specific position of art theory in the field of artistic and intellectual activities and in the culture of the period, and then briefly analyze its relationship to neighboring domains. [7]

Art theory is, of course, closely related to actual art. To a considerable degree it consists of practical workshop experiences. Another significant part of art theory consists of descriptions of works of art, mainly of contemporary paintings which stir the curiosity of the public. Art theory thus reflects both the practices and the problems which have occupied the artists of a period or region. It is also the domain in which continually renewed attempts were made to clarify the foundations and norms of artistic creation.

However, art theory is not simply a reflection of artistic practices but has directions and propensities of its own. While both the artistic production and the art theory of a given period always clearly belong to the same broad cultural type, one frequently discerns some differences in emphases and tendencies between them. It has been noticed that the theoretical views of an artist can have a character somewhat different from his own actual work.

It is perhaps also true that art theory has a different pace of development, sometimes tending to be more conservative, and more strictly adhering to once established norms than the style of contemporary painting.[8] But the most important difference between art and art theory is that the latter has a broader – and in any case a different – range of sources. While – to stress this again – there is never a basic hiatus between the iconography and stylistic tendencies of art on the one hand and the art theory of the same age or cultural region on the other, art theory has, by its very nature, a deeper and more extensive connection to philosophical and general cultural trends, and to literary traditions than does actual art. In this book, particularly in the chapters dealing with the sixteenth century, we shall frequently have occasion to see that art theoretical treatises contain long discussions of subjects which could have been of only limited use for the painter. The impact of such extra-artistic sources may have been one of the motives of the process in which, to use a classic formulation, art theory developed from a theory for artists into a theory of art.

But it would also be wrong to describe art theory as simply a branch of science, or as a ramification of the history of ideas lacking any intrinsically specific character. Needless to say, while speaking of Renaissance science we cannot apply modern criteria of abstraction. Renaissance science, as everybody knows, not only held animistic views (i.e., of a "world soul") but also, more important in our context, was never as separated from practical purposes and applications as would sometimes seem to be suggested by modern scientific attitudes. Whatever the particular domain – from Machiavelli's rules for the prince and Castiglione's prescriptions for the gentleman's behavior to the science of physiognomics, and Cardano's investigation of subtlety in matter – the practical uses of learning were rarely completely disregarded by Renaissance scholars and scientists. For an understanding of the intimate relationship between art theory and science it should further be kept in mind that, as has become increasingly clear during recent decades, some of the achievements of the arts should be considered as vital contributions to the progress of science in the Renaissance period. Moreover, authors of art theoretical treatises frequently spoke of the "science of art" or "science of painting" and thus further suggested a connection between them.

Yet in spite of all these affinities, art theory was never transformed into a science, not even into a science of the Renaissance type. This not only follows from the fact that the subject matter of art theory is art (and not nature), but it also follows from the specific attitude of art theory. Originating in the workshops, in the early fifteenth century it had already outgrown the intellectual horizons and habits of thought of master and apprentice. But, with a few notable exceptions, it never completely severed its links with the workshops. The question of how to produce a picture (or how was a certain picture produced?) remained in the forefront of art theory, even when it was permeated by science or symbolic traditions. Whatever the impact of geometry and astrology, of optics and medicine on the theory of art, they were seen from the point of view of the artist producing a work of art (the Renaissance image of the artist being of course radically different from that of our own age) and were usually adapted to this point of view. In the following chapters we shall indeed frequently try to show in detail that authors of art theoretical treatises had the artist in mind when selecting ideas and motifs from the vast scientific and cultural heritage, and that these ideas and motifs, which in their original contexts usually had nothing to do with art, were transformed into concepts significant for the artist in his work.

Art theory, then, holds a particular position in Renaissance culture; it is a phenomenon *sui generis,* and in spite of its close relation to art it has a structure and a history of its own.

While the specific position of art theory as a phenomenon in its own right is fairly clear when seen in the context of Renaissance culture as a whole, its outlines grow dimmer and become blurred when looked at from closer range. Italian art theory in the fifteenth and sixteenth centuries was the meeting ground of disparate heritages, tendencies, and interests. Developing without a common institutional framework, with no common social background, and not even within a unified cultural tradition – in other words, without factors that could assure its intrinsic unity – it grew into a phenomenon characterized perhaps more by diversity than by any other feature. The authors of the treatises came from different social strata; they were variously educated; and, while all of them were speaking of the art of painting, they were in fact often pursuing widely differing aims.

Some of the treatises are based almost completely on the practical experience accumulated in the workshops and set out to transmit that experience for direct application by painters. While this type is most characteristic of the earliest stage of Renaissance theory of art (Cennini), we shall have occasion to show that the same attitude also appears in later periods, although combined, or merged, with different dispositions. Another group of treatises was composed by university-educated humanists, whose acquaintance with, and understanding of, the painter's actual procedures in his work were rather limited. Bringing with them scientific knowledge and a broad literary erudition, they aimed at building up a systematic "science" of painting which was opposed to the workshop approach. Beginning with Alberti, this "scientific" trend played a major part in art theory of the fifteenth and early sixteenth centuries, and it contributed systematic patterns of discussion which persisted in the Baroque period. Still another group of texts was written by *letterati;* fascinated by the aesthetic charms of painting, frequently referring in detail to contemporary painters and pictures—and occasionally containing valuable information—their approach was basically that of the critic and the delighted spectator, although usually they followed the "system of painting" proposed by Alberti. We find these texts mainly in sixteenth-century Venice, but their characteristic attitude is also represented in other regional traditions. A large group of Renaissance treatises on painting, composed in the last decades of the sixteenth century in Milan (mainly by Lomazzo), is perhaps the most problematic of all. Overburdened with only half-digested humanistic learning and leaning heavily on direct or indirect quotations from ancient and medieval sources and esoteric doctrines, they nevertheless show a sometimes surprisingly intimate knowledge of the painter's craft.

The difficulties arising from this great diversity, of which we have mentioned only the major types, are increased by the literary character of the treatises. As may be expected, both the exposition of ideas and the style of writing differ enormously. However, what is of greater concern for the historian is the extreme repetitiveness which characterizes this literature as a whole. This repetitiveness and the use of common formulas may sometimes obscure profound changes. That two widely differing authors use the same formulations or expound their ideas according to almost the same pattern does not of course necessarily mean that they actually hold the same views.

Reviewing these difficulties, one asks whether these sources can be made the subject of historical treatment. Can one say that texts written in a later period represent a more "advanced" stage in the development of ideas on art than those composed earlier? Can we treat the different approaches of art theory as stages in a concrete historical continuity, as parts of a basically coherent tradition?

These questions become more clearly focused when we investigate a specific problem, such as views on light and color in painting. But in undertaking such an investigation we also discover that the very diversity of art theoretical treatises is often helpful in making evident both the specific tendencies of a particular "school" or cultural region (e.g., Venice) and the different facets of the problem (e.g., color symbolism, technique of shading). More important, however, is the fact that precisely in the investigation of a specific problem do the outlines of a continuity emerge. One notices, of course, that the problem itself continually persists even where the approaches differ and change; its treatment, therefore, necessarily mirrors these changes. Moreover, when carefully reading a late author (e.g., Lomazzo), one sees, perhaps with some surprise, that he knew most of the earlier treatises—though he only casually refers to them—although what may be termed his basic approach differs radically from that of his predecessors.

Notes

1. Modern scholarship has not paid sufficient attention to light and color in Renaissance painting. For general surveys, cf. Theodor Hetzer, *Tizian: Die Geschichte seiner Farbe,* 2d ed. (Frankfurt, 1948), esp. pp. 25 ff., and Wolfgang Schöne, *Uber das Licht in der Malerei* (Berlin, 1954), esp. pp. 82 ff. (with a rich, though obviously not exhaustive, bibliography).

2. I don't feel competent to speak about psychology, but the subject has been discussed by E. H. Gombrich in *Art and Illusion: A Study of Psychology of Pictorial Representation* (London, 1960). Schöne gives in an appendix (pp. 222-241) a survey of psychological theories and experiments that have a bearing on color and light in painting. Erwin Panofsky, *Problems in Titian: Mostly Iconographic* (New York, 1969), p. 13, calls attention to the fact St. Thomas Aquinas said "sensory perception, too,

is a kind of reason" ("nam et sensus ratio quaedam est"); cf. *Summa Theologica*, I, qu. 5, art. 4, ad. 1.

3. The example of the Negro portrayed in white chalk is found in Philostratus, *Life of Apollonius of Tyana*, book II, chap. 22. For light and color in painting as a "translation," see the interesting remarks by Hermann von Helmholtz, *Vorträge und Reden*, II (Braunschweig, 1903), pp. 95-135 ("Optisches über die Malerei"). On p. 111 Helmholtz says that what the painter gives is "nicht mehr eine reine Abschrift des Objekts, sondern die Übersetzung seines Eindrucks in eine andere Empfindungsscala."

4. Panofsky, *Problems in Titian*, pp. 14 ff.

5. From the very diffuse literature on color symbolism I should like to mention only Edwyn Bevan, *Symbolism and Belief*, London (1938), pp. 125 ff. Some of the studies of the symbolism of light and color in ancient times and the Middle Ages may be helpful for a study of Renaissance views. I shall mention here only the *Eranos Jahrbuch X: Alte Sonnenkulte und die Lichtsymbolik in der Gnosis und im frühen Christentum* (Zurich, 1944); Franz Cumont, *Lux perpetua* (Paris, 1949); R. Bultmann, "Zur Geschichte der Lichtsymbolik im Altertum," *Philologus*, XCVII (1948), 1-58. For the Middle Ages, cf. C. Baeumker, *Witelo: Ein Philosoph und Naturforscher des XIII. Jahrhunderts* (Beiträge zur Geschichte und Philosophie des Mittelalters, III, Heft 2, esp. pp. 357 ff.); Joseph Braun, "Zur Entwicklung des liturgischen Farbenkanons," *Zeitschrift für christliche Kunst* (1902), cols. 80-88, 111-120, 143-152, 171-176.

6. The well-known standard works on Renaissance theory of art are J. von Schlosser, *La Letteratura artistica*, terza edizione italiana aggiornate da O. Kurz (Vienna, 1964), orig. ed. *Die Kunstliteratur* (Vienna, 1924); Anthony Blunt, *Artistic Theory in Italy: 1450-1600* (Oxford, 1940). Useful for the sixteenth century is K. Birch-Hirschfeld, *Die Lehre von der Malerei in Cinquecento* (Rome, 1912), and Denis Mahon, *Studies in Seicento Art and Theory* (London, 1947). For the more philosophical aspects cf. the important discussion by Erwin Panofsky, *"Idea": Ein Beitrag zur Begriffsgeschichte der älteren Kunsttheorie* (Leipzig-Berlin, 1924).

7. It is a curious fact of art historical scholarship that so far no attempt seems to have been undertaken to discuss systematically the position of art theory in relation to art and to the intellectual trends of the period. Needless to say, our brief observations do not represent such an attempt.

8. Cf. Walter Friedländer's interesting observations in his review of Panofsky's *Idea*, in *Jahrbuch für Kunstwissenschaft* (1928), pp. 56-63, esp. p. 62.

CENNINI AND ALBERTI

I. Cennini

(1)

IN THE ART literature of the late fourteenth and early fifteenth centuries, that is, before Alberti wrote his *Della pittura,* one seldom finds light and color discussed in relation to painting. The only theoretical document that enables us to get a notion of the views held at this early stage of our story is Cennino Cennini's *Libro dell' arte.* The *Libro* cannot be considered a "source" in a precise historical sense; in the Renaissance period it was apparently known only to a few readers in manuscript, and it did not appear in print before the nineteenth century.[1] But scholars have never doubted that the *Libro* clearly reflects concepts and attitudes that were common to artists, craftsmen, and probably the public in Cennini's generation. In the following pages, therefore, we shall discuss Cennini's views as representative of a historical type rather than as an individual source.

Modern scholarship has frequently stressed Cennini's intimate relationship to medieval traditions, particularly as they were preserved in the workshops of his day.[2] But it has also been noticed, though less frequently, that in fact he occupies an almost unique position, differing both from the typical medieval attitude and from that characteristic of the fully developed Renaissance.[3] Cennini's observations on light and color make this specific transition stage manifest with particular clarity. Art historians and scholars of Renaissance culture have not paid much attention to these observations, and it will therefore be the task of the following discussion to emphasize the neglected aspects rather than to repeat the well-known facts about the *Libro* and its author.

A characteristic feature of Cennini's doctrine, noticed in a first reading of the *Libro,* is the separation of light and color and their different treatment. Cennni himself has divided a part of the *Libro* into five chapters (drawings; colors; fresco paintng; oil painting and embellishments for the wall; and glues, sizes, and cements). [4] Given the empirical, not strictly systematic character of the *Libro,* this division should not be taken too seriously. Nevertheless, we may infer from it a certain general attitude. It is therefore interesting to notice that while color has a chapter of its own, light has not, the few remarks on light appearing either in the section devoted to drawing or in the sections dealing with a specific technique (fresco, oil painting, etc.).[5] Later we shall come back to the origin and historical significance of this fact; [6] here we note only that, following Cennini's exposition, we too shall have to discuss light and color separately.

(2)

Compared to the medieval fascination with light, brilliance, and shining materials, Cennini's views seem disappointingly dull and restricted in scope. The rather dry tone of his scattered remarks does not suggest that he was enraptured by the magic of light. It is, however, exactly in this restraint that his new approach first becomes manifest. Cennini does not inquire, as did his medieval forerunners, into the essence of light, its symbolism, and the fascination it radiates, but he does ask, although in a way that is not yet fully articulate, how figures and objects should actually be illumined, and what good conditions of lighting in the painter's workshop are. Speaking summarily, we may say that Cennini deals with illumination of objects rather than with light per se.

Cennini was aware of the significance of light for the painter, but the ideas conjured up by his use of the term "light" are derived from different sources and are far from unambiguous. In a chapter in which he advises the artist how to start drawing Cennini says: "And let the helm and steersman of this power to see be the light of the sun, the light of your eye, and your own hand: for without these things nothing can be done systematically."[7] The terms "light of the sun" and "light of your eye" probably refer to theories of vision as they were developed in antiquity and revived in fourteenth-century Padua, where Cennini lived and worked.[8] As has been pointed out by several scholars, Cennini sometimes includes in his text references to humanistic learning,[9] and the terms he mentioned may be another example of this fact. Scientific optical theory does not play any significant part in his treatise. Neither the general context of the chapter from which the above-quoted sentence is taken nor the reference to the painter's "hand" indicate scientific intentions. He discusses light, as he discusses all other problems, from the point of view of things that should be "done"; that is, he speaks as an artist-craftsman.

But while Cennini's comments on light do not display any fundamental scientific interest, as was to be the case in later generations, they clearly reflect the naturalistic tendencies that prevailed in late Trecento workshops, and perhaps also show the problematic, vague character of the concept. In a famous passage of the *Libro* we read: "If you want to acquire a good style for mountains, and to have them look natural, get some large stones, rugged and not cleaned up; and copy them from nature, applying the lights and darks as your system requires."[10] This passage has rightly been interpreted as one of the earliest literary descriptions of the use of a natural model in the Renaissance workshop.[11] It has, however, been overlooked that it also constitutes an interesting statement on light, characteristic of the early stage of Renaissance art and art theory. While the intention to produce a convincing illusion of nature is evident in the passage quoted, it is not clear to which "system" Cennini refers. Does he mean the illumination in the picture itself, that is, the system of lights and darks as produced by the artist? Or does he mean the conditions of light prevailing in nature in which the rock is actually seen? In a consistent naturalism such a question would not arise, as the two systems—the artistic and the natural—would completely overlap; but then, of course, there would also be no need for Cennini's advice that the painter apply the lights and darks "as your system requires." In his period, different systems of light were possible. The distributions of light as required by iconography is but one example of an additional possible system.[12] It would, then, seem that Cennini here has in mind the system of light within the picture itself, and it is to this system that the artist should adapt the isolated piece of rock.

Other passages in the *Libro* suggest a close relationship between light in painting and light in nature. Thus he advises the painter to represent distant hills in dark colors, whereas they should be rendered in brighter hues if they are near.[13] Whether or not this observation is correct,[14] the statement indicates that Cennini conceived of light as a part of nature. Like the human figure and the material object, the phenomenon of light becomes, however vaguely, a model for the painter's imitations.

The accommodation of light as represented in the picture to the conditions of illumination prevailing in nature plays a significant part in Cennini's thought. The few passages pertaining to this scheme contain far-reaching ideas. In a passage which is worth close analysis he says:

> If, by chance, when you are drawing or copying in chapels, or painting in other adverse situations, you happen not to be able to get the light off your hand, or the way you want it, proceed to give relief to your figures, or rather, drawing, according to the arrangement of the windows which you find in these places, for they have to give you the lighting. And so, following the lighting, whichever side it comes from, apply your relief and shadow, according to this system. And if it happens that the light comes or shines through the center straight ahead, or in full glory, apply your relief in the same way, light and dark, by this system. And if the light shines from one window larger than the others in these places, always follow the dominant lighting; and make it your careful duty to analyze it, and follow it through, because, if it failed in this respect, your work would be lacking in relief, and would come out a shallow thing, of little mastery.[15]

This short chapter indicates several ideas and problems that were to achieve central prominence in the following generations. The background of the whole chapter is of course the awareness of the significance of light for the artist (and therefore of the painter's duty to "analyze" it). But from the passage quoted a distinction between different types of light also emerges. Here the criterion for distinguishing between one light and another is the degree of brightness, and perhaps also the angle of incidence. Of further historical significance is the connection between light and modeling, so clearly expressed by Cennini. Light is understood as a means of making bodies visible and naturally represented; in other words, the connection between light and relief leads to the concept of "functional light," a concept that was reiterated innumerable times in the Renaissance.

Cennini's demand for consistency in illumination ("always follow the dominant lighting") also announces the rational, systematic application of light in Quattrocento and early Cinquecento paintings and its discussion in the art theory of the period. But probably the most interesting aspect of the chapter is Cennini's thought on the interrelation between actual light and painted light. His insistence on achieving consistency between the "natural" light which actually prevails in the chapel and the "artistic" light as represented in the murals (a requirement which, incidentally, also recurs in later stages of the Renaissance) [16] can be understood only as an expression of a naturalistic tendency. Through the adaptation of the painted light to the natural, the latter helps to intensify the convincingly illusionistic, "natural" character of the painting as a whole.

As far as can be inferred from Cennini's fragmentary remarks, he conceived of light mainly as a means of naturalistic representation and of modeling. But in reading the *Libro* one sometimes feels that he also assumed, however vaguely, a relationship between light and what we would call "aesthetic values" in art. In this respect, too, the specific historical stage of the art of his times becomes manifest. In indicating a relationship between light and artistic values Cennini does not mention any of the examples typical of the Middle Ages, such as glittering materials, the radiance of gold, and so on, but rather ideas that were to reach full materialization only in sixteenth-century art. Interesting in this respect are his precepts for the representation of drapery in the technique of ink and washes. The chapter starting with "when you have mastered the shading" may probably be considered the earliest formulation of the tonal style. First, Cennini says, the painter should apply the deepest shadows with an almost dry brush. Then, adding washes, and "without trying to hurry, go on shading little by little, always going back with this brush into the darkest areas. Do you know what will come out of it?—If this water is just a little tinted, and you shade with enjoyment, and without hurrying, you will get your shadows well blended just like smoke." [17] One can easily imagine the effect of such a drawing which clearly anticipates *sfumato*. In another precept, to which we shall come back later, he gives practically the same advice in relation to color. These soft, toned-down shadows, "almost imperceptible" as they will be called later, are not aimed at fulfilling only the function of making visible the form and structure of bodies; it is for their own inherent beauty, and for the satisfaction they give to the painter ("and you shade with enjoyment") and probably also to the spectator, that they are recommended. In other words, Cennini conceives of them, however vaguely, as possessing aesthetic value.

(3)

In contrast to his discussion of light, Cennini's treatment of color is not haphazard and fragmentary but constitutes a coherent and integral part of the *Libro*. It contains very few theoretical reflections or even generalizations from empirical observations. Clearly, Cennini's interest is centered on individual colors and on concrete, specific questions, such as the blending of hues, the application of color on different surfaces, and so on; that is, on problems which arise from the painter's actual handling of color materials. It is also in this field that he offers solutions that may be useful to the artist in his work. Cennini's concrete, practical approach, alien to any philosophical reasoning, is usually considered a testimony to his origin in the pre-Renaissance workshop, but in some observations he anticipates the problems dominant in later stages of the Renaissance. The concrete details of his color doctrine are, of course, beyond the scope of the present study; I shall, therefore, attempt only to bring out some of the underlying assumptions of his theory and to analyze some of the major problems which are of significance for the understanding of future developments.

One of his few theoretical statements concerns the number of colors. He opens his discussion of color by saying: "Know that there are seven natural colors, or rather, four actually mineral in character mainly, black, red, yellow, and green; three are natural colors, but need to be helped artificially, as lime white, blues—ultramarine, azurite—giallorino." In this opening sentence we observe the collision between two traditions reflected in the criteria used in reducing the wealth of hues to a few basic colors. We know that neither the seven-color scale nor the four-color scheme originated in the workshops but in ancient and medieval science. The seven-color scheme was derived from the system of seven planets; the four-color pattern, from the system of four elements.[18] But when scientists in antiquity and in the Middle Ages spoke of primary colors, they obviously did not have pigments or other materials in mind (although in a more complex sense a connection with certain materials was present in their thought); [19] they were referring to the look or appearance of colors. Seen against this background (which was Cennini's immediate source), his use of the term "natural color" is indicative of his practical attitude. When he speaks of *colori naturali* he does not refer to the optical impression, to the pure appearance, but to material pigments. A "natural color" is one that is found ready in nature and needs no further blending and adaptation.[20] Natural colors are opposed to colors which are "manufactured by alchemy," that is, colors which are the result of blending.[21] He even speaks of "half-natural" colors.[22] Even in the list of the seven natural colors quoted above, their material qualities are stressed. Cennini, then, absorbs the theoretical statement into his workshop attitude and thus confers on them a new meaning.

The *Libro dell'arte* is not only a document attesting to the persistence of traditional workshop procedures; it also reveals the emergence of new tendencies which reached their full expression in later generations. In the discussion of color the new tendencies are indicated mainly in two themes: the use of color in the imitation of nature, and the articulation of stylistic values of coloring.

In the *Libro* several examples can be found to illustrate the first theme. The body of a dead figure, for instance, should be represented in greenish tones, and without applying "any pink at all because a dead person has no color. . . . And manage the hair in the same way, but not so that it looks alive, but dead, with several grades of verdaccio." [23] This precept, with its strong naturalistic flavor, clearly reflects some fourteenth-century usages. In Trecento painting the convincing representation of decaying corpses played, as we know, a significant part,[24] and the greenish corpse color is frequently found. To the same group belongs the precept that the face of an old person should be darker than that of a youthful figure.[25] These examples are hardly derived from Cennini's own observations of nature, although to some limited extent his attentive perception of reality might have been of some significance for his theory. Basically, he here adduces *exempla;* that is, he refers to both works of art and to well-established workshop conventions. It is the *exempla* themselves that are permeated with a naturalistic tendency.

More novel and daring are his observations on the representation of textures. In these observations, time-honored conventions and bold innovations are curiously blended. We shall briefly discuss two examples: the application of gold, and the representation of woolen fabric.

Needless to say, in the art reflected in Cennini's work the use of gold in panel painting was common. In fact, his chapters help explain some of the technical aspects of this procedure. Gold was used mainly as an embellishment of the panel (with a decorative or expressive meaning), or as an iconographic device.[26] Cennini conceives of gold, not only as fulfilling these functions, but also as a device for representing certain textures. In a group of chapters he gives detailed advice on how to paint brocades interwoven with gold, or "a mantle, or a gown, or a little cushion, out of cloth of gold."[27] In representing such an object the painter should apply actual gold in his picture. The application of gold, especially in garments, is of course well known from the *maniera greca*. There is, however, a significant difference between the *maniera greca* and Cennini. While the artists belonging to the *maniera greca* used the spots of gold in the picture to represent lights,[28] Cennini intends them only as a representation of the texture of golden objects. The appropriate depiction of texture is warranted by the fact that both the object and its painted equivalent actually consist of the same material. This solution reflects a clash of tendencies characteristic of the late fourteenth century. The very fact that Cennini is aware of the problem of representing textures makes him a predecessor of a naturalistic art; his avoiding of a specifically pictorial solution, that is, creating the illusion of gold without applying actual gold metal, characterizes him as an heir of medieval practice.

The conflict between traditional habits and new tendencies is even more obvious in the other example, in which Cennini discusses "how to do velvet, wool and silk." Here he is faced with the problem of representing the texture of a fabric (wool) which lacks the precious quality and noble character of gold. The attempt to represent the texture of such an everyday substance would seem to betray a naturalistic attitude. How should the texture of such a fabric be rendered?

Sometimes on a wall a lining has to be simulated, or a drapery which shall really look like woolen cloth. And for this, when you have plastered, smoothed down, and done the painting, put off whatever you want to do until afterwards. And take a little block, not much bigger than a checker and, sprinkling clear water into or over this part with the brush, work over it, around and around, with this little block. The mortar gets rough and poor surfaced. Let it stay so, and paint it as it is, without smoothing down. And it will really look woolen stuff or cloth.[29]

What Cennini proposes is not to "simulate" the way wool looks but to reproduce on the wall the actual texture of the woolen cloth. There is a basic affinity between his solutions for representing golden objects and woolen cloth. In the case of gold the painter uses the same material; in the case of wool he reproduces the same texture. In both cases it is a material duplication rather than an optical representation.[30]

These solutions are of course typical of a medieval attitude which is concerned with the "essence" of objects (or figures) rather than with their visual appearance. Yet the problems which Cennini poses, and which he tries to solve in this traditional way, announce some of the major themes of Renaissance theory of art. Throughout the Renaissance, and particularly in sixteenth-century Venice,[31] the problem of textural representation was one of the focal points of discussion of light and color.

Cennini also suggests other concepts which held a significant place both in the artistic production and aesthetic thought of later generations. One of them is modeling in colors of different shades. In advising the painter "how to do draperies in blue and purple," he says:

If you want to do a blue, that is, for a drapery, neither wholly modeled with lights nor all just laid in flat, take some of three or four divisions of ultramarine blue: for you will find various grades of it, one lighter than another. And paint according to the lighting of the figure, as I have shown you above.[32]

Even in the Trecento workshop there is, of course, nothing new in this precept. Yet it is remarkable that Cennini consciously distinguishes it from two other possibilities. These, I believe, are monochrome modeling, on the one hand, and the application of fully saturated but unmodeled ("flat") colors, on the other.[33] Cennini advises the painter to avoid the extreme possibilities and to combine light and color. What he here proposes is modeling in *Lokalfarbe*. He has translated this general concept in the well-known precept that the painter prepare three (sometimes more) shades of the same color: one for the illumined parts, another for those covered by shadows, and the third consisting of an intermediary tone. This precept should be applied in the rendering of faces, of nude bodies and draperies,[34] and generally for any object that has mass and volume. This precept is one of the most persistent in Renaissance theory of art; wherever it appears in later generations it usually suggests a close connection of the author with the workshop tradition.[35]

The requirement of soft modeling and of gradual transition of color, implied in this and in many other Cennini precepts, indicates a general aesthetic attitude, the preference of a taste. It leads to avoiding, or at least to restricting, the application of pure colors. This is already implied in the idea that each color should be graded in brighter and darker hues. But sometimes Cennini is more explicit: in painting cheeks, the artist should not use *cinabro puro* but blend it with some white;[36] the main emphasis should be placed on *incarnazion mezana*.[37] In general, the delicate blending of hues is considered as attesting to the skill of the artist.[38] In the final result of such blending the colors are fused and softened "like a puff of smoke" *(chome un fummo)*, an image which, as we already know, indicates not only the acme of naturalism but also an aesthetic value.[39]

The naturalistic and aesthetic attitudes suggested in the requirement to blend light and color bring us back to the question with which we started. At the beginning of this chapter we said that Cennini discusses light and color separately, color having a set of consecutive chapters, and the remarks on light appearing in contexts other than the investigation of color. Seen against a historical background, this arrangement can easily be understood. In medieval treatises on painting (like Theophilus's *Schedula diversarium artium* or the *De coloribus et artibus Romanorum* attributed to Heraclius),[40] we find extensive discussions of color but no investigation of light in the specific sense in which it occurs in the *Libro,* that is, as an illumination of objects. In devoting a large part of the *Libro* to color as well as in avoiding any discussion of light in this context Cennini, then, follows tradition. On the other hand, his observations on light reflect, as we have seen, the naturalistic tendencies of Trecento painting. It seems natural, therefore, that these observations do not occur in the traditional realm of color but rather in connection with *disegno* and the different techniques of painting. This may also explain why Cennini does not have a consistent and well-rounded theory of light in painting. But it is precisely this context which lends to some of his motifs (illumination instead of light per se, textural representation, the softening of colors by light as naturalistic and aesthetic value, and perhaps the image of the smoke screen) a particular significance. Given the fact that the *Libro* precedes the full impact of humanism and scientific explanation on the theory of art, and particularly in view of Cennini's close association with actual painting, one may say that the specifically Renaissance problems of light and color were born in the workshop.

II. Alberti

(1)

The juxtaposition of Cennini and Alberti has become a commonplace in the study and teaching of Renaissance art. Although Cennini's *Libro* may have been composed only a few years before Alberti wrote his *Della pittura*, the two works, we are often told, represent radically different stages in the history of ideas on art, and they reflect different styles and workshop practices. While Cennini belongs to the medieval past, Alberti is considered, in his theory of art as in so many other fields, the founder and representative of a new era. In this context one usually mentions his formulation of perspective, his system of proportions of the human body, and his concept of expressing emotions by means of gestures. In these fields Alberti did indeed outline some of the major developments of Renaissance theory of art. But is the characterization of Alberti as the founder of a new era also a correct description as far as light and color in painting are concerned? How are new ideas and old concepts blended in his doctrine of *lume* and *colore?*

Alberti's theory of light and color, of course, cannot be separated from the wider aspects of his personality and thought or from the specific historical situation in which he lived. Before entering into a discussion of our subject, we shall therefore briefly outline some of these aspects.

As is well known, Alberti did not grow up in a painter's workshop, and his own painting endeavors were rather limited. It is generally agreed that he did not have the firsthand experience that lends Cennini's *Libro* such a high degree of authenticity and makes it an important source for the study of the late Trecento workshop. Alberti, educated at one of the traditional and scholastic universities of his time (Bologna), where he read canon law for a degree and studied the "mathematical sciences," apparently on his own,[41] developed an attitude to painting which was fundamentally different to that which a painter apprentice of his time would have acquired in a *bottega.* Alberti's new position may have yielded significant results in rationalizing the representation of space (his much-quoted theory of perspective) and in similar subjects, but it must have created serious problems in the discussion of light and color. As we have seen, in the artistic workshops with their traditional methods, and in the treatises reflecting them, a comprehensive and intimate knowledge of colors, of their material nature, and of methods of handling them, was accumulated. But this was an empirical knowledge consisting of many isolated observations and precepts which lacked the theoretical and systematic spirit so characteristic of Alberti's thought.

Whatever the difficulties inherent in the conjunction of a workshop based largely on experience and a humanism that sought to transform painting into a "science," Alberti assigned light and color a specific, definite, and important place by making them one of the "three parts of painting." The presentation of the theory of art under a few headings, although perhaps vaguely intimated slightly earlier, is one of Alberti's most significant contributions.[42] Departing from the empirical workshop traditions which, even when written down in a *trattato* or a *libro,* usually lacked a principle of overall organization, he proposed a structure of the theory of painting which prevailed throughout the Renaissance. As is known, Alberti's doctrine of painting is composed of three parts: "Circumscription" (mainly outline, what later in the Renaissance was called "drawing"), Composition (including "invention" and *istoria),* and the "Reception of Lights." [43] It is in keeping with Alberti's outlook that this tripartite scheme was not taken from even the most progressive Quattrocento workshop practices but probably originated in the study of ancient and medieval rhetorics. Roman, and particularly medieval rhetorics, were taught under three main headings: invention, disposition, and elocution. Some scholars have convincingly argued that Alberti transformed "invention" and "disposition" into *circomscriptione* and *compositione* while "elocution" became in his system the *receptione de lume.*[44] The famous "color of rhetorics" belonged to *elocutio,* and this may have made more easy the transfer of rhetorical terms into concepts of the theory of painting.

What is the actual contents of the third part of Alberti's theory of painting? Rhetorics could provide the theory of painting with a model of the general structure, but clearly it could not furnish the actual contents. It is, of course, likely that Alberti was acquainted with some basic texts of medieval optics dealing with light and color.[45] But these texts do not refer to art and do not discuss the problems encountered by the painter in his work. The absence of any relationship, direct or indirect, between the medieval scientist and artist is well known, and needs no further comment. How far, then, could Alberti draw from medieval optics in his discussion of light and color in painting? And if there was not too much in these texts for an author of pedagogic tendencies who, as he himself says, wrote his treatise "in Tuscan" so that the artists of his time could benefit from it,[46] to what extent was he, after all, influenced by the tendencies that began to take shape in the art of his period?

These are some of the questions which form the background of any investigation of Alberti's theory of light and color.

(2)

The "Reception of Lights," the third part of Alberti's theory of painting, encompasses both light and color. This does not mean, however, that Alberti treats them as a unity. Although some of his observations suggest an interrelationship between light and color, they are in fact discussed separately and are assigned different functions in the picture. Moreover, even those few passages which seem to point at a unity of *lume* and *colore* are so ambiguous in formulation that, as we shall later try to show, they may also be understood as confirming their separation.[47] For these reasons we shall discuss Alberti's view on light and color separately.

Alberti's theory of light indeed represents a major departure from the concepts and practices of the preceding centuries. In order to understand where his original contribution lies and the reasons for his continuing influence in the Renaissance, we may start with a brief characterization of his general approach to light.

The new, "modern" character of Alberti's treatment of light is indicated by two main features: first, by the very fact that he discusses light (as distinct from color) as one of the central problems of painting; and second, by what may be described as the mood or emotional level of his discussion.

The first characteristic is simple, but it points to a major revolution in the history of painting and of the philosophical ideas of art. In medieval theology and literature one of course finds innumerable passages describing the fascinating power and symbolic meaning of light. These texts, however, rarely have anything to do with art, and certainly they were never meant to be practical instructions for the artist. Medieval theory of art, on the other hand, did not discuss light as one of the artist's concerns. Even in this rather technical literature we find many observations on brilliance and splendor, which are part of the general medieval concern with luminescence. As far as they betray any specific relationship to art they usually refer to the resplendence which is a characteristic quality of certain materials such as those used in mosaics or stained glass.[48] Medieval theory of art did not refer to the lights and shadows of an object in nature, and to the creating of the illusion of such an object on a flat surface (a panel, wall, or piece of parchment) by the proper application of lights and shadows. Seen against this background, Cennini's remark on "modeling" a piece of rock by applying lights and shades according to a system (and without mentioning color) does indeed indicate a major change.[49] But while in Cennini such an observation remains isolated, the question of how to apply lights and shades becomes a central theme in *Della pittura,* a major "part" of the theory of painting. We may, then, simply say that Alberti was the first author to make light per se an object of investigation.

The other general characteristic, Alberti's "emotional attitude" to light, is more difficult to pinpoint than the first one. I believe, however, that it can be described, and once it is recognized it should be considered a significant feature of his approach.

In carefully reading the text of *Della pittura* one gains the impression that Alberti's tone is particularly restrained when speaking of light. This restraint is of course immediately evident when we compare his text with medieval descriptions of light. In the medieval tradition (with which

Alberti was certainly familiar) the fascinating power of light is often expressed by the literary style. Whether they describe a mystical experience of the "supernatural light" or a piece of glittering silk, these texts tend to use superlatives and to employ dramatic metaphors. Compared with the style of this tradition, Alberti's sober, almost prosaic tone becomes particularly obvious.

It is of course true that Alberti's discussion of any subject is sober and that he usually avoids an emotional pitch. But a careful reading of his treatise on painting reveals significant differences in the emotional levels. When we compare his discussion of *receptione de lume* with that of other subjects—for example, of *istoria,* of the expressive movements of figures and draperies, of the shape of hair and of branches, or of the expressive power of the portrait [50] —we notice a perceptible difference in tone. While in the discussion of the other topics Alberti's style is lively and sometimes emphatic, light is dealt with in a definitely detached manner.

Della pittura probably offers yet more positive proof of this attitude. Toward the end of the second book of the treatise Alberti condemns the use of gold in painting. His reason for rejecting the gold ground is that the shining quality of the gold cannot be controlled by the artist; [51] in other words, the inherent and autonomous radiance of the gold, which in the Middle Ages was considered as its very value, is the reason for Alberti's rejection of it.

In the same passage we also find the advice that the painter use white— which stands for light—sparingly. Alberti wishes white to be made of the most precious material available so as to impede its excessive use. His formulation, suggesting the psychological reason for the fascination with light, expresses almost a fear of too much light. "Certainly by nature we love open and clear things; therefore, close more tightly the way in which it is most easy to sin." Clearly, these precepts had specific and more practical meanings for the painter (to which we shall later return), but they also indicate a general attitude to light which is dominated by restraint and a purposeful detachment from that fascination with it which is characteristic of medieval culture.

These typical features of Alberti's attitude lead us to, and are explained by, his basic concept of light. Alberti does not give a simple, brief definition of his fundamental concept of light, but a careful reading of the passages in

Della pittura in which the *receptione de lume* is discussed enables us to describe it. Although Alberti discussed light at length and was, as we have said, the first author of an art theoretical treatise to do so, he did not consider *lume* as an end, but as a means to an end. He never regarded light itself (i.e., dazzling brightness, glitter, radiance) to have an aesthetic value of its own, either in expression or in symbolism. Its specific value for the artist lies in its ability to make the world surrounding us—or what in the Renaissance was called "nature"—visible and representable in painting. In short, Alberti formulated, or at least clearly indicated, what we would call the "functional" concept of light in painting. In so doing he outlined a major theme in the theory of art of the whole Renaissance period. However deep and extensive the transformations which ideas on art underwent between the early fifteenth and the late sixteenth centuries, the assumption that light was principally a means for representing nature in painting was never abandoned.

Before going into a more detailed investigation of Alberti's text, an additional general observation should be made. It is obvious that a concept of light such as Alberti's cannot be isolated from a wider context; it necessarily belongs to a philosophy of art and is intimately related to a definite view of what should be the proper aims of painting. Clearly the functional approach to light presupposes a realistic style of painting (whether actually in existence or envisaged as desirable); in other words, a style in which the picture is conceived as an "imitation" of nature. Only an art which aims at representing nature will consider light as an all-important factor and will yet conceive of it only as a means.

Alberti's functional view is even more sharply focused than such a general description would suggest. Speaking in abstract terms, light used as a means has a rather wide range of possible applications. In producing an illusion of texture or in conjuring up atmospheric effects, light is not less a "means" than in revealing the form and structure of bodies. The impressionistic painter can also regard light as a means for rendering in paint his unstable, immaterial vision of nature. To Alberti light is not simply the condition of visual experience, regardless of what is perceived; he conceives of it as of the revealer of form, of the structure and volume of material bodies. Attaching the functional view of light to the revelation of the form and the volume of solid bodies may be a limitation (in terms of philosophy), but it articulates attitudes and tendencies inherent in Florentine painting since Giotto which reached perhaps their clearest expression in the work of Alberti's contemporary and friend, Masaccio.[52]

As we have said, Alberti did not give a clear formulation of his views, but we believe that several passages in *Della pittura* support our interpretation. Perhaps the most important passage is the one in which Alberti sets forth the general outline of his system. "Since painting strives to represent things seen, let us note in what way the things are seen." Three aspects of the "things seen" are singled out and arranged in hierarchic order, according to their value and importance to art. First is the space occupied by the object, the general outline of that space being rendered by the artist by drawing an outline. Second is the fact that the body is composed of many planes, their rendering being termed by Alberti as *compositione*. "Finally, we determine more clearly the colors and qualities of the planes. Since every difference in them is borne from light, we can properly call their representation the reception of light." [53]

Several features in this text demand our attention. Both from the place of *receptione de lume* in the hierarchy of the "parts" of the art of painting and from the specific function assigned to it, it clearly follows that light is not considered to have an independent value.[54] Its function is to reveal to the eye the qualities and colors of the planes. It does not even affect the basic shape of the object seen and represented, since this shape is rendered by the outline. Light only shows the modeling and colors of the body within its outline. It is also worth noticing, if we may draw from an *argumentum ex silentio,* that in this programmatic text nothing suggests a concern with texture, atmosphere, or any other effect light can produce (although in other passages of *Della pittura* he refers to some of these effects).[55] Alberti here thinks light should show the sculptural solidity, the material firmness of the body.

The central function of light in the picture is to produce the equivalent of the solid material body, namely, the illusion of projecting mass, of relief. This simple and basic concept, reiterated innumerable times in the later stages of the Renaissance, was set forth and systematically discussed for the first time by Alberti. It was to prove an important element in his legacy to the theory of art.

The illusion of projecting mass on what is in fact a flat surface is of course to be achieved by a proper arrangement of lights and shadows, or by the skillful application of white and black (white and black, not being considered as colors, stand for light and shade).[56] The appearance of relief is one of the main values of painting, and its creation is one of the painter's major achievements. "It is worth all your study and diligence," says Alberti to the young painter, "to know how to use these two [black and white] well, because light and shade make things appear in relief." [57] In antiquity the painter Zeuxis was praised for "knowing the force of light and shade." But Alberti apparently considers his own times more advanced. "I almost always consider mediocre the painter who does not understand well the strength of every light and shade in each plane." [58] In his brief remark on monochrome painting he again extols the value of relief created by light and shade. Combining a reference found in classical literature with the problems of art in his own time, Alberti says: "Aglaophon was marvelled at because he liked to paint with one simple color. . . . I certainly agree that copiousness and variety of colors greatly add to the pleasure and fame of a painting, but I should like the (highest level of attainment) in industry and art to rest, as the learned maintain, on knowing how to use black and white." [59]

Alberti's basic concept of light naturally follows from his broad view of painting as imitation of nature. As has frequently been said, in formulating his doctrine he articulated the actual tendencies of early fifteenth-century Florentine painting. But does Alberti here express only the "spirit" of Florentine painting, its broad tendencies and general aims, or does he also draw on the actual workshop experience and artistic procedures of his time?

In scholarly literature it has become commonplace to emphasize the abstract nature of Alberti's treatise on painting; and in this respect, too, his *Della pittura* is often juxtaposed with Cennini's *Libro,* which is so full of authentic detail. While Alberti's treatise on painting is indeed theoretical and abstract, one nevertheless finds in it some details which could not have derived from his scholastic literary sources; nor do they necessarily follow from his overall philosophical concepts. These details indicate a relationship to the artistic workshops which goes beyond a mere understanding or articulation of general and broad tendencies of style. In his discussion of light one finds several descriptions and precepts which bear witness to his close acquaintance with artistic procedures. Although Alberti suggests that his source is the observation of nature, a careful reading of the respective passages makes it clear that they are derived from established workshop traditions rather than from looking at nature.

An interesting passage of this kind is the suggestive description of how the artist should proceed in shading so as to achieve the desired effect of relief. To create the illusion of projecting mass, Alberti says, the artist should carefully balance the lights against the darks. Shading is described as a slow and gradual process in which the painter, proceeding with restraint, carefully adjusts the bright and the dark spots, adding as he goes hue after hue.[60] Obviously we can look nowhere for the source of this description but to the atelier itself, where Alberti might have observed such a procedure. In Florentine painting of his time we find, in fact, many examples of such soft transition from light to dark. Moreover, this passage of *Della pittura* vividly recalls, both in its tone and in the actual contents, Cennini's precept for shading.[61] It seems that both Cennini and Alberti reflect in their writings the same pictorial tradition.

Another example is that curious precept that in each figure represented in a painting the shadows should correspond to the lights "so that no part of a body is lighted without another being dark." [62] The balancing of the two sides seems so important to him that he suggests the artist make a fine line in the center of the figure so as to ensure a perfect symmetry of its lighted and shaded parts. Alberti suggests that this advice is based on observation of nature, but it need hardly be said that in our visual experience we do not perceive in each object a lighted and a shaded part, and even less are those sides balanced against each other. But while Alberti's device is not derived from an observation of nature, it certainly points to the pictorial tradition of his time. Examples of such artificially lighted figures can be found in Florentine painting from the early fifteenth century.[63]

Another passage should be mentioned, although its origin in workshop practice is not as clear as that of the former ones. Alberti notices that cast shadows differ according to the source of light. Natural light (i.e., the light of the sun, the moon, "and that other beautiful star Venus") "makes the shadow equal to the body, but fire makes it longer." [64] This passage is of considerable interest both because it is probably the first suggestion in art theory of the different types of light and because it specifically mentions cast shadows. Here, however, we shall consider it only as a possible testimony to

Alberti's relationship to the workshops. Awareness of the irrational, unstable shape of shadows produced when an object is illumined by fire may have been based on observation of nature, but this procedure could hardly have informed Alberti that the shadows cast in the light of the sun are as a rule of the same shape and length as the bodies casting them. Nor is it likely that he could have found such an unqualified statement in optical literature. On the other hand, we know that cast shadows were an important, and apparently newly discovered, theme in early fifteenth-century painting.[65] From a sixteenth-century source we learn that the representation of an object and the shadow cast by it as of equal length (apparently in natural light) was considered a sign of rational illumination, worthy of praise and recommended to the painter.[66] Since traditions of this kind usually have a long life, it is quite possible that what was recorded in the sixteenth century goes back to the early fifteenth century. If this is the case, Alberti's curious observations may well be based on workshop practice.

Considering these examples one feels that Alberti incorporated some observations of actual workshop procedures in his philosophical and abstract theory of light in painting. It is, however, worth noting that all these references to workshop procedures are made to support his basic concept of light as a means of portraying mass and making visible sculptural form.

Some of Alberti's remarks suggest that he actually did observe nature, relating what he saw to his theory of painting. An interesting example of this is provided by his observations on reflected light. "Reflected light," of course, was a well-established scientific category in medieval optics with which Alberti certainly was acquainted. Yet the brief observations he made on reflected light in *Della pittura* show, we believe, that he not only drew from traditional optics but also looked at nature. In accordance with optical science he describes reflected light as rays interrupted by one object and thrown onto another, adding that "these rays carry with themselves the color they find on the plane" from which they are reflected. But his examples reveal an immediate observation of nature. Thus he notices the reflection of rays from the surface of water onto the rafters of a house, and also observes "that anyone who walks through a meadow in the sun appears greenish in the face." [67]

In art theory Alberti was the first author to notice the merging of light and color in reflected rays. In the next generations, especially in Leonardo's notes and in the Venetian treatises, this observation became a major theme in artistic thought and seriously questioned the division between light and color. Alberti, however, did not draw any far-reaching conclusions from his observations, continuing to think of light as neutral in regard to color.

Two passages in *Della pittura* suggest that Alberti may have been aware of still another function of light in painting in addition to producing the illusion of projecting mass; namely, the representation of textures. While he sharply criticizes the application of gold foil in a picture, he considers the pictorial representation of at least some textures an important achievement of the painter.

> Even though one should paint Virgil's Dido whose quiver was of gold, her golden hair knotted with gold, and her purple robe girdled with pure gold, the reins of the horse and everything of gold, I should not wish for gold to be used, for there is more admiration and praise for the painter who imitates the rays of gold with colors.[68]

Earlier in *Della pittura* Alberti also speaks of the "force" of white placed next to black, "so that vases by this means appear of silver, gold, and glass and appear to be shining in the picture." [69]

As we know,[70] Cennini was already aware that textures can, and probably should, be represented in a picture. His very desire to capture in painting the material nature of wool and velvet, linen and silk shows a tendency toward naturalism which, in a very broad sense, leads to Alberti's philosophy of art as imitation of nature. But probably nothing better illustrates the crucial transformation which both art and art theory underwent in the first third of the fifteenth century than a comparison of Cennini's and Alberti's advice for representing textures. While Cennini envisages an actual duplication of the "represented" texture in the painting, Alberti clearly recommends an illusionistic representation of texture by means of depicting its reaction to light.

Alberti's views on the representation of textures do not seem to be derived from, nor even influenced by, Cennini's. This is shown not only by the radically different means of representation recommended by the two authors but also by the specific textures they mention. While Cennini speaks of different fabrics, Alberti refers only to solid and glittering objects made of glass; silver; and, of course, gold (the only exception being Dido's "golden hair knotted with gold"). All textural effects mentioned by Alberti, then, belong to what we call "highlight" and what the Renaissance called *lustro*. This is further supported by what he says when admonishing the painter to be cautious in the use of white. "The painter has nothing other than white with which to show the highest luster of the most polished sword." [71] These observations by Alberti seem to be a new beginning.

What, then, are Alberti's sources, and what is the precise scope of his observation of *lustro* and its significance in his system? Since observations on highlights constantly recur in Renaissance theory of art, it may be useful to survey briefly the earlier history of this problem in connection with its first formulation in the fifteenth century.

The history of highlight in painting is not easy to trace. In Pompeian still lifes and in mummy portraits from El Fayum we find unmistakable representation of highlights on glass, grapes, pearls, and the tips of noses.[72] Pliny also speaks of luster, leaving no doubt that in the paintings which he saw, *splendor* was different from *lume*.[73] In the Middle Ages these highlights vanished as luster and brightness merged. The radiance of medieval mosaics and stained glass is probably unsurpassed by the works of any other period, but it is not a textural quality and therefore not a *lustro* in the sense of both antiquity and Alberti. While Italian painters of the early Renaissance were not attracted by highlights, they were revived in the northern art of the time. Van Eyck's representations of mirrors, weapons, crowns, and brocades show that highlights are a quality of textures, and they are clearly distinguished from regular brightness.[74]

Alberti knew Pliny's text, and he might have paid attention to the sentence on *splendor,* although he does not mention it. But he did not know the examples of highlight in ancient painting; and his acquaintance with the most advanced northern painting, although it cannot be definitely excluded, does not seem likely.[75]

The image of splendor, however, had not only a pictorial but also a literary history. A long, continuous series of texts, from remote antiquity onward, reflects the fascination with brilliance of all types. But, as a rule, in the literary traditions no distinctions are made that might be useful to the painter. Although what we here call highlight was noticed on innumerable occasions, it is usually not regarded from the painter's point of view; it is considered part of the overall phenomenon of radiance. This may even be seen in the terms applied. In the ancient texts available to a humanist in the early fifteenth century, mainly Latin translations of Greek writings, the term *splendor* designates a high degree of brightness, without any reference to texture. This is the meaning of the term in texts as important to our study as Plato's *Timaeus* and the pseudo-Aristotelian *De coloribus*.[76]

In medieval theology, and in related literary works of the Middle Ages, *splendor* came to designate a metaphysical principle, but for this very reason the term does not denote the gleaming light seen at a specific angle in an object of metal or glass. Even the sparkling glitter of gold, as is well known, is considered a reflection of divine light rather than a quality of simple texture. It is for this reason that gold can, in Abbot Suger's words, carry "his mind from the material to the spiritual world." But the highlight, being detached from texture, is confused with brightness and radiance in general.[77]

These views persisted in the fifteenth century. Thus, to give but two examples, the *Margarita philosophica,* a popular encyclopedia of that period, describes *splendor* as a reflection of the supranatural light whose meaning cannot be exhausted by empirical observation.[78] In the late fifteenth century, Ficino uses the term *splendor* to designate the highest degree of brightness in a light-and-color scale, again without any reference to texture.[79]

This literary tradition was of course common knowledge among the educated. Alberti must have been acquainted with at least part of it, and we may assume that it had some influence on him both in his observation of nature and in his formulation of what he saw. There is indeed a certain ambiguity in his descriptions which makes one wonder just how far he distinguished between dazzling brightness as such and the highlights on a golden object or on a glass, that is, as a characteristic feature of certain textures. In fact, the sentence opening with the statement that the painter has nothing but white "with which to show the highest luster of the most polished sword" concludes by saying that he has "only black to show the deepest shadow of the night." [80] The white spot in the picture, then, could be meant both as a proper highlight showing the smoothness of the polished sword, and simply as a bright spot correctly juxtaposed with the "dark shadow of the night" which has no texture quality. This ambiguity clearly corresponds to a similar ambiguity in the traditional literary formulations. Though it seems likely that Alberti did indeed observe the bright flash on the polished sword illuminated by the sun, it seems equally likely that his acquaintance with the literary tradition, in which *splendor* denotes both luster and any other brightness, molded his understanding of what he saw. Seen in a larger context, this is a good illustration of Alberti's historical position between the Middle Ages and the Renaissance.

But observations of individual types of illumination (such as reflected light) and of specific effects (such as luster) are marginal to Alberti's basic concept *lume*. Fundamentally, he conceived of light, as we have already said, as revealing solid, massive form, and the structure of the represented bodies. In his thought, however, the functional concept of light was related to an aesthetic attitude, to an idea of what a "beautiful" aesthetically valuable illumination should look like. The aesthetic aspect of light is never separately discussed, but a careful reading of *Della pittura* shows that it is inherent in Alberti's views on the correct representation of nature.

Alberti's aesthetic attitude, intimately related to other aspects of his theory, is suggested in his request for restraint in the representation of strong lights and deep shadows. "Never make any plane so white that it cannot be made whiter. If you should dress a figure in whitest robes, it is best to stop much below the highest whiteness." [81] Alberti does not spell out the reasons for his request, but they can be inferred by analyzing the context of the passage and by seeing it against an historical background. The request for moderation, one might argue, so well conforms with Alberti's aesthetic attitude and moral philosophy that the search for further explanation would seem to be superfluous. But we know that in his discussion of art Alberti did not always adopt a moderate attitude. As we have already had occasion to see, in treating emotional movements he clearly conceived of dramatic forms not only as better means of expression but also as an aesthetic value (the embodiment of *varietà*).[82] His request for moderation in light, therefore, is not simply a result of his general attitude; it must have specific reasons.

One possible reason of this particular request might have been the fact that Alberti was aware, as Gombrich puts it, "that the painter's gamut of relationships can never match the range of light intensities that can occur in nature." [83] The scaling down of light intensities would, then, be a consciously applied method of translating visual experience into the more limited language of painting.

Another motive of Alberti's asking the painter that he restrain himself in the representation of pure light may be inferred from later formulations in the theory of art. Since Leonardo it has been commonly accepted that a moderate, subdued light is more appropriate than glaring light both for the observation of voluminous bodies in nature and for their representation in painting. While glaring light renders invisible the *minutezze* of material bodies and tends to flatten (in the beholder's impression) bulging masses, a subdued light reveals even slight modulations and is a powerful agent in creating the illusion of a projecting mass. Even in the late sixteenth century the representation of glaring, dazzling light was recommended only in specific themes and for definite symbolic and iconographic reasons.[84] As a medium, subdued light was preferred throughout the Renaissance period. It seems at least feasible that Alberti, who laid the foundations of Renaissance theory of art in general and anticipated many of its major developments, was also the first to understand the specific value of subdued light.

But with Alberti, the functional is also the aesthetically valuable. Behind his request for moderation in the representation of light there is, indeed, an aesthetic attitude. The shrinking back from harshness in the rendering of light suggests the soft style, and especially the soft transitions, as an aesthetic ideal. It is interesting that in order to indicate these soft, gradual transitions Alberti, like Cennini before him and Leonardo and others afterward, uses the metaphor of smoke: where light is fading out, "white is lost as if in a smoke." [85] We have already seen in Cennini, and we shall see again in later chapters, that the smoke metaphor carried an aesthetic tone.

But the aesthetic character of restrained light is more clearly indicated in the passage where Alberti makes his request. If white were more expensive than precious gems, he says, the painters would be "miserly and good managers and their work would be truthful, sweet and pleasing." [86] Here, then, the functional ("truthful") is at the same time also the aesthetically valuable ("sweet and pleasing"). The aesthetic qualities of the restrained light, although inherent in the correct representation, are nevertheless specifically mentioned. Moreover, Alberti stresses that the hand of the painter who follows his precept will become "more delicate in grace and beauty."

(3)

While what Alberti has to say about light betrays a certain, even if only slight, influence of workshop experience, his treatment of color seems to be completely detached from the artist's actual endeavors. A comparison of the respective parts of *Della pittura* and Cennini's *Libro* makes this particularly clear. What the two authors say under the common heading of "Color" shows that they not only aim at different ends but that they in fact discuss different subjects.

As we have seen earlier in this chapter, Cennini's detailed and expert discussion of color is intimately and constantly related to concrete materials and their specific properties. Only in a few instances does he speak of color in more general terms, particularly when presenting the lists of "true colors." But we have had occasion to notice that even in these cases the connection between colors and materials persists in his thought: of the seven, or eight, "natural colors," some are *di natura terrignia,* and others "need to be helped artificially." [87] In brief, then, Cennini, who is deeply immersed in workshop practice, does not abstract color as an immaterial phenomenon (the contents of our visual experience) from the pigment which produces that color sensation. Whenever he thinks of red, he thinks of minium (or of another appropriate pigment). Colors are treated from the point of view of the artist who handles them.

Alberti's discussion of color, on the other hand, does not contain a single hint of their material nature. With total disregard of pigments, he considers color exclusively as visual sensation, as pure phenomenon. His lack of acquaintance with, and interest in, pigments and the properties of color materials is interesting for more than merely biographical reasons. Alberti's concentration on color qua appearance shows, we believe, that in this specific field, as in so many others, he derived his concepts from the scientific tradition rather than from his painter friends. In the early fifteenth century the science of optics was of course known to the university-trained humanist, but it was still a sealed book to the workshop apprentice.

In ancient and medieval optics color was viewed purely as a phenomenon, and, needless to say, no consideration was given to the pigments which the painter must use to create an appropriate appearance. Moreover, in the scientific tradition Alberti might have found the statement of a venerated authority expressly rejecting the painter's experience as a source of understanding the nature of colors. The author of the pseudo-Aristotelian *De coloribus* says that knowledge of colors is not gained

> ... by blending pigments as painters do, but rather by comparing the rays reflected from the aforesaid known colors [in nature], this being the best way of investigating the true nature of colors.[88]

Alberti knew, of course, that his sources were far removed from the painter's actual concern. In the Latin edition of his work on painting he says:

> Let us omit the debate of the philosophers where the original source of colors is investigated, for what help is it for a painter to know in what mixture of rare and dense, warm and dry, cold and moist color exists? However, I do not despise those philosophers who thus dispute about colors and establish the kinds of colors at seven. White and black are the two extremes of color. Another is established between them. Then between each extreme and the middle they place a pair of colors as though undecided about the boundary, because one of the colors more resembles the extreme than the other. It is enough for the painter to know what the colors are and how to use them in painting. I do not wish to be contradicted by the experts, who, while they follow the philosophers, assert that there are only two colors in nature, black and white, and all the others are created from mixtures of these two. As a painter I think thus about colors. From a mixture of colors almost infinite others are created.[89]

In the Italian version of his work, which postdates the Latin text,[90] he omitted this passage, but his actual discussion of colors remained basically unchanged.

The very starting point of Alberti's discussion of color shows his dependence on the scientific tradition. He begins with an attempt at establishing the primary, or "true," colors. The actual contents of his color scales will be discussed in the last chapter of this book, in connection with the development of other color scales in the Renaissance. Here we shall consider Alberti's views of primary colors only as far as they reveal his general approach to the subject of color.

The establishment of primary colors may, of course, have an eminently practical aspect for the painter, and, as becomes evident from the passage just quoted, Alberti was aware of it. However, in spite of his assertion that he speaks "as a painter" he proposes, in fact, a scientific classification of primary colors without adapting it to the painter's needs.

The quest of reducing the infinite number of hues to a few primary colors has, of course, a long history. From the pseudo-Aristotelian *De coloribus* (and even earlier) up to late medieval and early Renaissance treatises it was constantly reformulated. The variety of scales that emerged in the process is partly reflected in Alberti's text.

Alberti obviously hesitated in deciding on an actual scale and the number of primary colors included in it. As we have seen in the passage quoted above, in the Latin version of his treatise he adopts the scale of seven primary colors which progresses from white to black. The seven-color scale was well known, and frequently commented on, in the Middle Ages.[91] In early Renaissance Italy it was so common that even Cennini, who was not well versed in science, had to bow to it.

In the Italian version of *Della pittura* Alberti offers another list of primary colors, consisting of only four colors which are related to the elements.

> Through the mixing of colors infinite other colors are born, but there are only four true colors—as there are four elements—from which more and more other kinds of colors may thus be created. Red is the color of fire, blue of the air, green of the water, and of the earth gray and ash.[92]

Like the seven-color scale, the scheme of four colors which are related to the four elements has a venerable history. *De coloribus* may again be quoted as an early formulation. The very first sentence of this treatise (which otherwise proposes the seven-color scale) reads: "Those colors are simple which belong to the four elements, fire, air, water and earth."[93] But although this tradition persisted, prior to Alberti no attempt was made to apply this assumption in art.

In ancient literature a four-color scheme is also mentioned in connection with painting. Alberti knew that the Greek painters Polygnotos and Timantes were said to have used only four colors.[94] He was probably also aware of the passage in Pliny where Apelles' palette is described as consisting of only four colors.[95] But although Alberti was aware of these particular texts, his own four-color scheme is not derived from them. What is missing in these classical texts is any connection between colors and elements. But it is precisely this connection, so clearly stated by Alberti himself, which is prominent in the scientific texts, both ancient and medieval. Since we know that the optical treatises were known to Alberti, we are safe in assuming that his four-color scheme was derived from the scientific tradition.

That Alberti should have changed from a seven-color scale to a four-color scheme is particularly interesting for his views of the relationship between light and color. The seven-color scale, progressing from white to black, suggests a unity of light and color; the four-color scheme, including neither white nor black and devoid of any gradation of colors in their degree of brightness, separates color from light. Since the Italian edition of *Della pittura,* which proposes the four-color scheme, most probably postdates the Latin version, which has the seven-color scheme, this shows that Alberti's thought changed from the assumption of a closer relationship between light and color to the granting of more independence to each of them.

In other passages of *Della pittura* one also detects signs of a certain hesitation between an attitude tending to fuse light and color, and a tendency toward separating them.

In the exposition of the first attitude Alberti bases himself on "the philosopher":

It seems obvious to me that colors take their variation from light, because all colors put in the shade appear different from what they are in the light. Shade makes color dark; light, where it strikes, makes color bright. The philosophers say that nothing can be seen which is not illuminated and colored. Therefore, they assert that there is a close relationship between light and color in making each other visible. The importance of this is easily demonstrated for when light is lacking color is lacking and when light returns the colors return. Therefore, it seems to me that I should speak first of colors; then I shall investigate how they vary under light.[96]

In modern scholarship this passage has been interpreted as showing Alberti's belief in the unity of light and color.[97] But a careful reading shows, we believe, that light is here considered as a condition for the perception of colors (as it is a condition for the perception of shapes and surfaces); it is, however, not conceived as identical with, or as the source of, colors. There is a "close relationship" between light and colors, but colors do not emanate from light.[98]

Alberti also notices, apparently referring to actual visual experience, "that one will never find black and white unless they are [mixed] with one of these colors."[99] Since white stands for light, the fact that pure white cannot be found means that what we actually perceive in nature is always a blending of light and color.

The tendency to differentiate between light and color is more clearly articulated. Speaking of the dependence of light and color, Alberti proposes to "study first of all light and shade, and remember how one plane is brighter than another where the rays strike, and now, where the force of light is lacking, the same color becomes dusky." According to the varying degree of light, a color may become brighter or more dusky; however, it does not change its basic chromatic quality. By adding white (light) a red will become brighter, and by blending with black (darkness) it will become darker, but it will always remain red. In this sense Alberti concludes the passages by saying: "Therefore, the mixing with white and black does not change the genus of the colors but forms species."[100]

The application of the terms "genus" and "species" is characteristic both of Alberti's general outlook and of his conception of colors. As is well known, the reference to "genus" and "species" is a basic principle in Aristotelian definitions and scientific procedure, and the meaning of the terms has become firmly established in the course of their long history. The species, as one knows, are subordinated to the genus and are unable to change it. Applied to our problem, it means that the addition of light (white) forms variations ("species") of a color but never causes a basic change. The use of the Aristotelian terms, attesting to the character of Alberti's education, proves that Alberti considered light and color as separate elements.

Some remarks in *Della pittura* concern only the aesthetic value of colors in painting. In a lengthy passage Alberti describes the desirable combinations of colors in a picture.

> I should prefer that all types and every sort of color should be seen in painting for the great delight and pleasure of the observer. Grace will be found, when one color is greatly different from the others near it. When you paint Diana leading her troop, the robes of one nymph should be green, of another white, of another rose, of another yellow, and thus different colors to each one, so that the clear colors are always near other different darker colors. This contrast will be beautiful where the colors are clear and bright. There is a certain friendship of color so that one joined with another gives dignity and grace. Rose near green and sky blue gives both honor and life. White not only near ash and crocus yellow but placed near almost any other gives gladness. Dark colors stand among light with dignity and the light colors turn about among the darks. Thus, as I have said, the painter will dispose his colors.[101]

This passage is a remarkable historical document, since Alberti here seems to go beyond all traditional sources. Obviously in this passage he abandons the scientific color theory; the criterion of selecting color combinations is purely aesthetic, "the greatest delight and pleasure of the observer." Characteristic of this lack of relationship between the scientific and the aesthetic consideration of color is the fact that here he makes no distinction between "true colors" (green) and mixed shades (rose).

But here also Alberti does not turn to the workshop tradition. He does not advise painters which pigments are good and how colors should be blended. He himself expresses his dissociation from the outlook of the workshops, although in this context he mentions Vitruvius rather than the contemporary *bottega*. In the sentence preceding the passage quoted he says that unlike Vitruvius he will not consider "where all good and tried colors are found . . . but in what way well ground colors are used in painting." [102] In other words, Alberti is not concerned with the technical procedures of producing and applying colors but only with their aesthetic appearance in the picture.

Alberti is vaguely aware of some expressive qualities inherent in given color combinations, as such terms as "dignity," "grace," and "gladness" indicate. The expressive qualities, however, are absorbed in a general aesthetic approach. Only in the late sixteenth century did a theory of color expression develop. [103]

Alberti's aesthetic ideal of coloring reflects, though only in a very general way, the taste and style of early Quattrocento painting. A beautifully colored picture consists of large stretches of clearly distinguishable colors. The very criterion of harmonious relationship–what he calls the "friendship of colors"–is not a gradual transition from one color to another, as in tonal painting, but juxtaposition and even contrast. Therefore, his description evokes the image of color variegation rather than of a subdued harmony. As these areas of contrasting shades coincide with the colors of different objects (in Alberti's example, with the robes of the nymphs), it is essentially the principle of *Lokalfarbe* which is here elevated to the rank of an aesthetic ideal.

It is interesting to notice that Alberti has different criteria in judging the value of the representation of light and shade, or of color. So far as light is concerned, he praises, as we have seen, [104] soft transitions, advising the artist to proceed with restraint and conjuring up the image of the smoke screen as the model of a beautiful rendering. For the application of color, on the other hand, he recommends a clear distinction, and even contrast, of the color surfaces as a guiding principle. The different criteria prove, we believe, that Alberti distinguished between light and color not only in scientific concepts but also in the aesthetics of painting.

Alberti seems to have been aware of the novelty of his aesthetic approach to color. He introduces the passage quoted above by saying: "They say that Euphranor, an ancient painter, wrote something about colors; it is not found today. Truly, if ever this was written by others, we have dug this art up from under the earth. If it was never written, we have drawn it from heaven. We will continue to use our intellect as we have done up to now." [105]

Notes

1. Except for Vasari, who discusses the *Libro* as a historical document rather than as an exposition of art theory (cf. *Le vite . . .,* ed. Milanesi, I [Florence, 1878], pp. 643 ff.), it does not seem to have been quoted by any sixteenth-century author. It was first published in print by Giuseppe Tambroni, *Di Cennino Cennini trattato della pittura, messo in luce la prima volta con annotazioni* (Rome, ·1821).

2. The rather limited number of studies of Cennini's doctrine are listed in J. von Schlosser, *La letteratura artistica,* Terza edizione italiana aggiornata da O. Kurz (Vienna, 1964), pp. 93, 710. So far as I know, no systematic study of Cennini's views on light and color has been undertaken.

3. Cf. Schlosser, pp. 93 ff., who stresses the combination of medieval and classical elements in Cennini which is characteristic of the "dawn of the Renaissance." And see also Karl Borinski, *Die Antike in Poetik und Kunsttheorie,* I (Leipzig, 1914), 96 ff., who emphasizes the influence of classical literature on Cennini (transmitted to him, as Borinski believes, by medieval traditions).

4. Cf. the editor's note to *Cennino d'Andrea Cennini, The Craftman's Handbook: "Il Libro dell' Arte,"* translated by Daniel V. Thompson, Jr. (Yale University Press, 1933), p. xix. Henceforth I shall quote the easily accessible paperback edition (New York, ca. 1960), which is a reprint of Thompson's translation.

5. The passage suggesting *sfumato* (see note 17) appears in the section on drawing; the brief chapter on the representation of mountains (see note 10) appears in the section of fresco painting. In the second section of the *Libro,* which is entirely devoted to color, Cennini does not touch on the subject of light.

6. See below, pp. 6 ff. See also pp. 160 ff.

7. Cennini, *Libro,* p. 5 (chap. 8).

8. The two concepts of vision that were known in classical times (that the rays proceed from the object to the eye and, as in Plato, that they proceed from the eye to the object) have often been studied and summarized. For a brief account see Vasco Ronchi, *Histoire de la lumière* (Paris, 1956). These theories, which have never been completely forgotten, were studied in Italian universities of the fourteenth

century. For the particular place of Padua in the intellectual life of the period and in the development of science, influenced of course by works of antiquity, see J. H. Randall, Jr., *The School of Padua and the Emergence of Modern Science* (Padova, 1961), pp. 15-68. Cennini, in spite of his workshop approach, was touched superficially by humanistic scholarship, as can be seen by his well-known use of humanistic *topoi*. See, e.g., the comparison between the painter and poet in the first chapter of the *Libro*. Cf. Schlosser, *Letteratura*, pp. 91-98, esp. pp. 93, 98. And cf. also Karl Borinski, *Die Antike in Poetik und Kunsttheorie*, pp. 96 ff.

9. Borinski, *Die Antike in Poetik und Kunsttheorie*, I, pp. 97, 274 ff.; Rensselaer W. Lee, *Ut pictura poesis: The Humanistic Theory of Painting* (New York, 1967) (originally in *Art Bulletin*, 1940), p. 5, note 14. Most of these and similar observations refer to Cennini's views on the status of painting and on the artist's imagination.

10. Cennini, p. 57 (chap. 88).

11. Schlosser, *La Letteratura*, pp. 95 ff.; Erwin Panofsky, *"Idea": Ein Beitrag zur Begriffsgeschichte der älteren Kunsttheorie* (Studien der Bibliothek Warburg, V) (Leipzig, 1924), pp. 23, 88, note 94.

12. Good examples of the iconographic meaning of light in fourteenth- and early-fifteenth-century painting (though mainly of the Lowlands) have been studied by M. Meiss, "Light as Form and Symbol in Some Fifteenth-Century Paintings," *Art Bulletin*, XXVII (1945), 175-181. In the last chapter of this book I shall come back to the iconographic meaning of light, as it was understood in the late sixteenth century. Schlosser, *Letteratura*, p.96, quotes the eighteenth-century Swiss painter Salomon Gessner *(Werke*, I, p. 176), who paraphrased Cennini's advice: "Ein Stein kann mir die schönste Masse eines Felsens vorstellen und ich hab es in meiner Gewalt, ihn ins Sonnenlicht zu halten, wie ich will, und kann die schönsten Effekten von Schatten und Licht, und Halblicht und Wiederschein, dabei beobachten." This passage is indeed very closely related to Cennini's *precetto*, but, characteristically, the ambiguity of the "system" is resolved for the eighteenth-century artist; the system of light is clearly only that prevailing in nature.

13. Cennini, *Libro*, p. 56 (chap. 85).

14. Cennini's precept reflects a common usage which had prevailed long before his time, as can be observed in many works. See, for instance, I. Tintori and M. Meiss, *The Painting of the Life of St. Francis in Assisi* (New York, 1962), p. 64. As E. Panofsky, "Die Perspektive als symbolische Form," *Vorträge der Bibliothek Warburg, 1924-1925* (Leipzig-Berlin, 1927), p. 319, note 56, has noticed, Leonardo still had to

CENNINI AND ALBERTI

argue against this precept. See Leonardo's *Treatise on Painting,* ed. McMahon (Princeton, 1956), pp. 103-104, 275-279.

15. Cennini, *Libro,* p. 6 (chap. 9).

16. In the late sixteenth century it was especially Armenini *(De veri precetti della pittura* [Ravenna, 1587], particularly in the third book), who placed much emphasis on the coordination between the light prevailing in the chapel and the light in wall paintings in that chapel. The main motive for such a coordination is, as with Cennini, the desire to achieve a convincing effect. See H. Voss, *Die Malerei der Spätrenaissance in Florenz und Rom* (Berlin, 1920), pp. 27 ff., who does, however, not mention the precedents for Armenini's attitude.

17. Cennini, *Libro,* pp. 17 f. (chap. 31).

18. In medieval and early Renaissance treatises the seven-color scale derives mainly from Aristotle, *De sensu et sensibili,* 4, 442a, although it had, of course, a much earlier history. Another important source was the Peripatetic *De coloribus,* which in the Renaissance was considered as an authentic work by Aristotle. The Aristotelian *De sensu* was translated twice into Latin in the Middle Ages, in the twelfth and in the thirteenth century (the latter by William of Moerbecke). Cf. S. D. Wingate, *The Medieval Latin Versions of the Aristotelian Scientific Corpus . . .* (1931), pp. 48 f., 92 f.

Four color schemes also go back to the ancient world, where at least some of them were connected with elements. To the European Middle Ages the concept was also transmitted, *inter alia,* by the *De coloribus* tradition. In the so-called *translatio vulgata* versions of this work (cf. Ezio Franceschini, Περι Χρωματων *Autour d'Aristote: Recueil d'études de philosophie ancienne et medieval offert à M. Auguste Mansion* [1955], pp. 451-469), it reads: "Simplices colorum sunt quicumque elementis consequuntur." A history of the seven-color scale and the four-color scheme has not yet been written, but cf. the interesting article by Samuel Y. Edgerton, Jr., "Alberti's Color Theory: A Medieval Bottle without Renaissance Wine," *Journal of the Warburg and Courtauld Institutes,* XXXII (1969), 109-134. Needless to say, Cennini did not have to study these treatises themselves in order to get acquainted with the ideas expressed in them, since these ideas belonged to the common cultural heritage which was not restricted to the educated.

19. In the sense that a certain metal corresponds to a certain planet, as, for instance, gold to the Sun, lead to Saturn, iron to Mars, etc.

20. This follows from Cennini's formulations. I give here only a few examples. "Natural blue is a natural color which exists in and around the vein of silver. It

occurs extensively in Germany" (chap. 40, p. 35). "A natural color known as sinoper, or porphyry, is red" (chap. 38, p. 32). It should be noticed that here the "natural color" is not the basic tone "red" but a quite specific nuance of it, sinoper. The same is true for other "natural" colors. See, for instance, "A natural color known as ocher is yellow" (chap. 14, p. 27). See, however, below, note 22, for "half-natural" colors which are artificially produced.

21. Cf. *Libro*, pp. 24, 25 (chaps. 40, 41).

22. I give again only a few examples. "A half natural color is green; and this is produced artificially" (chap. 52, p. 31); "A color known as verdigris is green. It is very green by itself. And it is manufactured by alchemy" (chap. 56, p. 33).

23. *Libro*, p. 95.

24. Cf. Millard Meiss, *Painting in Florence and Siena after the Black Death* (Princeton, 1951), pp. 74, 83.

25. *Libro*, pp. 47 ff. (chap. 68).

26. Cf. Erwin Panofsky, *Early Netherlandish Paintings: Its Origins and Character* (Cambridge, Mass., 1953), p. 167 and note 2, for a discussion of gold as a means for achieving a hieratic effect. For gold ground, cf. also Wolfgang Schöne, *Uber das Licht in der Malerei* (Berlin, 1954), pp. 91 ff. Detailed information is to be found in J. J. Tikkanen, *Studien über die Farbengebung in der mittelalterlichen Buchmalerei* (Helsingfors, 1933), passim, esp. pp. 311 ff. (Carolingian art) and pp. 422 ff. (Ottonian art). See also E. Gombrich's review of the Vienna dissertation by J. Bodonyi, "Entstehung und Bedeutung des Goldgrundes in der spätantiken Bildkomposition," which appeared in *Kritische Berichte zur kunstgeschichtlichen Literatur* (1932-1933), pp. 65-76.

27. *Libro*, pp. 86-89.

28. Cf. E. H. Gombrich, "Light, Form and Texture in XVth Century Painting," *Journal of the Royal Society of Arts*, CXII (1964), 826-850.

29. *Libro*, pp. 89 ff.

30. I have not been able to investigate how far this precept reflects an actual procedure of fourteenth-century mural painting. Since Cennini in general does not innovate techniques but describes those actually in use, examples of such a method of representing textures in fresco should be found. Unfortunately, I am unaware of them; as far as I know, they are not mentioned in literature, and many colleagues, who have generously given of their time to answer my questions, also could not

point out any examples. It would be interesting to investigate this problem in detail.

31. See below, the chapter on Venetian theory of art.

32. *Libro,* p. 93.

33. A rather circumstantial confirmation of our interpretation may be found in Cennini's precept for grisaille painting *(Libro,* pp. 121-122), where the modeling is strongly suggested.

34. *Libro,* pp. 46, 92-94.

35. See, for instance, G. P. Lomazzo, *Trattato dell'Arte della Pittura, Scultura, ed Architettura* (Rome, 1844), II, pp. 109 ff., and Armenini, *De veri precetti,* pp. 108 ff.

36. *Libro,* p. 94.

37. *Libro,* p. 46.

38. This can be inferred from such formulations as the following: "And take great care, if you want your work to come out very fresh: contrive not to let your brush leave its course with any given flesh color, except to blend one delicately with another, with skilful handling" (chap. 67, p. 47). "And in this way go back once again to the first dark folds of the figure with the dark color. And carry on as you began, with these colors, over and over again, first one and then the other, laying them in afresh and blending them skilfully, softening delicately" (p. 92).

39. *Libro,* p. 94.

40. Medieval treatises on the craft of painting and of related arts either disregard light altogether (see, for instance, Villard de Honnecourt's model book), or they discuss light as a material quality of the picture or the wall decoration as objects. Needless to say, there are some passages vividly describing the fascination emerging from glittering materials (see Theophilus's *Schedula,* particularly the introduction to the third book) and betraying an amazing sensitivity to light effects in paintings. All these texts, however, do not ask how an object is illumined in nature and how it should be represented by the painter. In another place ("Quelques remarques sur l'esthetique chez Theophile le Moine," *Revue d'Esthetique,* XIII [1960], 257-272), I have tried to show the basic difference between Theophilus's views on light and those of the theory of art of a practical type, as found in the Renaissance.

41. Cf. Girolamo Mancini, *Vita di Leon Battista Alberti* (Rome, 1911), pp. 47-64, still the most authoritative biography of Alberti.

42. Most medieval treatises in the theory of art show, of course, some kind of systematic arrangement. But Cennini seems to have been the first author to arrange his treatise according to artistic problems. As we have seen above, however, he was inconsistent, dividing his *Libro* according to widely varying criteria; besides such general problems as "drawing," and colors we find specifically technical and much narrower criteria and "fresco painting," "oil painting and embellishments," and even "glues, sizes and cements."

The literature on Alberti as the founder of Renaissance theory of art is conveniently summarized in Schlosser, *La Letteratura,* pp. 128 ff., p. 712. I limit myself to a few titles: H. P. Michel, *La Pensée de L. B. Alberti* (Paris, 1930), pp. 333-503; A. Blunt, *Artistic Theory in Italy: 1450-1600* (Oxford, 1940), pp. 1 ff.; Kenneth Clark, *Leon Battista Alberti on Painting (Proceedings of the British Academy,* XXX (London, 1940); I. Behn, *Leone Battista Alberti als Kunstphilosoph* (Strasbourg, 1911). A classical formulation of Alberti's new approach to art may be found in E. Panofsky, *Idea* (1924), pp. 31 ff. In all these studies, however, Alberti's views on light and color attract but little attention. The only studies that analyze Alberti's views of light and color in some detail seem to be those of H. Siebenhühner, *Uber den Kolorismus der Frührenaissance vornehmlich dargestellt in dem Trattato della pittura des L. B. Alberti,* diss. (Leipzig, 1935), and Samuel Y. Edgerton, Jr., "Alberti's Colour Theory: A Medieval Bottle without Renaissance Wine," *Journal of the Warburg and Courtauld Institutes,* XXXII (1969), 109-134.

43. *Leone Battista Alberti, on Painting,* trans. J. R. Spencer (henceforth quoted as Spencer) (Yale, 966), pp. 67 ff.; *Leone Battista Alberti, Della pittura,* ed. L. Malle (henceforth quoted as Malle) (Florence, 1950), pp. 81 ff.; Leone Battista Alberti, *Kleinere kunsttheoretische Schriften,* ed. H. Janitschek (henceforth quoted as Janitschek) (Vienna, 1877), pp. 99 ff. For an interesting interpretation of Alberti's categories see R. W. Lee, *Ut pictura poesis: The Humanistic Theory of Painting* (1967) (originally appeared in *Art Bulletin,* XXII [1940]), pp. 70 ff.

44. Cf. Creighton Gilbert, "Antique Frameworks for Renaissance Theory of Art: Alberti and Pino," *Marsyas,* III (1946), 87-106, and E. Panofsky, *Renaissance and Renascences in Western Art* (Stockholm, 1960), p. 26.

45. For Alberti's general acquaintance with medieval authors, cf. the important study by V. Zoubov, "Leon Battista Alberti et les auteurs du Moyen Age," *Medieval and Renaissance Studies,* IV (1958), pp. 246 ff. For his knowledge of medieval optics, cf. Edgerton, "Alberti's Colour Scale," passim, esp. p. 112.

46. See Alberti's famous prologue to his *Della pittura.*

47. See below, pp. 17, and pp. 29 ff.

48. See, e.g., Giraldus Cambrensis's description of the radiant colors in a manuscript (O. Lehmann-Brockhaus, *Lateinische Schriftquellen zur Kunst in England, Wales und Schottland vom Jahre 901 bis zum Jahre 1307* [Munich, 1955-1960], III, no. 5940, p. 217) and the description of light effects in the *Versified Life of Saint Hugh of Lincoln* (reprinted in Lehmann-Brockhaus, II, no. 2372, pp. 27 ff.) Cf. E. Panofsky, "The Ideological Antecedents of the Rolls-Royce Radiator," *Proceedings of the American Philosophical Society* CVII (1963), 273 ff., esp. 285 ff.; see also M. Schapiro, "On the Aesthetic Attitude in Romanesque Art," *Art and Thought* (London, 1941), pp. 130 ff.

49. See above, p. 3.

50. For *istoria* Alberti requests variety (Janitschek, p. 117; Spencer, p. 76), while for light he seems to prefer uniformity. In the enumeration of body movements and emotions Alberti is very detailed and varied. His famous programmatic formulation of expressive movements points to variety: "We weep with the weeping, laugh with the laughing and grieve with the grieving. These movements of the soul are made known by movements of the body" (Janitschek, p. 121; Spencer, p. 77). Even more dramatic is his style and imagery when he speaks of the forms of hair and of branches. The hair "turns in spirals as if wishing to knot itself, waves in the air like flames, twines around itself like a serpent. ... In the same way branches" (Janitschek, p. 129; Spencer, p. 81). No similar description is given of light. Warning the painter against being seduced by the charm of light, Alberti says: "Certainly by nature we love open and clear things; therefore, close more tightly the way in which it is most easy to sin" (Janitschek, p. 137; Spencer, p. 84).

51. "Et anchora veggiamo in una piana tavola alcuna superficie ove sia l'oro, quando deono essere obscure risplendere et quando deono essere chiare parere nere" (Malle, p. 102; Spencer, p. 85). For the broader context, cf. Jan Bialostocki, "Ars auro prior," *Mélanges de litterature et philologie offerts à Mieczyslaw Brahmer* (Warsaw, 1966), pp. 55-63.

52. For a general discussion of light in Florentine painting, cf. Schöne, *Uber das Licht in der Malerei*, pp. 82 ff., 119 ff. (but for Masaccio concentrating mainly on cast shadows); Theodor Hetzer, *Tizian: Geschichte seiner Farbe*, 2d ed. (Frankfurt, 1948), pp. 25 ff. (but as a rule not distinguishing between color and light). More specific is Siebenhühner, *Uber den Kolorismus der Frührenaissance*, pp. 50-56, 61 ff., 67 ff.

53. Malle, p. 82; Janitschek, p. 99; Spencer, p. 68.

54. Alberti is quite outspoken in this respect: "In qual cosa cosi affermo debbano

molto exercitarsi. Niuna compositione et niuno ricevere di lumi si puo lodare ove non sia buona circonscriptione aggiunta" (Malle, p. 82; Spencer, p. 68).

55. See below, pp. 21 ff., 24 ff.

56. Cf. Malle, p. 98; Janitschek, p. 131; Spencer, p. 82. That white and black are not colors also follows from the assumption that their mixing with other colors forms "species" but does not change the "genus" of these colors.

57. Loc. cit. The high esteem of relief is clearly expressed: "I say the learned and the unlearned praise those faces which, as though carved, appear to issue out of the panel, and they criticize those faces in which is seen no other art than perhaps that of drawing."

58. Malle, p. 99; Janitschek, p. 133; Spencer, p. 82.

59. Loc. cit. This is probably based on Quintillian, XII, x, 3, who praises Aglaophon, together with Polygnotus, for "simple coloring" *(simplex color)*. Interestingly, Alberti turns the "simple coloring" into painting in one color only. His text reads: ". . . et Aglaophon si maravigliano si diletasse di dipingere in un solo semplice colore." In this passage Alberti clearly distinguishes between light and shade (represented by black and white) and chromatic colors.

60. Malle, p. 100; Janitschek, p. 133; Spencer, p. 83. It is perhaps symptomatic that Alberti here uses the verb *bilanciare,* which he does not seem to use in other contexts.

61. Cennini, *Libro,* pp. 17 f. (chap. 31).

62. Malle, p. 99; Janitschek, p. 133; Spencer, pp. 82 ff.

63. Gombrich, "Light, Form and Texture," fig. 14, adduces a painting by Fra Angelico, done in 1437, as a pictorial example of Alberti's device. But such a procedure can be found already in Masaccio's work. Some figures in Masaccio's *Tribute Money* (see esp. the figure of the tax collector seen from the back) show a careful balancing of light and shade which conforms to Alberti's prescription.

64. Malle, p. 64; Janitschek, p. 67; Spencer, p. 50.

65. Cf. Millard Meiss, "Some remarkable early shadows in a rare type of Threnos," *Festschrift Ulrich Middeldorf* (Berlin, 1968), pp. 112-118. For cast shadows in the north (Konrad Witz), cf. Miriam Schild Bunim, *Space in Medieval Painting and the Forerunners of Perspective* (New York, 1940), p. 173.

66. See, e.g., R. Borghini, *Il Riposo* (Florence, 1730), p. 143 (original edition [Florence, 1584], p. 182): ". . . ed il lume vuol esser preso alto, di maniera che ogni corpo faccia tanto lunga l'ombre sua per terra, quanto è la sua altezza." It should

also be noted that the unpredictable length and direction of shadows caused especially by open fires and other artificial lights was considered a manifestation of the irrational character of this type of light. See below, the chapter on Lomazzo and note 62.

67. Malle, p. 64; Janitschek, p. 67; Spencer, p. 51.

68. Malle, p. 102; Janitschek, p. 139; Spencer, p. 85.

69. Malle, p. 100; Janitschek, p. 137; Spencer, p. 84.

70. See above, pp. 8 ff.

71. Malle, p. 100; Janitschek, p. 135; Spencer, pp. 83 f. Alberti here uses the term *lustro.*

72. Cf. Gombrich, "Light, Form and Texture," pp. 826 ff. For ancient painting, see also A. Rumpf, "Classical and Post-Classical Greek Painting," *Journal of Hellenic Studies,* LXVII (1947), pp. 10-21, esp. pp. 14 ff.; for Hellenistic painting cf. G. Hanfmann, "Hellenistic Art," *Dumbarton Oaks Papers,* XVII (1963), pp. 89 ff.

73. "Splendor, alius hic quam lumen." *Natural History,* XXXV, 29. Pausanias's description of a painting representing a transparent crystal cup (II, xxvii, 3) may suggest, but does not explicitly mention, splendor. See, however, W. Seibt, *Helldunkel, I: Von den Griechen bis zu Correggio* (Frankfurt, 1885), pp. 9 ff.

74. Cf. Panofsky, *Early Netherlandish Painting,* pp. 151 ff., 418. A comprehensive history of highlight in painting still remains to be written.

75. For Alberti's journey to northern Europe, only a few years before he wrote his treatise on painting, cf. Mancini, *Alberti,* p. 87. However, it seems unlikely that Alberti was acquainted with the art of Van Eyck, created in these years. During his journey Alberti made careful and extensive notes, but nothing in them refers to northern art. Given the originality of the new Flemish painting, it would certainly have struck Alberti and have been mentioned in his notes.

76. For some discussion of this problem in ancient philosophy cf. J. Walter, *Die Geschichte der Ästhetik in Altertum* (Leipzig, 1893), pp. 216 ff. As an example I refer to Plato's *Timaeus,* 68 a-b, where "bright," "dazzling," and "brilliant" are used as synonyms. In the pseudo-Aristotelian *De coloribus* (which was regarded in the Renaissance as an authentic work by Aristotle), the identity of brightness and brilliance is particularly clear where the author juxtaposes the "bright and shining" to the "dark and dull." "Shining is nothing but the continuity and intensity of light" (793 a). See the remarks by Walter, pp. 660 ff.

77. Cf. *Abbot Suger on the Abbey Church of St. Denis,* ed. and trans. by Erwin Panofsky (Princeton, 1946), pp. 46 ff., 62 ff.

78. For a late example, cf. *Margarita philosophica* translated into Italian by Giovan Paolo Gellvoi (Venice, 1600), p. 591. It should be mentioned that the *Margarita philosophica* was a widely read encyclopedia in the Renaissance. Between 1486 and 1583 fourteen editions of this work appeared. For sixteenth-century editions, cf. James Wilbenforce, *A List of Editions of the 'Margarita philosophica' 1503-1599* (New York, 1884). Vasco Ronchi, *Histoire de la lumière* (Paris, 1956), p. 49, believes that the *Margarita philosophica* reflects most clearly the Renaissance concepts of light.

79. For a discussion of the color scale, cf. below the chapter on Milanese theory of art, section IV.

80. Malle, p. 100; Janitschek, p. 135; Spencer, pp. 83 f.

81. Malle, p. 100; Janitschek, p. 137; Spencer, p. 84.

82. See above, note 50.

83. Gombrich, "Light, Form and Texture," pp. 831 ff.

84. For the recommendation of subdued light, see below, pp. 59 ff., 73 ff.; for glaring light, pp. 150, 155.

85. ". . . mancando il lume il bianco si perderebbe quasi in fumo." Janitschek, p. 135; Spencer, p. 83. Cf. also Malle, p. 62; Janitschek, p. 65; Spencer, p. 50, where Alberti uses the term *vapore,* which is closely related to smoke. For the smoke metaphor in Cennini, cf. above, p. 10; for a discussion of *sfumato,* cf. below, pp. 73 ff.

86. Malle, p. 100; Janitschek, p. 137; Spencer, p. 84.

87. *Libro,* chap. 36.

88. *De coloribus,* 79 a.

89. Spencer, p. 49. Malle and Janitschek do not give the Latin text, but Janitschek quotes the respective passage in his notes, pp. 227 ff. The generation of colors was frequently discussed by Greek philosophers. Cf. Plato's *Timaeus,* 67d-67e, and Aristotle's *De plantis,* ii, 8, 827b; *Physica,* i, f, 188b; *Meteorologica,* iii, 374b; and *De generatione et corruptione,* passim. Cf. W. Kranz, "Die älteste Farbenlehre der Griechen," *Hermes,* XLVII (1912), 126-140, and Edgerton, "Alberti's Colour Theory," p. 114.

90. Cecil Grayson, "Studi su Leon Battista Alberti," *Rinascimento,* IV (1953), 45-62, has proved that the Latin version of *Della pittura* is the earlier one.

91. See above, note 18.

92. Malle, p. 63; Janitschek, p. 65; Spencer, pp. 49 f.

93. But both in the precise color lists and in the attribution of each color to an element Alberti and Aristotle do not agree. The comparison looks as follows:

Element	Aristotle	Alberti
Fire	red	red
Water	white	green
Earth	white (ashes)	gray (ashes)
Air	white	blue

94. Malle, p. 98; Janitschek, p. 131; Spencer, p. 82. Cf. Spencer's note 73, p. 128. Alberti's references to Polygnotus and Timantes probably come from Cicero's *Brutus,* xvlii, a copy of which Alberti naturally owned.

95. Cf. Pliny, *Natural History,* XXXV, xxxii, 50. Spencer has shown that numerous references in *Della pittura* prove Alberti's familiarity with the thirty-fifth book of Pliny's *Natural History.* Edgerton, "Alberti's Colour Theory," note 32, believes that Pliny's mention of the four colors had no influence on Alberti's color vocabulary.

96. Malle, p. 62; Janitschek, p. 65; Spencer, p. 49.

97. Cf. John Shearman, "Leonardo's Colour and Chiaroscuro," *Zeitschrift für Kunstgeschichte,* XXV (1962), 13-47, esp. p. 13 and note 5. See also Siebenhühner, *Über den Kolorismus der Frührenaissance,* pp. 18 ff.

98. It should, however, be noticed that even here Alberti only says that the colors take their *variations* from light; he does not say that the colors are produced by light. It is, therefore, consistent that he concludes this passage by announcing his intention to "speak first of colors; then I shall investigate how they vary under light."

99. Malle, p. 64; Janitschek, p. 67; Spencer, p. 50.

100. Malle, p. 63; Janitschek, p. 65; Spencer, p. 50.

101. Malle, p. 101; Janitschek, pp. 137 ff.; Spencer, pp. 84 ff.

102. Malle, p. 101; Janitschek, p. 137; Spencer, p. 84. Alberti's reference to Vitruvius is probably to *De architectura,* VII, vii-xiv.

103. See below, chapter on Milanese Theory of Art, pp. 165 ff. See also p. 188.

104. See above, pp. 24 ff.

105. Malle, p. 101; Janitschek, p. 137; Spencer, p. 84.

2

LEONARDO

(1)

THE PROBLEM of light and color central to Leonardo's conception of art stands in marked contrast to the comparatively slight importance accorded to it by Alberti, a contrast that also reflects the different character of their respective periods. The early fifteenth century, deeply interested in the "true" representation of bodily structure and mass, regarded light mainly as a medium of visibility, and hence set the highest value on the simplest type of illumination—the clear, evenly distributed daylight which permits objects to stand out most distinctly. At the end of the fifteenth and the beginning of the sixteenth century, painters in Flanders, Venice, and to some extent also Florence represented through coloristic values and atmospheric conditions the texture of objects, "soft" transitions and "sweet" shadows, and the play of light on the surface of colored things. The importance that Leonardo attached to light in his artistic and scientific work reflects this general historic development.

Although Leonardo's concepts of light and color have often been discussed, the principles underlying his theory are not easy to grasp, and the interrelation between its different parts and aspects is not easily clarified. His paintings, in their present state, cannot serve as conclusive documentation for his ideas on this subject, although those few works that have been preserved in somewhat better condition may help us reconstruct his concepts. The transparent shadows in the portrait of *The Musician* (in the Ambrosian Library in Milan), the infinitely fine gradations of light and shadow in the hazy atmosphere of the *Madonna of the Rocks* give us an idea of what he considered the essential values of light and color in the art of painting. Looking at these works we can understand Vasari's assertion that the toning down in Leonardo's paintings became a model for Giorgione and influenced Venetian painting.[1] The main source for studying Leonardo's theory of light and color, however, remains his written legacy.

Leonardo's so-called *Notebooks* provide ample evidence of his absorbing interest in this subject. They abound in scientific investigations of optics; show his recurrent preoccupation with the luminaries, the sun, the moon, and the stars;[2] and contain the elaborate formulation of his observations, sometimes interspersed with religious and mythical images and ideas. It is therefore not surprising that we should find in his notes the most comprehensive theory of light and color that had so far been developed by a Renaissance artist. At first glance this theory is by no means a coherent and unified whole. Although Leonardo reformulated his views and observations many times, his conception of light and color is in part replete with ideas that have not been worked out to their conclusion; and it often betrays the divergent, if not conflicting, interests and attitudes of the painter and the student of optics. We shall, however, try to show that despite its fragmentary character, a coherent set of ideas underlies Leonardo's views on the subject. It is from this standpoint that we shall first outline some of the general aspects of his theory of light and color and then examine more closely some of its specific problems.

It is almost superfluous to say that in Leonardo's preoccupation with light and color, scientific interests merged with the painter's concern for representation. A considerable part of his numerous observations on the phenomena of light and color grew out of his desire to understand their natural constitution and to grasp their underlying mathematical principles and is, prima facie, only loosely connected with the problems and tasks of painting. While a division of his notes into "scientific" and "pictorial" cannot be accepted, they can perhaps be classed in two groups according to their emotional "tone." The first group contains analytical observations which suggest a detachment; the other is written in a more passionate tone, and it is interesting that here we find more detailed reflections on light.[3] Following a long tradition, Leonardo describes optics as the "blood of physics," that is, of all natural sciences.[4] Quoting a medieval scholastic almost verbatim, he writes that "among the various studies of natural processes, that of light gives most pleasure to those who contemplate it."[5] With an absorbing interest, he investigated the effects of different lights,

45

the light of the sun and the stars, the light reflected on the surface of the sea, and the luminescent quality of the air itself. The study of these empirical phenomena is also frequently permeated with an emotional quality. On seeing lightning he thinks of "creative nature" and describes it as that "mighty and once living instrument of formative nature." [6] This emotional attitude prompted him to set forth the outlines of an aesthetics of grace, which is intimately related to the phenomenon of light and to the appearance of colors.

His scientific interests also persist, of course, in the notes connected more immediately with painting problems. Here, however, one can also see his dependence on the aesthetic norms of his time and his close relationship to the workshop tradition. Impressive relief effects were for him, as for most painters of the fifteenth century, the highest aim of painting and the basis of its esteem among the learned. The illusion of material solidity in the representation of bodily forms is achieved by the proper distribution of lights and shadows, and thus illumination is relied upon to produce the most important aesthetic value in painting. This point of view is aptly formulated by Leonardo as follows:

> The primary purpose of the painter is to make a plain surface display a body in relief, detached from that plane and he who in that art most surpasses others deserves most praise, and this concern, which is the crown of the science of painting, comes about from the use of shadows and lights, or, if you wish, brightness and darkness. Therefore whoever avoids shadows avoids what is the glory of the art for noble minds, but gains glory with the ignorant public, who want nothing in painting but beauty of color, altogether forgetting the beauty and marvel of depicting a relief on what in reality is a plane surface. [7]

In view of the importance that Leonardo attached to such projected forms, it is not surprising that he attempted to determine and exactly to describe the various conditions under which illumination produces the boldest relief.[8] It is mainly in this sense that he regards light and darkness as elements of painting.[9]

The modification of color by light is another significant theme of

Leonardo's observations. The best-known formulation of this problem is the so-called aerial perspective, which plays an important part in his general conception of painting. A considerable portion of his notes treats of colors that grew dim or faint as the rays are filtered in the air. The observation of the diminution of the color intensity of distant objects is connected with the pictorial category of *sfumato* and is made into a paramount aesthetic value.

A focusing of interest on illumination rather than on color is common in the art theory of the early Renaissance. But, in contradistinction to most artists and writers of this time, Leonardo sometimes also valued illumination higher than outline. In a page of the *Notebooks* the question arises as to whether design is more difficult than the application of lights and shadows.[10] Leonardo often returns to this question. A famous passage in the *Treatise on Painting* says that "Light and shadow together with foreshortening constitute the ultimate excellence of painting." [11] Again, in another passage, where he draws up a scale of values for the representation of figures, good relief is placed before good drawing. "Of the first four parts that are required of the figure, attitude is the first and most important part . . . the second important part of the figure is to have relief; the third is good drawing; and the fourth is good coloring." [12] Correct illumination (i.e., one that produces relief) is put before outline, and in another passage it is made a condition for the comprehension and representation of the contour itself. The "form" of the body is most clearly perceived when it is seen in a certain type of illumination.[13]

For Leonardo, however, light is more than the natural indispensable condition for painting whereby the object to be represented is made visible to the eye; the use of illumination, and to a lesser degree of color, in painting has an autonomous artistic value and makes demands on the virtuosity of the artist that are more exacting and perhaps superior to those of the scientist. Although Leonardo himself made numerous shadow constructions with the compass, he insists that shadows in painting cannot be constructed with instruments. "The shadow in a picture is matter for much greater investigation and reflection than its outlines. The proof of this is shown by the fact that the outlines can be traced by means of veils or glass panes placed between the eye and the thing to be traced, but shadows are not attained by any such method because their edges are indistinguishable and usually confused." [14] The fact that shadows cannot be measured nor their "correctness" ascertained by technical means makes their representation a definite manifestation of that artistic talent which, unlike "rules," cannot be learned. The same would seem to apply to certain subtle modifications of colors by light. In thus bringing illumination into a direct, specific relationship with artistic genius, Leonardo anticipated some important intellectual trends that became prevalent in the second half of the sixteenth century.

(2)

Before we examine some of the significant problems in Leonardo's theory of light and color, we shall attempt to outline roughly the sources and origins of his views.

It is first necessary to recall that in contradistinction to Alberti, who had come to deal with the problems of art after having absorbed the scientific and humanistic culture of his day in the circles of the learned and at the University of Bologna, Leonardo grew up in a Florentine workshop. As is well known, the artistic workshops of the fifteenth century not only served the practical needs of the artist but were also storehouses of theoretical knowledge accumulated over generations and handed down from teacher to pupil. Despite the large literary legacy (textbooks, biographies, and anecdotes) that has come down to us, we should keep in mind that in the workshops knowledge was to a large extent transmitted by oral teaching, a fact that obviously presents the historian with grave difficulties. In trying to define the sources from which Leonardo drew, one is bound, therefore, to attempt to re-create the intellectual views of artists in the workshops and the different cultural trends of the period that were connected with them. Just how much importance should be granted to a particular artistic trend or specific doctrine very often remains a matter of conjecture. The main groups of Leonardo's sources, however, can be established by such a procedure.

Andrea Verrochio, in whose workshop Leonardo was trained, represents the versatile artistic culture of Florence in the second half of the fifteenth century. Verrochio was not only a goldsmith, sculptor, and painter, but was also considered a reputable scholar in the fields of mathematics, geometry, perspective, and optics.[15] The teaching in his workshop, we may assume, included a great deal of theoretical, "scientific" matter. In optics, however, as well as some of the other sciences, Leonardo did not remain within the confines of the workshop's oral tradition. To be sure, he called himself "uneducated," an "omo senza lettere," but Leonardo scholars have long since ceased to take this half-ironical self-characterization seriously.[16] Especially in his study of the various aspects of nature Leonardo did not rely solely on oral teaching and immediate experience but read some classical works of science. His preoccupation with Galen and Archimedes is a good example.[17] Despite many valuable accounts, we have no definitive knowledge of the extent of Leonardo's literary education or of his familiarity with the published works of scientific theory. This general statement also applies to his knowledge of optics.[18] The humanistic circles of Florence and Milan in which he moved undoubtedly introduced him to some of the significant works of optics which then animated the intellectual world. In his youth he had studied in the school of Benedetto dell'Abbaco, called "Benedetto aritmetico." [19] Later Paolo Toscanelli, the famous Florentine astronomer, mathematician, physician, geographer, and mete- orologist, probably influenced him.[20] When Leonardo came to Milan, the jurist, physician, and mathematician Fazio Cardano was beginning his edition of Peckham's *Perspectiva,* an important medieval book on optics, and Leonardo knew at least parts of it.[21]

Another group of Leonardo's possible sources has to be considered. It has often been said (and in the opinion of this writer, correctly) that Leonardo was no Neoplatonist and that Neoplatonism had but little influence on his spiritual development. Nevertheless, we may assume that isolated ideas and images, familiar to the Neoplatonic trend, could have affected his thought. This is perhaps especially applicable to his views on light. The overwhelm- ing importance that Neoplatonism gave to light need not be discussed here. In the Florentine Neoplatonic circle, active in Leonardo's time, certain pantheistic conceptions were largely based on the image of light, and metaphysical significance was granted to the sun and other luminaries. Giovanni Francesco Nesi, a poet who lived at the court of Lorenzo the Magnificent and who was apparently on friendly terms with Leonardo (whom he called "il mio Vinci"), wrote Neoplatonic hymns to the sun and might have imparted to his friend something about the Neoplatonic metaphysics of light.[22] Michele Marullo, a refugee Greek poet from Byzantium who also lived at Lorenzo's court, likewise composed hymns to the sun in which he expressed in an elegantly turned language his pagan adoration for the awe-inspiring power of nature.[23]

But besides Leonardo's learned friends, his notes show ample evidence of his wide knowledge of scientific and literary sources as well as of his acquaintance with the currents of thought of his time. His library was probably not that of an *omo senza lettere*. He is said to have frequented public libraries, [24] and, if so, he could not have failed to consult some scientific manuscripts. The authors and works he mentions, directly or indirectly, form an impressive list. He was apparently familiar with most of the significant works on optics extant in his day. Although he mentions but a few authors by name (among them, Roger Bacon, Vitello, and Avicenna), [25] it may be assumed that he was acquainted with many more. A number of these authors or books were such well-known authorities (for example, Ibn-alhaitam, known as Alhazen, the great Arab mathematician) [26] that Leonardo perhaps did not feel that it was necessary to mention them by name when he set forth their views or cited whole paragraphs from their works. As we know, he quoted an important paragraph from Peckham's work without mentioning the name of the author.[27] In view of all this we may say that Leonardo, besides relying on the oral traditions of the workshops, also drew on the established scientific traditions.

In the following sections I shall not touch the much-discussed question of Leonardo's originality or merits as a scientist. I shall, however, attempt to show that his attitude toward the scientific traditions, at least as far as light and color are concerned, was largely determined by the interests and exigencies of the painter. It is from this point of view only that I shall discuss some scientific aspects of his theory or some of his borrowings from the scientific knowledge of his time.

(3)

It is a significant fact that Leonardo's copious notes concerning luminaristic phenomena deal not so much with light and darkness as separate entities as with their mutual dependence and interpenetration. He makes the intermediary area, which he calls *mezzo* (the middle or in between), the peculiar province of his observation. "Brightness and darkness, that is, light and shadow, have an intermediary which can neither be called bright nor dark, but participates equally in the bright and in the dark; it is sometimes nearer the one than the other." [28] The focusing of his interest on that intermediary zone indicates Leonardo's particular position. Medieval speculations on light centered around the abstract notions of light and darkness in their isolated state and, so to speak, pure form. This is especially true for the Platonic trends which tried to apprehend and formulate the "essence" of light and darkness. Leonardo's interest in the *mezzo* reflects the non-Platonic attitude of the empiricist who is fascinated, not by the abstract idea of a pure light and an absolute darkness, but by a graduate middle area whose individual phenomena can actually be observed and experimentally investigated.

The *mezzo* is, furthermore, the peculiar province of the painter, the domain of the visible and the representable. Both deep darkness and pure light transcend the realm of what can be represented. Leonardo, on one occasion, perhaps influenced by the study of medieval literature, says that pure, bright light makes the eye smart.[29] Since Cennini, Renaissance theory of art did in fact concentrate on that "middle," setting the problem of real, natural illumination of bodies in the center of discussion on light. In concentrating on the *mezzo,* Leonardo thus follows the tradition of art established several generations before him. The investigation of the phenomena pertaining to the "middle" area is, therefore, intimately connected with the painter's work. It can, I think, even be shown that there is a certain chronological correlation between his preoccupation with *chiaroscuro* in his work as a painter and his theoretical studies of the "intermediary" zone. As has often been said, Leonardo almost never used the bright, shadowless colors of the Quattrocento, and even his early works are distingushed by their mysterious half tones and twilight effects.[30] The drawings that date from the late 1480s, shortly before the composition of the so-called manuscript C (1490) with its series of diagrams illustrating the effects of light falling on spheres, cylinders, and so on, show how much he was occupied in this period with the distribution of masses of light and shade. The text that accompanies one of the Alp drawings (Windsor, p. 285 b) contains many detailed annotations concerning the color of the mountain flowers seen through a dense layer of air. Some of the pages of manuscript C (composed mainly in 1513) are devoted to observations on illuminated trees, a half-transparent arbor, reflections in the air, and the *prospettiva di colore,* which bear the unmistakable mark of a painter's eye. These observations were set down a short time after he had painted *The Virgin and the Child with Saint Anne* which, in its rich landscape background, represents these half-transparent, atmospherical appearances. These are some of the examples that illustrate the close relationship between Leonardo's artistic development and his study of optics, and the deep impact of the interests of the painter on those of the scientist.[31]

For the painter, the *mezzo* crystallizes in a particular phenomenon, the shadow, and this is indeed the most important single theme discussed in Leonardo's investigations of different light phenomena. It is inherent in the nature of a shadow that it is neither pure light nor absolute darkness but a product and a blending of the two. In Leonardo's words: ". . . shadow is a mingling of darkness with light, and it will be of greater or lesser density as the light with which it is mingled is of lesser or greater strength." [32] Leonardo is familiar with the techniques of the artists who adhere to workshop practices, and whom he calls "the practitioners" *(li pratici).* These artists divide all represented objects into four areas of light and darkness, but Leonardo insists that on a continuous surface these gradations are infinite.[33] He believed that between darkness and brightness there is no essential or qualitative break or gap, but only transitions and quantitative differences that can be infinitely varied. This can be seen clearly in his formulations of what he calls "compound light" and "compound shadows." The short passage reads: "what is the difference between compound light and compound shadow? Compound shadow is that which participates more in the shadowed body than in the luminous. Compound light is that which participates more in the luminous body than in the shadowed. We shall say then that compound shadow and compound light take their names from that in which they participate most." [34] In contradistinction to some metaphysical conceptions, Leonardo believes that darkness is nothing but the deepest shadow and that light is nothing but the weakest shadow. Every diminution of pure light, be it ever so slight, is already a shadow. He evokes in the reader's mind the famous image of emanation when he says: "With the name of shadow in the proper sense of the word we designate every diminution or weakening of the light applied to the surface of bodies, which begins where the luminary [*luce*] ceases and ends in full darkness." [35] We shall have occasion to return to the distinction between *luce* and *lume;* for the present it suffices to point out that *luce* does not mean simply light or brightness but refers to the source of light. The most intense brightness in nature, unless it is a body that itself gives light (like the sun), already belongs, according to Leonardo, to the realm of shadow.[36] The shadow, then, with its innumerable variations, ranges over the entire domain of visibility, and in a sense symbolizes that domain.

Although Leonardo is principally interested in the various manifestations of individual shadows, he is curious about the nature of shadow in general. The explanations recorded in his *Notebooks* sometimes reveal a peculiar combination of scientific observation and a mythology of nature.

Shadow is first explained as a deficiency or "withdrawal" of light which arises when an opaque body interrupts the movement of the rays of light and hinders their progression in a certain direction. This naturalistic or scientific explanation of shadows, which rests on personal observation as well as on the accepted doctrine of optics, is elaborated by Leonardo in great detail and forms the basis for all his shadow constructions.[37] His subtle distinctions between the various categories of shadows and his discriminating terminology reveal an empirical turn of mind.[38] But, together with many explanations based on empirical observation, we also find some notes that reflect a mythical conception where shadows are understood not simply as the absence of light but as a positive power. This conception, of course, is not set forth as clearly as the former; ambiguous formulations and images suggest, however, that in Leonardo's world view there was a mythical undercurrent which also had an effect on his doctrine of light.

There are some indications that Leonardo took shadows to be not merely optical phenomena whose existence is exhausted in the world of appearances but semiautonomous dynamic forces that dwell in a world beyond visual experience. The surface of all bodies, he observed, is wrapped up in light and darkness; [39] and the enveloping darkness he here speaks of seems to refer, not to the absence of light, but to an element with an independent existence. Leonardo divides shadows into "adhering shadows" *(ombra congionta)* and "separate shadows" *(ombra separata),* the former being the shaded side of a body and the latter being chiefly personified by the cast shadow. The description of the "separate shadow" is often ambiguous, since Leonardo seems to regard it not only as an absence of light but also as something that potentially exists in the body and, under certain conditions, is realized as a visual phenomenon. He assumed a propagation of shadows, analogous to the propagation of light. Every shaded body *(corpo ombroso)* sends forth its images *(similitudini)* in all directions, [40] and these must be understood as some kind of dark, shadowy images. Some shadows wander through space and materialize only when they collide with an object; that is, they become visible as shadows or as darkness; and if they fail to collide with an object, they are lost in infinite space.[41] In misty or dusty air . . . when the sun penetrates through small holes into dark places, the shadows are partly seen between the rays of the sun even when they do not collide with opaque objects.[42] Leonardo also speaks of "shaded rays" *(razzi ombrosi)* that wander through the atmosphere.[43] He explains the gradual diminution of the intensity of shadows which become brighter the further they are removed from the bodies that cast them by the assumption that the luminous air fills them with light and, so to speak, tints them bright.[44] All these passages suggest that for Leonardo shadows are not only visually perceived phenomena but have a kind of real existence of their own; they take part in the nature of darkness.[45] Leonardo thinks of the relation between light and darkness as a struggle. In one place he describes light as the hunter of darkness; [46] in another he says that obscurity is stronger than light which is unable to subdue the shadows completely.[47] The invisible struggle between light and darkness conforms with Leonardo's general view of nature as an arena of warring powers.[48] Most of these formulations can be interpreted as figures of speech; I believe, however, that they also indicate a deep layer in Leonardo's thought in which mythical elements dimly persist.

A certain Neoplatonic overtone may perhaps be discerned in Leonardo's habit of associating light with the spiritual and darkness with the corporeal. Shadow is explained as being derived "from two dissimilar sources of which one is corporeal and the other spiritual; the body that is shadowed is corporeal and the light is spiritual. Light and body are the cause of shadow." [49] The body that here produces the shadow is, of course, the material object that interrupts the progression of light rays; light is spiritual because it is not embodied in a solidly material object. While the source of this distinction is not a Neoplatonic one, it is likely that such terms, used in late-fifteenth-century Florence, evoked, however vaguely, Neoplatonic associations.

Having discussed Leonardo's views concerning shadows, the typical representative of the *mezzo,* we now turn to his conception of light itself. Here we also find the influences of former periods and a fluctuation between empirical observation and mythical imagery. A medieval influence can be detected in his distinction between *luce* and *lume.* In the same fragment where shadow is described as partaking in the nature of darkness, Leonardo says that "lume è di natura della luce." [50] This distinction could not have arisen from the workshops, and it goes beyond the actual needs of the fifteenth-century painter. In fact, it occurs neither in Cennini nor in Alberti. Needless to say, the difference between *lux* and *lumen* was a common distinction in theological literature of the Middle Ages, and it appears in the teachings of the fifteenth-century Florentine Neoplatonists.[51] These were presumably the sources from which Leonardo derived his distinction between *luce* and *lume* which, indeed, have for him a somewhat similar meaning; as *luce* is the pure, undimmed brightness inherent in the nature of the illuminating body itself, the source of light, *lume* is a light that emanates from this luminous source, of lesser intensity and mixed with shadows. Although Leonardo's terminology is not always consistent, the distinction is clear.[52] Sometimes limited apertures through which light penetrates, such as windows or eyes, are also termed *luce* by Leonardo, [53] perhaps because they impress us as if they were sources of light. Even though *luce* is not understood by him as a mystical radiance, as with medieval theologians and Renaissance Neoplatonists, the very making of the distinction attests to the power of these intellectual traditions and to their impact on Leonardo's thought.

Mythical images become predominant in another context, concerning the sun. In a passionate eulogy to the sun replete with learned allusions, written in 1508, he inserts the outline of a treatise on light that he had planned for more than twenty years. The interpenetration of these two seemingly disparate elements—a religious adulation of the sun and the outlines of a scientific treatise—indicate an important aspect of Leonardo's attitude to light.

> I can never do other than blame those many ancients who said that the sun was no larger than it appears—among these being Epicurus. ... I could wish that I had such power of language as should avail me to censure those who would fain extol the worship of men above that of the sun, for I do not perceive in the whole universe a body greater and more powerful than this, and its light illumines all the celestial bodies which are distributed throughout the universe.
>
> All vital principle descends from it, since the heat there is in living creatures proceeds from this vital principle; and there is no other heat or light in the universe as I shall show in the fourth book, and indeed those who have wished to worship men as gods, such as Jupiter, Saturn, Mars and the like, have made a very great error seeing that even if a man were as large as our earth he would seem like one of the least of the stars, which appear but a speck in the universe; and seeing also that these men are mortal and subject to decay and corruption in their tombs.[54]

This fragment bears the superscription *Lalda del sole,* and it has been justly observed that the word *Lalda,* derived from the liturgical *Lauda,* retains in this new context something of its original exalted connotation.[55] Reading this fragment one perceives, I believe, that in spite of all his meticulous empirical observations Leonardo's attitude to light was imbued both with traditional images and with a high emotional tension. Other light motifs that recall theological symbols and imagery can be found in Leonardo's notes, such as the identification of the sun with the rays that emanate from it, one of the important symbolic images in early Christian and medieval literature.[56] More often, however, Leonardo's descriptions of the sun suggest the attitudes and motifs of ancient pagan culture. "Quality of the sun: The sun has substance, shape, movement, radiance, heat and generative power; and these qualities all emanate from itself without its diminu-tion." [57] The description of these qualities which make of the sun a kind of god recall ancient sun-cult ideas. While the value of these descriptions as testimonies to Leonardo's thought should not be exaggerated, they can also not be altogether overlooked.

Leonardo's conception of light appears in clearer outline when looked at in its larger historical context. On the one hand, he is primarily interested in shadows and in the "intermediary zone," both being the proper sphere of the scientist and the painter; on the other hand, he sometimes alludes to mythical and theological concepts that lie outside the proper province of painting or science. This complexity, besides reflecting Leonardo's personal nature, mirrors a critical turning point in the cultural development of the age.

(4)

Leonardo's intellectual and emotional sources and attitudes, which we have only outlined, constitute an underlying stratum of his conception of light and color. The large mass of his notes on this subject is dedicated to a detailed investigation of the individual categories of light and of specific phenomena of the illumination of color. In the following pages I shall try to show that Leonardo's detailed discussion of light and color reveals an artist's approach and that the themes discussed and the aspects emphasized are in accordance with specific painting problems. It is true that in his descriptions and analyses he often borrowed categories that bore no relation to art, nor had any specifically expressive character, from ancient and medieval works on optics. In his own application of these categories, however, the expressive aspects and the problems arising from the artistic representation of these types of light are in the forefront of the discussion. His transformation of the categories of scientific optics into expressive forms of art is not always obvious at a first glance; the artistic tendencies are often concealed beneath geometric constructions. To understand this transformation, which is an original contribution to the theory of light and often anticipates many of the significant problems of late-sixteenth-century theory of art, we must take into consideration not only the texts which deal explicitly with the subject of light and color but also the miscellaneous observations concerning mirrors, varnishes, rainbows, and so on, which, in their entirety, constitute Leonardo's aesthetic of the chiaroscuro.

The study of light and of optical literature occupied Leonardo throughout his life, but it was intensified in his old age. In the late manuscripts he several times systematically formulated his views on the types of light. In a passage of manuscript B, also quoted in the *Treatise on Painting,* he says:

> The lights that illuminate opaque bodies are of four kinds: that is, universal, such as the air which is within our horizon; specific, as that of the sun, or of a window, or door, or other opening; the third is reflected light; while the fourth is that which passes through translucent matter such as linen, paper, or similar things, but not transparent matter, like glass, or crystal, or objects which produce an effect as if nothing were lying between the shadowed body and the light which illuminates it.[58]

The main characteristic of "universal light" *(lume universale)* is that it streams in from all directions and produces pale, blurred shadows. In nature it occurs on cloudy days. Landscapes, Leonardo says, "should be represented in such a manner that the trees are half illuminated and half in shadows, but it is better to paint them when the sun is covered by clouds, for then the trees are illumined by the universal light of the sky and by the universal shadow of the earth." [59] Here one of the basic elements of *plein air* painting is recognized, namely the dispersion and brightening of the deep shadows. Leonardo is aware of the far-reaching implications of this light for painting. He gives us an interesting insight into the problems arising from the clash between traditional workshop procedures and newly acquired knowledge, based on observation of nature: he criticizes those artists who paint a figure or an object indoors, where the light enters through a window or a door and is necessarily a "specific light," and then places it against a landscape background, "as though it were in the general light of the open air of the country, where the air embraces and illuminates equally all sides of the thing seen. Thus they make dark shadows where there cannot be a shadow, or if there is, it is so light that it cannot be distinguished." [60] As is well known, Leonardo himself frequently applied this type of light in his paintings. The pale, soft, hardly discernible shadows in his works impart to them that peculiar quality which Vasari describes as "lo splendor dell'aria sua." [61]

The source of Leonardo's concept of universal light is more difficult to trace than that of his other types. Whereas the other three categories are common, and are often used in medieval books on optics, a separate category of illumination similar to the *lume universale,* does not seem to have been usual in his scientific sources. On the other hand, we know that the Italian workshop tradition was familiar with "diffuse light" which shows the same characteristics as the *lume universale.* As we remember, "diffuse light" was described by Cennini with surprising accuracy.[62] It might well have been this workshop concept that influenced Leonardo in his notion of the "universal light."

Such an interpretation is perhaps reinforced by the fact that Leonardo recommends "universal light" as eminently suitable for painting, often stressing both its practical value and its expressive quality. A broad (that is, a diffused) and not too intense light in the artist's workshop permits the object that is to be represented to appear "very agreeable." [63] The painter's courtyard, Leonardo says in one of his notes, should be covered with canvas in order to shut out direct light and produce a "soft" distribution of rays. "Or when you want to take a portrait do it in dull weather, or as the evening falls." [64] The expressive qualities are further stressed and combined with practical precepts:

> An object seen in a moderate light displays little difference in the light and shade; and this is the case towards evening or when the day is cloudy, and works then painted are tender and every kind of face becomes graceful. Thus, in everything extremes are to be avoided: too much light gives crudeness; too little prevents our seeing. The medium is best.[65]

The character and quality which universal light imparts to a painting played a significant role in his artistic oeuvre. Since his first landscape drawings he had been occupied with the problem of how to combine and unite the forms of various objects by means of the luminous atmosphere. His later paintings attest, as has often been said, to his repeated attempts to solve this problem in different ways. The brightening of the shadows (especially in the distant parts of the background) as well as the representation of several sources of light within one painting were intended to contribute to the overall distribution of lights and to the brightening of the atmosphere which are the most important characteristics of the *lume universale*. In this luminous atmosphere, as Vasari points out in another connection, the forms hover between the visible and the invisible, imparting to Leonardo's work that specific double character of naturalistic representation and immaterial appearance which Séailles has described as "rêverie intellectuelle." [66]

The category of "universal light," which in painting is intimately related to the half tones and conveys the moods of softness and gracefulness, was the background for Leonardo's conception of the aesthetic meaning of *sfumato,* a subject to which we shall return later in this chapter.

In contradiction to "universal light," "specific light" *(lume particulare)* is concentrated, comes from but one direction, strikes the body directly along the shortest path, and produces intensive lights and deep shadows. This light, which Leonardo also calls "restricted," [67] can have various sources: outdoors it is principally the direct light of the sun unmediated by any intervening bodies; indoors it comes from a single opening (a window, door, or some other aperture in the wall), and it can also emerge from an artificial light, like an open fire. Its essential value resides in the fact that it produces strong effects of relief.[68] This evaluation reveals a painter's attitude. The creation of a convincing illusion of corporeal solidity on the flat surface of a picture occupied, as we know, a central place in the scale of pictorial values accepted by Leonardo and his contemporaries. Specific light capable of producing this excellent value readily becomes an important type of illumination for the painter. This type of light is particularly suited for anatomical observation. Muscles can best be seen in direct light, while the universal light is unsuited to this purpose.[69] When we consider the high esteem generally granted to correct anatomical representation, we find further reason for the importance of specific light.

The instrumental function of "specific light," however, is not its only value; it also has an expressive character that bears little relation to its nature as a medium of visibility. Dramatic effects of illumination are especially related to "specific light," probably because it produces the most vivid contrasts between bright and dark. It is interesting to note that

Leonardo sometimes describes "specific light" in scenes which, apart from their illumination, are inherently dramatic in subject matter.[70]

The clearest indication of the expressive quality of "specific light" is Leonardo's description of it as "crude and without grace" and his admonition to artists against its excessive use.

> That body will cause the greatest contrast between shadows and lights which is exposed to the greatest light, such as the light of the sun, or the light of a fire at night. But this device is to be employed seldom in painting, because such works are crude and without attractiveness. That body which is in a medium light causes little contrast between the lights and the shadows, and this happens at twilight or when it is cloudy. Such works are soft and give grace to every kind of face. As in everything, extremes are faulty; too much light makes for crudeness, while too much darkness does not allow anything to be seen; the median is good.[71]

The few attempts that Leonardo made to combine the "specific" and "universal" lights do not invalidate the different expressive characters of these two categories,[72] nor does the use of "specific light" as a means of emphasizing certain parts of the painting[73] negate its emotional nature.

If we consider all the attitudes to "specific light" set forth in the passages cited above, we cannot fail to perceive certain contradictory tendencies. We started by noting that "specific light" is the most suitable means for depicting the form and bulk of a body, that is, its principal objective characteristics, and we concluded with the observation that this light has an expressive character of its own that enables it to perform a significant function in conveying a certain mood. The expressive character, however, does not follow from the correct representation of nature; direct light will retain its striking, dramatic quality even in scenes which, in themselves, are not dramatic. The question here, I believe, is not one of Leonardo's development. We cannot discern whether one aspect appeared earlier in his thought and another later. "Specific light" always had for him both the function of representation and of expression, although these functions were not defined with equal clarity and might even collide. This tension reflects, I think, an antagonism inherent in a type of painting that attempts to be both art and science. Leonardo's thought, which clearly represents the culmination of the attempt to fuse art and science, also indicates the antagonism inherent in such a fusion.

Leonardo's treatment of the third type of illumination, reflected light, constitutes the most original part of his doctrine. The phenomenon of reflection fascinated him and appears in his notes in various contexts. The "sixth book" of his contemplated work on light and shade would have been devoted to the subject of reflections.[74] The wealth of penetrating observations contained in his preserved manuscripts indicates the great effort he expended in the realization of this intention.

It is at times difficult to determine exactly Leonardo's views on certain aspects of the problem of reflection. In his paintings the representations of reflections have suffered more than other elements of his art, such as drawing or modeling, through darkened varnishes and later overpaintings. His literary remains certainly contain a wealth of observations concerning reflections, but the formulation is not always free of ambiguities. He speaks of reflections in cosmic space; the reflection of the sunlight in the moon and in the stars; of the brilliance of the sun's rays on the ocean; [75] and, above all, of reflections that can be observed in landscapes and in our immediate environment, without clearly differentiating between these different types. In spite of all this, however, the significance which he granted to reflections cannot be disputed.

Leonardo's sources are varied, and for the most part known. "In no area of physics," says Werner in his instructive study *Zur Physik Leonardo da Vinci's,* "is the influence exerted by the ancients on Leonardo and his works seen as clearly as in that of catoptrics, in the reflections of both flat and curved surfaces." [76] We know that he was also acquainted with medieval works on optics. He mentions, indeed, the so-called Alhazen's problem, that is, to find the point of reflection in spherical, cylindrical, and conical mirrors, and in its solution exhibits the same shortcomings as Alhazen himself.[77] Leonardo's acquaintance with such ancient and medieval sources has even led some scholars to assume that he felt no need of propounding a theory of reflections, since he had before him the well-known and generally accepted doctrines of Euclid, Alhazen, and Vitello.[78]

But important as the scientific tradition of optics must have been for Leonardo, it could not have been his only source. Side by side with the great works of optics we must place the living workshop tradition. To be sure, as far as reflections are concerned, the influence of this tradition is particularly difficult to estimate. The paintings of the fifteenth century were, judging from their present condition at least, not rich in the representation of reflections. The earlier art literature does not provide much information either. The two sentences by Alberti, describing the reflection of the sun's rays on the rafters of the roof and the green shadows on a man's face as he walks across a meadow, [79] are an isolated example. One of Leonardo's own notes, however, provides unmistakable evidence that the problem of reflection was a subject of vehement discussion among the painters of his day. The passage reads:

> The reflected lights from the illuminated sides rebound to the shadows opposite, more or less relieving their obscurity, depending on how near or far they are, and how bright. This theory has been put into practice by many, but there are many others who avoid it, and each side laughs at the other.[80]

This isolated but highly instructive passage not only proves that reflection was a much-debated theme, but it also suggests that the painters were aware of the fact that it poses a specific problem in their craft. In the workshops it was certainly not the question of determining the essence and the scientific laws of reflection that led to a violent dispute and to the subsequent formation of two rival camps, but the question of whether and how to represent it. Leonardo's interest in the pictorial aspect of reflection was not an isolated instance.

Leonardo's lines, however, also indicate that the problem was still a new one and that no definite attitude had as yet been formed with respect to it. His numerous precepts for the representation of reflections obviously show that he belonged to that group of artists who "put reflections into practice." Although his observation of reflections was never divorced from scientific considerations, it seems clear that he conceived of them as a specific problem of the painter. In the following remarks we shall deal with reflections mainly from this point of view.

What did reflected light mean to Leonardo, and what did he consider to be its proper scope in painting? His descriptions are sometimes ambiguous in terminology. In one passage, for instance, he says that "lume derivatiuo fia il lume riflesso." [81] We have seen that *lume,* in contradistinction to *luce,* could be termed as "derived light," that is, a light emanating from a source. If we adhere to the above definition, reflected light would lose its specific characteristics and would be identified with emanated light in general. The equivocation may, of course, be explained by the fact that the most obvious characteristic of reflected light is its derivation from the reflecting body; but it may also indicate some analogy between simple emanated light *(lume)* and reflected light, their common feature–their origin–being particularly marked in the latter. Emanated light is dependent on its source, the luminous body *(luce);* reflected light is dependent light par excellence, being dependent not only on the source of light *(luce),* but also on the illumined body which reflects the rays. Reflected light is, therefore, the clearest example of the dependent character of every emanated light. It is perhaps for this reason that Leonardo sometimes uses the same terms in designating these two types of light. The ambiguous designation, however, does not mean that he believed the two types to be identical in their appearance.

Reflected light is one of the most frequent phenomena in visual experience. No shadow, Leonardo says, "is without a reflection which augments or weakens it. . . ." [82] In other places he restricts this far-reaching assertion. In universal light the reflections, with few exceptions, remain invisible; on dark bodies they emerge clearly but on bright bodies they are hardly noticeable.[83] Under "specific" illumination reflections are weaker, since the direct light outshines them.[84] But despite these reservations Leonardo understood reflected light as a universal phenomenon.

A characteristic feature of reflected light, as it appears in ordinary visual experience, is its coloring. Alberti had already recognized, as we have noted, that reflected lights are saturated with the color of the reflected object.[85] In a large number of notes Leonardo discusses colored reflections, stressing time and again that the surface of every opaque body is affected by the color of the surrounding objects.[86] This view, which is encountered in many formulations, is of such general validity that it raises the question of how to determine the "true color" of an object, or even whether the "local color" of an object can be established at all. "Almost never can we say that the surface of the illuminated bodies is of the true color of those bodies." [87] If the painter wishes to represent the "true color" of an object, Leonardo says, he must avoid multicolored reflections by having the environment of the represented object in the same color as the object itself [88] or by having it white or black, since these are not real colors, and their reflections would therefore not alter the color of the object.[89]

Leonardo was aware that such instances can be produced only under artificial conditions. In nature, the multicolored reflections produce a baffling network of relations between the represented figure or object and all the projects, partly or completely invisible, which constitute its environment. This network constantly produces color mixtures; in fact, each reflection is a mingling of colors. "No color that is reflected on the surface of another body will tinge that surface with only its own color, but it will mingle with a concurrence of the other reflected colors which rebound on the same place." [90] Reflections, therefore, often produce hues that exist neither on the body which reflects the rays nor on the body on which the reflected rays fall, but are the result of the blending of the two colors. Thus, for example, we see a green tone where a yellow reflection falls on a blue object.[91] Nor are reflections simply a relation between only two objects. There are double or triple reflected lights.[92] Moreover, they are also influenced by the colored rays that wander about in the atmosphere and slightly tinge the reflected lights with their own color.

All these observations lead Leonardo to far-reaching philosophical and aesthetic conclusions. He is well aware that the tangled web of relations produced by reflections creates an illusion, an optical substitute for the corporeal reality, which exists only in the eye of the beholder. The reflection of a body seen in water can never coincide with the shape of the body itself.[93] Bodies seen at a distance appear other to us than they really are because of the intervening air layers their "images" must traverse before they reach our eye. The reflections that intensify or diminish shadows or alter their color show that this law is also valid for objects not so far removed. There is thus a necessary divergence between the actual body and its "image" as it is perceived by our eyes. What the painter represents, then, is not the object itself but the "image" which is mingled with, and to some extent constituted by, all reflections. It is this problem which lends crucial significance to the concept of the "image" *(simulacro)*. This concept applies to Leonardo's theory of light, and indeed of painting as a whole, but it emerges most clearly in his view on reflected light. The *simulacro* is the crystallization of the specific optical pseudo-reality.[94]

The observation of reflections also has specifically artistic meaning. As reflections create a comprehensive coloristic relationship in nature they are, for the painter who represents nature, necessarily also a means for uniting the colors in his work. It is characteristic of Leonardo that he turns the observation of a natural appearance into an artistic device. It is here that we can perceive the existence of certain divergent tendencies which, although concentrated in the question of representing reflected lights, reach far beyond that natural phenomenon and reveal something of the basic problems of Renaissance art. On the one hand Leonardo adheres to a faithful representation of reflections in nature, conceiving of them only as a phenomenon to be depicted, and without attaching to them any additional value.[95] On the other hand, he points to the aesthetic element of color composition, which is connected with the representation of reflected lights. This aspect is suggested, for instance, by the requirement that the painter arrange the colored objects arbitrarily so that the pattern that results from the reflections may produce a harmonious effect.[96] Reflections here are no longer merely a means of representing nature but have become the bearers of an autonomous aesthetic value. This general problem, which is by no means restricted to the theory of light, is brought out clearly in the theory of reflection.

In conclusion we may thus say that Leonardo's doctrine of reflections contains *in nuce* the concept of impressionism. His notion of the universality of color reflections anticipates the impressionistic doctrine that all things are reflected in one another. In this concept a tendency is implied that is bound to lead to an overturning of the well-established Renaissance views on light as a medium of unhampered visibility and faithful representation of material nature. This, however, was only an implication, which Leonardo himself does not seem to have fully realized.

The fourth type of light, which is produced when light rays penetrate semitransparent matter, was the subject of considerable scientific investigation in the history of optics.[97] In the theory of art it did not play a significant part. Leonardo's observations on this particular phenomenon are meager, and he seems to have devoted little attention to the subject. He defines transparent light as the light that shines through "cloth or paper," but in his notes we find no examples of light penetrating these materials. It is only when we consider the air, which sometimes contains "grossness and moisture" as a half-transparent matter, that this category becomes important. In this case, of course, the fourth type becomes of vital significance in Leonardo's doctrine of light. The atmosphere as a semimaterial medium (i.e., when the air is "dense") causes the contours and colors of distant objects (whose images must travel through the air layers) to appear unclear and their proportions distorted.[98] But Leonardo did not describe the air as "translucent matter," and indeed it does not seem likely that he was referring to the air when he spoke of the fourth category of light, taking it over, apparently, from optical science.

(5)

It has been rightly stressed by art historians that Leonardo did not elaborate a theory of color apart from his theory of light; wherever he treats of light he also treats of color.[99] While the truth of this statement need not be demonstrated, its historical significance and the questions it raised should be briefly discussed. By discussing color together with light, Leonardo went beyond what was known and accepted even in the advanced artistic workshops of his time. His tendency toward a merging of light and color may have been influenced, to a certain extent, by some scientific notions which he inherited from the past, but it follows mainly, I believe, from his own observations of nature, which were largely focused on the painter's task of representing visual reality. In discussing his views on reflection we have already seen that Leonardo in fact reached the conclusion that the proper color of an object can never be seen exactly, as both the reflections from other objects and the colored air that lies between it and the observer's eye obscure the object's color or tinge it with their own hue. Hence the great emphasis he placed on reflections on the one hand and on aerial perspective on the other. Both of these concepts, which are the foci of Leonardo's theory of light and color and probably his most original contributions to the doctrine of painting, are the specific areas where the blending of light and color attains its fullest realization.

This merging of light and color crystallized in Leonardo's thought in several ideas, the most characteristic being the notion of "accidental color." Accidental color is, in a certain respect, the very opposite of what seemed both to the fifteenth-century artists and to the Aristotelian natural science of the period to be the very essence of color. Color, as we know, was regarded by Quattrocento painters and scientists as a constant property of natural objects, inextricably linked to the object's surface. It was often said in this period that light can brighten or darken colors but cannot produce them. This view was also characteristic of the workshops of the century, and the masters working in them believed, as we know, that the painter should not alter colors under the impact of illumination.[100] Needless to say, Leonardo was deeply immersed in the workshop tradition. Some of his technical precepts for the production of colors and for the blending of pigments are very similar to those enunciated by Cennini, [101] attesting both to the fact that these precepts had persisted in oral workshop instruction throughout the whole period of the Renaissance and to the fact that Leonardo had drawn from this living tradition. When, however, Leonardo deals with the visual appearance of colors in nature, he oversteps the limits of workshop thought and goes beyond the generally accepted scientific views of the time. He recognizes the existence of "accidental colors," that is, of temporary coloristic appearances which are not linked with the material nature of the object on whose surface they are observed.

It is instructive to consider carefully the notes in which he uses this concept. Two of these brief comments read:

> The accidental colors of the leaves of trees are four, namely shadow, light, luster, and transparency.

> The accidental parts of the leaves of plants will at a great distance become a mixture, in which the accidental color of the largest part will predominate.[102]

These passages are characteristic for Leonardo's thought in more than one respect. It should first be noted that here he is concerned with the painter's work, and intends to establish what the painter observes and what he should represent when painting a landscape. In speaking of "accidental colors," then, he has the painter in mind.

Not less important are the specific elements which constitute the "accidental color." All four characteristics or elements mentioned by Leonardo ("shadow, light, luster, and transparency") do not belong to the traditional realm of colors, as the fifteenth century understood it. Rather they are either light itself, or the results of illumination (shadow, luster), or a quality of the air in which the objects are actually seen (transparency). "Accidental color" is thus neither a "true" nor a constant property of a body, but it is the sum of modifications of such "true colors" when seen in different conditions of illumination and atmosphere. It is this type of color which we actually perceive in nature and which, subsequently, the painter should represent in his work. In this concept, therefore, the "impressionistic" tendency in Leonardo's theory becomes clearly visible.

This tendency, although of major significance, does not exhaust the whole of Leonardo's views on colors. Side by side with the "impressionistic" views, the notion of "true colors" is easily discerned in his notes. He believes, of course, that "among colors of the same quality, the second will never be of the same color as the first" because of "the multiplication of the color of the medium interposed between the object and the eye;" but he equally believes that the nearer the object (i.e. the less of the interposed medium of the colored air) the more it will display its "real color." [103] He further stresses that colors become indistinguishable in darkness, but in the light "they keep their essence unchanged." [104] This is also shown by way of example. "Of bodies clad in light and shade," Leonardo says, "it is the illuminated part which reveals the true color." [105] The painter is required to show "the true quality of colors in the parts which are in light." [106] He even expressly distinguishes between the natural and accidental colors, [107] granting equal reality to both of them.

Considering these quotations, one cannot doubt that Leonardo, in spite of certain impressionistic tendencies which by their nature tend to eliminate plain "local" colors, assumed the existence and even perceptibility of "true" colors. Contrary to attempts to transform Leonardo into a modern scientist, I think it should be emphasized that he did not conceive of color as a purely optical phenomenon, as the reaction of the eye to certain stimuli from the outside world; rather, he believed that natural objects have their own inherent color. The actual conditions of visual experience only distort their appearance and usually render them inaccessible to the eye.

Besides the more philosophical question of the existence of "true colors" in nature, pure colors also raise another purely artistic problem for Leonardo. It is the problem of the coloristic beauty of the picture. Leonardo sometimes conceives of such a beauty in terms of pure colors. Isolated pure colors are not held in high esteem; they are not the merit of the painter but of him who manufactures them.[108] But the proper arrangement of several pure colors is an artistic achievement and enhances the beauty of the picture. Leonardo suggests two principles for the arrangement of pure colors. One is that of contrast. Colors look most vivid when set against contrasting colors.[109] The few passages in which he puts forward this principle perhaps betray the influence of Alberti in suggesting a carpetlike arrangement of colors. The other means of enhancing the vividness and beauty of colors is their arrangement according to the principle of complementarity. Of course, Leonardo does not know this term, but, led by experience, he finds a complementary combination of colors to be the most satisfactory. He seems to have perceived a law behind these experiences and speaks of the "harmony" of these arrangements. "Colors which go together harmoniously are green with red or purple or violet, and yellow with blue." [110]

In these arrangements, both according to contrast and to "harmony," it is, I think, obvious that Leonardo had pure colors in mind, that is to say, colors which are unaffected, or only slightly affected, by the conditions of illumination. The concept of the beauty of pure colors stands in marked contrast to the principle of tonal unity and *sfumato* which prevail in Leonardo's theory. Vaguely reminiscent of certain medieval concepts, it is a residue of the past which does not merge organically with his main tendencies and views.

The assumption both of pure color as a natural property of objects and as an aesthetic element in painting is interesting for the understanding of Leonardo's historical position rather than for his own contribution to the problems of light and color in painting. They remind us that we should not expect a consistent doctrine of color and light from a Renaissance artist and theoretician of art, even if he was Leonardo.

(6)

Apart from the more comprehensive types of illumination Leonardo was also interested in more limited phenomena. One of these themes, of great significance for the development of the concepts of painting, is that of luster *(lustro)*.

Before attempting to analyze this problem, a certain distinction, which is often overlooked, should be made between brilliance and luster. In the sense used in this study, brilliance is a quality of materials which may also be used in painting. When medieval artists covered certain areas in their paintings with radiant materials like gold, or when Renaissance painters covered their works with varnish, they intended to impart to their pictures the quality of brilliance by making proper use of natural materials. Usually, however, brilliance of this type is not part of the object represented, and has no representative, mimetic function.[111] Luster, on the other hand, is a rather limited phenomenon which is perceived in nature itself and which can be represented in the same way as everything else contained in our visual experience. Luster is a dazzling bright point (or a very small area) seen on objects or a certain texture and under certain conditions of illumination. Luster is thus a subject of representation, but it is not a material quality of the painting itself. The following remarks deal with luster in this limited sense.

Leonardo's notes contain only a few observations on luster. The significance of these observations lies in the fact that they show us how deeply he was influenced by specific pictorial problems when studying light and color. In his description of *lustro* he stresses its difference from light. This difference comprises, I think, three essential points: (1) For the scientific study of optics, luster is nothing else than a specific instance of the reflection of light rays; for Leonardo, and for the painter in general, however, it is basically different from reflected light (the third type of illumination), a difference which is not explainable by additional scientific considerations but which constitutes a further sensual quality of the object of visual experience. We have noted that for Leonardo reflected light is always saturated with the color of the reflecting body. He regards luster, however, as colorless; it is a "saturation of white," and since white is no color, luster is impervious to all colors.[112] (2) Contrary to reflection in general, luster appears only when the object is of a certain texture; that is, it becomes visible only on objects with a smooth surface, while objects with a rough surface never show luster.[113] This Leonardo believes to be true also of cosmic bodies–the luster of the moon is rendered possible because of its smooth surface. (3) The position of luster on an object bears no necessary relation to the structure of the object and need not occupy the center or any other given area "but moves as and where the eye moves in looking at it." [114] Contrary to the four basic types of light in which the point of view of the beholder is of no major significance, luster is dependent on the accidental position of the beholder.

The foregoing chapter contained a brief sketch of the history of *lustro* in art and thought.[115] Seen against this background, Leonardo's description of *lustro* seems to be the first literary formulation of this phenomenon, as seen from the painter's point of view, and the first analysis of its characteristic features.

When we consider Leonardo's brief observations on luster in the context of his general theory of light, we discover certain tendencies which partly contradict and partly complement one another. On the one hand luster, although in a limited sense, performs the function of a medium, since it tells us something about the material quality and the texture of the represented bodies. The presence of luster indicates a smooth, and its absence a rough, texture of the represented bodies. But this function may conflict with the functions of the other main types of illumination, which are to reveal to the eye the structure and volume of those bodies. When the *lustri* break through the tonal continuum of light and shade they tend to create a scale of textures, extending from the dazzling precious stones to the pale woolen materials, and to introduce a new dimension of nature; but they also tend to conceal the structure and volume of the bodies. The representation of luster, although based on the objective reality of texture, denotes the painter's inclination to pay greater attention to immediate visual experience. We have seen that Leonardo was aware of the fact that the unstable, "accidental" character of *lustro* and its dependence on the position of the observer makes it a quality of the immediate visual experience not less than an element of the object itself. In this sense we can perhaps understand Leonardo's dictum: "Illumination is the participation in light, luster is the reflection of light." [116]

(7)

It has often been said that Leonardo placed art in the service of science and that his pictorial and graphic representations were also meant to be scientific statements. While this is undoubtedly true, in the study of his conception of light the opposite tendency also emerges, reaching its high point in the concept of *sfumato*.

Sfumato, as we know, is a technical workshop expression, used in the sixteenth and seventeenth centuries in Italy as well as in other European countries. The word conjures up the image of a "veil of smoke" and was used to designate the fine gradations and transitions of tones and shadows.[117] The concept of *sfumato* seems to have been known in Italian Renaissance workshops, even though only vaguely and in a more limited application, long before the time of Leonardo. Cennini speaks of "shadows well blended, just like smoke." [118] His precept is restricted to shading in only one color and is not elaborated in detail, but it nevertheless shows that the concept of *sfumato* as an ideal for the representation of soft transitions was known in the workshop several generations before Leonardo. The art theory of the fifteenth century hardly alludes to it; and considering the artistic tendencies of this period, governed by an "idealism of the line," this is hardly surprising. This does, of course, not exclude the possibility that the concept persisted in the practical, oral teachings of the workshops. *Sfumato* was, however, not recognized as a comprehensive principle of painting until Leonardo.

Leonardo did not clearly define the meaning of *sfumato.* In the course of recent discussions in connection with the restoration of Renaissance paintings, some writers have gone so far as to question altogether the use of *sfumato* as a principle in Leonardo's paintings. Several aspects have been distinguished in the concept of *sfumato,* the more important being: (1) the soft transitions of light and shadow within *one* object; (2) soft contours and blurred outlines between different objects, as, for instance, between a figure and its background; (3) indistinctness as a result of distance. *Sfumato* was taken by restorers to apply only to the first category.[119] As can be seen from Leonardo's notes, and from the views of certain authors in the sixteenth and seventeenth centuries who were influenced by Leonardo, the general function of *sfumato* was to unify the painting as a whole by overcoming the tension between the local colors and thereby diminishing the significance of contour.

Leonardo's few notes, which hint at rather than formulate his concept of *sfumato,* show that it is intimately connected both with his observations of nature and with his belief in certain aesthetic values. It is impossible to isolate the principle of *sfumato* from his observation of nature, especially of distant objects and of views seen in mist and fog. What we call Leonardo's concept of *sfumato,* is, to a large extent, the transformation of these observations into a principle of style. In nature the air performs a function similar to that of the imaginary smoke screen in painting. The blurring of distinct colors and sharp contours, which are essential properties of *sfumato* as a stylistic principle, is perceived when looking at distant objects. It is, indeed, in connection with the representation of distant objects that Leonardo says: ". . . do not fail therefore to paint so that a smoky contour can be seen, rather than contours and profiles that are sharp and hard. Hence it is to be concluded that the work to which the eye of the observer can approach closely should be finished with extreme diligence in all its parts, and moreover, those in the foreground should be defined against the background with clear, sharp contours, and those that are more distant should be well finished but with more smoky edges, that is, edges that are more indistinct, or if you wish, less clear." [120] Here the "smoky edges" are clearly derived from observations of nature.

Leonardo, however, uses the image of smoke to describe a certain quality of the painter's work itself, without referring to an observation of nature. He advises the painter to look at the outlines of his picture, "which way they tend; and which part of the lines is curved to one side or to another, and where they are more or less conspicuous and consequently broad or fine; and, finally, that your light and shade blend without strokes and borders [but] looking like smoke [*a uso di fumo*]." [121] It is evident that here the "smoky contour" is a purely artistic device, detached from the observation of nature. This was indeed the meaning *sfumato* acquired in the following period. Filippo Baldinucci, for example, defines *sfumare* as "unire i colori;" [122] and a French writer of the seventeenth century, Dupuy de Grèz, says that "Les teints se doivent perdre, se noyer insensiblement les unes dans les autres. . . . Les Italiens appellent cela 'sfumato.' " [123]

As I have said, the concept of *sfumato* was not developed by Leonardo in detail. The few notes that mention this principle do not discuss its stylistic functions, but these, I believe, can be inferred. The smoke screen promotes the unification of the picture by diminishing the force of the isolated colors. Just as the colors of distant objects, seen through many layers of air, will be less distinct and powerful, so will the colors of all objects be if seen through the screen of smoke. In this respect Leonardo's views are clearly opposed to those of Alberti, and his conception signifies a new era in painting as well as in the theory of art. In the sixteenth century the stylistic meaning of *sfumato* was developed mainly in Venice.

Another result of the application of *sfumato* as a general principle in the painter's work is the—at least partial—replacing of sharp contours by soft transitions. The comparison with the "aerial perspective" again provides many parallels which constitute a kind of commentary to the meaning of *sfumato*. [124]

As a workshop device, *sfumato* is of a practical character without any pronounced expressive quality. Nevertheless, a certain unformulated expressive tendency would seem to be inherent in it. It is true that such a tendency can only be conjectured and that Leonardo did not state it. Considering, however, the results necessarily following from an imaginary "screen of smoke," this tendency can be inferred. Inherent in *sfumato* there would seem to be the propensity to impart to the picture a soft quality, expressing, or at least favoring the expression of, a "soft" mood rather than a "hard" one. As we have seen, Leonardo used the term "smoky contour" in contradiction to "sharp and clear," thereby suggesting the affinity of vagueness and softness. Such synesthetic comparisons are, of course, of a very general nature, but nevertheless they indicate a certain inclination. Sixteenth-century authors, who reflect the opinions held in the period, stress softness and sweetness as general characteristics of Leonardo's work. They do not expressly relate these qualities in his work to his use of *sfumato,* but this characterization agrees with what seems to be the general stylistic effect of a "smoke screen." Their description may, therefore, be taken as an additional indication that *sfumato,* as conceived and practiced by Leonardo, had indeed a predisposition to evoke a certain mood.

Notes

1. Vasari, *Le vite,* ed. Milanesi, IV, p. 92 (at the beginning of the *Vita* of Giorgione). For the problem of light and color in Leonardo's artistic work, cf. John Shearman, "Leonardo's Color and Chiaroscuro," *Zeitschrift für Kunstgeschichte,* XXV (1962), 13-47, esp. p. 26 for light in the two versions of the *Virgin of the Rocks.*

2. J. P. Richter, *The Literary Works of Leonardo da Vinci* (Oxford, 1939) (henceforth quoted as Richter), pp. 857-918. In quoting Richter I shall refer to the numbering of fragments, not pages. Particularly important for light are fragments 868-870 (air and perspective); 879-880 (praise of the Sun); 885 (brilliance of the Sun); 892-902 (light of the Moon); 911-912 (light of the stars). For Leonardo's views of the stars cf. P. Duhem, *Etudes sur Leonardo de Vinci: Ceux qu'il a lus et ceux qui l'ont lu,* 2d ed. (Paris, 1955), II, pp. 255-269, and I, pp. 42 ff. However, Duhem does not discuss Leonardo's views of the stars in connection with the problem of light. From the vast literature on Leonardo I shall quote only a few studies which deal to some degree directly with the problem of light and color.

3. This has been noticed by A. Chastel, *Art et humanisme à Florence au temps de Laurent le Magnifique* (Paris, 1959), pp. 413 ff. While no conclusion can be reached on the basis of "tone" or mood of the discussion, these should not be altogether disregarded. For a discussion of Leonardo's literary style see L. Olschki, *Die Literatur der Technik und der angewandten Wissenschaften vom Mittelalter bis zur Renaissance,* I (Heidelberg, 1919), pp. 345 ff., esp. pp. 378 ff.

4. Codice Atlantico, 207r. See E. Solmi, *Leonardo da Vinci: Frammenti letterari e filosofici* (Florence, 1908), p. 91.

5. Cod. Atl., 203r. See Fumagalli, *Leonardo: Omo senza lettere* (Florence, 1943) (henceforth referred to as Fumagalli), p. 72. Here Leonardo's source, which he translates literally, is John Peckham's *Perspectiva communis,* as has been well known for a long time. See recently L. H. Heydenreich, *Leonardo da Vinci* (1954), p. 113; cf. V. P. Zubov, *Leonardo da Vinci* (Cambridge, Mass., 1968), p. 43.

6. "O potente e gia animato strumento dell'artificiosa natura," Richter, 1217. For Leonardo's concept of "creative nature" see Chastel, *Art et humanisme,* pp. 414 ff.

7. Leonardo da Vinci, *Treatise on Painting,* trans. and annotated by A. Philip McMahon (Princeton, 1956) (henceforth referred to as McMahon), p. 434. In the German edition of Leonardo's *Buch von der Malerei (Quellenschriften für Kunstgeschichte,* XV-XVII, [Vienna, 1882], ed. H. Ludwig (henceforth referred to as Ludwig), 412. In quoting the editions of McMahon and Ludwig I shall always refer to the number of the fragment, not of the page.

8. Richter, 155, 157. See also E. MacCurdy, *The Notebooks of Leonardo da Vinci* (New York, n.d.) (henceforth quoted as MacCurdy), I, p. 265.

9. See, e.g., McMahon, 135-138; Ludwig, 120, 87, 93, 155.

10. Richter, 486. This is a rhetorical question. Since it is obvious that Leonardo preferred drawing after nature to drawing after the classical models, the superiority of light and shadow over outline is implied or is supposed as self-evident. See also McMahon, 107; Ludwig, 124. As is well known, however, Leonardo sometimes considered outline superior to light and shadow. See, e.g., McMahon, 106; Ludwig, 121. For the general image which the fifteenth century formed of classical style, it is interesting that classical art is coupled with outline and opposed to a style based on light and shadow.

11. McMahon, 840; Ludwig, 671.

12. McMahon, 430; Ludwig, 403.

13. "The outlines and form of any part of bodies in shadow are hard to recognize, but the parts of those bodies placed between the lights and shadows have the greatest degree of clarity" (McMahon, 445; Ludwig, 488). The frequent comparisons of Renaissance writers of a style of painting based on outline and one based on light and color deserve closer examination than they have received. For some observations on the significance of outline is early Italian theory of art, see J. von Schlosser, "Lorenzo Ghibertis Denkwürdigkeiten: Prolegomena zu einer künftigen Ausgabe," *Jahrbuch der K. und K. Zentralkommission für die Kunst- und Denkmalpflege* (Vienna, 1910), pp. 135 ff.

14. McMahon, 435; Ludwig, 413. For the transformation of this and similar observations into a principle of style see the last section of this chapter.

15. Verrocchio's versatility is stressed by Vasari, *Le vite,* III, pp. 357 ff. As Vasari says, Verrocchio studied the sciences in his youth, particularly geometry; besides being a sculptor, painter, and musician (the last occupation probably having a

broad, though perhaps vague, cultural meaning), he was also a *prospettivo,* which means both a master in perspective representation and in perspective (optical) science. On Verrocchio's technical activities cf. Heydenreich, op. cit., pp. 115 ff. The extensive discussion of Verrocchio in J. Thiis, *Leonardo da Vinci: The Florentine years of Leonardo and Verrocchio* (London, n.d.; ca. 1900), passim, esp. pp. 43 ff., 89, is limited to the artistic work. Similarly also W. R. Valentiner, "Leonardo as Verrocchio's Co-Worker," *Art Bulletin,* XII (1930), 43 ff. On the scientific aspects see O. Werner, *Zur Physik Leonardo da Vincis* (Erlangen, 1910), pp. 6 ff., who unfortunately gives no sources. See also the brief remark by Olschki, *Literatur der Technik,* I, pp. 270, and the observation of Chastel, *Art et humanisme,* p. 190, on the cultural atmosphere in Verrocchio's workshop.

16. Richter, 10 (I, p. 116); Fumagalli, p. 38. In the same fragment Leonardo discusses an ancient author, Demetrius. As far as I know, the identity of this Demetrius has not been established; it is, however, obvious that Leonardo refers here to a classical author. For an evaluation of Leonardo's statement, cf. A. Chastel, "Leonardo et la culture," *Léonard de Vinci et l'experience scientifique au seizième siècle (Colloques internationaux du Centre National de la Recherche Scientifique)* (Paris, 1953), pp. 251-263. (This book will henceforth be referred to as *Colloques.)* See also E. Panofsky, "Artist, Scientist, Genius: Notes on the Renaissance-*Dämmerung,"* *The Renaissance* (New York and Evanston, 1962), p. 139.

17. Vasari, *Le vite,* IV, p. 35, says that Leonardo was "among the first who began to illustrate the things of medicine with the doctrine of Galen, and to give true light to anatomy." Leonardo's studies of Galen have often been discussed. Cf. K. D. Keele, *Leonardo da Vinci on the Movement of the Heart and the Blood* (London, 1952), pp. 52-56, 124-125; G. Sarton, "Léonard de Vinci, ingenieur et savant," *Colloques,* pp. 11-22. It is doubtful whether Vasari's statement, according to which Marcantonio della Torre, a student of Galen, found "marvellous aid in the brain, work, and hand of Leonardo," is correct. Cf. Zubov, *Leonardo da Vinci,* pp. 34, 187. On Leonardo's study of Archimedes, cf. M. Johnson, "Pourquoi Léonard de Vinci cherchait-il les manuscripts scientifiques d'Archimède et comment les trouva-t-il?," *Colloques,* pp. 23-29. See also Panofsky, "Artist, Scientist, Genius," p. 139. For Leonardo's study of Archimedes, cf. also Zubov, *Leonardo,* p. 44 (with a collection of Leonardo's texts mentioning Archimedes) and p. 175.

18. The fundamental discussion of Leonardo's erudition, mainly in the sciences, remains the three volumes of P. Duhem, *Etudes sur Léonard de Vinci.* This work has often been criticized (e.g., E. Garin, "La cultura fiorentina nel età di Leonardo," *Belfagor* (1952), pp. 272-289, reprinted in the author's *Medioevo e Rinascimento;* R.

Klibansky, "Copernic et Nicolas de Cues," *Colloques,* p. 227); and many details should certainly be corrected. See also Werner, *Zur Physik Leonardos, passim;* Olschki, *Literatur der Technik,* pp. 280 ff.; G. de Santillana, "Léonard et ceux qu'il n'a pas lus," *Colloques,* pp. 43-59. For Leonardo's knowledge of optics cf., besides Werner's book, the brief studies of V. Ronchi, "L'optique de Léonard de Vinci," *Colloques,* pp. 115-120, and "Leonardo e l'ottica," *Leonardo: Saggi e ricerche,* ed. A. Marazza (n.d.), pp. 161-185; Zubov, pp. 131, 143 ff.

19. Cf. Vasari, *Le vite,* IV, p. 18. And see also W. von Seidlitz, *Leonardo da Vinci: Der Wendepunkt der Renaissance* (Berlin, 1909), p. 8, and *Colloques,* p. 44. Leonardo mentions Bendetto dell'Abbaco in his notes (cf. Richter, 1439).

20. Leonardo mentions Toscanelli only once—cf. Richter, 1439 ("maestro Pagolo medico," in the form in which he appears in contemporary Florentine documents). Curiously, Richter says (II, p. 107) that Leonardo does not mention him. In modern scholarship there has been considerable fluctuation in the evaluation of Toscanelli's influence. G. Séailles, *Léonard de Vinci: L'artiste et le savant* (Paris, 1919), believes that Toscanelli's influence can be assumed with certainty; Müller Walde, *Leonardo da Vinci* (Munich, 1889), p. 28, speaks of Leonardo's friendship with Toscanelli; and so does E. Solmi, *Leonardo da Vinci* (1908), pp. 15 ff. Heydenreich and Kenneth Clark do not mention him at all. C. Pedretti, *Studi Vinciani* (Geneva, 1957), pp. 118 ff., does not speak of "friendship" but discusses in detail the framework of Toscanelli's possible influence on Leonardo.

21. Peckham's treatise, revised by Fazio Cardano, appeared in Milan under the title *Prospectiva communis,* with no date. An unknown hand appears to have written in the book: "Milano 1496" (cf. Werner, p. 28), which would be the time when Leonardo lived in Milan. Leonardo writes: "Get Messer Fazio to show you the book on proportion," Richter, 304. See also Richter, 1448. E. Solmi, *Le fonti dei manoscritti di Leonardo da Vinci* (Turin, 1908), p. 252, thinks of the treatise on proportions by the Arab mathematician Alkindi, which was known as *Libellum sex quantitatum;* but Zubov, *Leonardo da Vinci,* pp. 16 ff., believes that Leonardo here refers to John Peckham's *Prospectiva.* Richter believes (I, p. 37) that one finds several similarities to Peckham's *prospectiva communis* in Leonardo's notes, besides the texts referred to in our notes 5 and 27. See also Duhem, I, pp. 227 f.; II, p. 445.

22. Cf. R. Bayer, *Léonard de Vinci: La grace* (Paris, 1933), pp. 135 f.

23. *Di hymni et epigrammata Marulli* appeared in 1497 in Florence, but was written between 1489 and 1494. The sun is acclaimed by Marullo as "sol pater." The preciosity of Marullo's language excited the derision of scoffers (cf. Olschki, *Literatur der Technik,* II, p. 164). For Leonardo's mention of Marullo, cf. Richter,

880; MacCurdy, I, p. 296. On Marullo, see A. Perosa, "Studi sulla formazione di raccolte di poesie del Marullo," *Rinascimento*, I (1950), 125-156, and Bayer, *Léonard de Vinci: La grace*, p. 418.

24. See, e.g. d'Adda, *Leonardo· da Vinci e la sua libreria* (Milan, 1873). That Leonardo used public libraries is attested by a fragment (Richter, 1448) which reads: "Try to get Vitelone which is in the library of Pavia and which treats of Mathematics." The library of Pavia was one of the famous libraries in Renaissance Italy.

25. Werner, *Zur Physik Leonardos*, pp. 22 ff., has collected the authors of optical treatises whose names are mentioned in Leonardo's notes.

26. Werner, pp. 29, 89 ff., 139 ff., has discussed Leonardo's familiarity with Alhazen's work in detail. See also C. Pedretti, *Studi Vinciani*, p. 75 (and p. 274 for bibliographical reference) on Leonardo's attempt to solve the so-called problem of Alhazen. Of Alhazen's extensive work on optics Leonardo could have known either the Latin translation by Gherardo of Cremona (d. 1187), which he mentions in Cod. Atl., 260 r, or perhaps an Italian translation.

27. Cod. Atl, 207 r. Cf. Solmi, *Le fonti*, p. 226; cf. above, note 5.

28. McMahon, 842; Ludwig, 672.

29. MacCurdy, i, p. 257. See also, in another context, Richter, 566: the sunlight that strikes a woman's white dress in the open air "dazzles the eyes like the sun itself." In medieval and Renaissance metaphysics of light it has often been said that the "true light" is too glaring for our sight and cannot be endured by our eye.

30. Vasari was probably the first author who noticed that this was a characteristic feature of Leonardo's style. Summing up Leonardo's merits as a painter he says: "Nel arte della pittura aggiunse costui alla maniera ad olio una certa oscurità, donde hanno dato i moderni gran forza e rilievo alle lono figure" *(La vite,* IV, p. 50). The same view has been repeated in numerous variations in modern literature. Cf., e.g., W. von Seidlitz, *Leonardo da Vinci: Der Wendepunkt der Renaissance,* I (Berlin, 1909), pp. 68 ff.; Kenneth Clark, *Leonardo da Vinci* (Cambridge, 1939), pp. 113 ff., stressing that Leonardo's use of light and shade "led away from the other styles of the world"; Heydenreich, *Leonardo da Vinci,* pp. 29, 35 (general observations on Leonardo's chiaroscuro). John Shearman, "Leonardo's Color and Chiaroscuro," esp. pp. 23 ff., studies Leonardo's development in this respect.

31. In the extensive literature on Leonardo, his concepts of light in painting and in scientific observations are usually discussed separately. There seems to be no

detailed study of the mutual influence of art and science in the particular realm of light that would also trace Leonardo's development from this point of view. The valuable study by Shearman, "Leonardo's Color and Chiaroscuro," discusses Leonardo's artistic work, and uses his notes only so far as they help to understand his paintings. The following remarks are, of course, not meant to be such a study. This chapter is based mainly on those of Leonardo's notes that have an immediate bearing on the problems of the painter and disregard the more purely scientific observations. For a clear and useful summary of the parts on light and color in Leonardo's *Treatise on painting,* cf. W. von Seidlitz, *Leonardo da Vinci: Der Wendepunkt der Renaissance,* I (Berlin, 1909). See the study by H. Rzepinska, "Light and Shadow in the Late Writings of Leonardo da Vinci," *Raccolta Vinciana,* XIX (1962), 259-266.

32. McMahon, 578; Ludwig, 558. Cf. Zubov, *Leonardo da Vinci,* p. 138.

33. Richter, 548. This practice is often recorded in Renaissance theory of art. Cf. Cennini, chap. 93 (p. 59); Lomazzo, *Trattato,* xi, pp. 109 ff.; Armenini, *De veri precetti,* p. 108.

34. McMahon, 593; Ludwig, 558.

35. McMahon, 575; Ludwig, 545. The Italian text reads: "L'ombra nominata per il proprio suo uocabulo e da esser chiamata alleuazzione di lume applicato alle superficie de corpi della il suoa principio e nel fine della luce et il suo fine e nelle tenebre." In the translation of this passage I have not followed McMahon.

36. Richter, 122. Here Leonardo says *lucie* instead of *lume.* Some of Leonardo's translators do not seem to have clarified the distinction between *luce* and *lume.* Where Leonardo, for instance, says *lume è di natura della luce,* McMahon (577) formulates "illumination is of the nature of light," although this otherwise excellent translation always renders *lume* as "light."

37. To mention only several passages, cf. McMahon, 578, 575, 577, 604; Ludwig, 665, 545, 549, 660; cf. also Richter, III, 120, 128. Also see Zubov, pp. 138 ff.

38. We list here only the most important terms: *ombre originali* (Richter, 111); *ombre derivative* (111, 152, 158 ff.); *razzi ombrosi* (111); *ombra primitiva* (123, 152); *ombra semplice* (124); *ombra congivnta* (125); *ombra separata* (125); *ombra fatta da'corpi* (138); *semplice ombra derivativa* (161). Cf. A. Agostini, *Le prospettive e le ombre nelle opere di Leonardo da Vinci* (n.d.), who unfortunately fails to give sources.

39. Richter, 111. "E per questo jo propongo nella prima propositione dell'ombre, dico in questa forma come ogni corpo fia circumdato e superfitialmente vestito d'ombre et di lumi. . . ."

40. Richter, 63; Fumagalli, p. 74. "Ogni corpo ombroso empie la circumstante aria d'infinite sue similitudine. . . ."

41. McMahon, 595; Ludwig, 616.

42. McMahon, 596; Ludwig, 597.

43. Richter, 111.

44. Richter, 176.

45. Richter, 119; McMahon, 577; Ludwig, 549. In this respect Leonardo's terminology is not always consistent. Darkness *(tenebre)* is sometimes called *priuation di luce* (Richter, 123), while shadow is only the "diminution of light," the difference being only one of size and proportion. In another fragment, however, shadow is defined as *priuation di luce,* but nevertheless it is distinguished from darkness (Richter, 128).

46. Richter, 128.

47. McMahon, 577; Ludwig, 549. "Shadow is of greater power than light, for it prohibits light of which it entirely deprives bodies, and light cannot dispel all shadow from dense bodies." The so-called Hand B has added to the original heading of this paragraph "what are shadow and light?" the phrase "and which is of greater power." See McMahon, p. 209.

48. He also sees *bellezze* in active conflict with *brutezze.* See McMahon, 277; Ludwig, 139. See also Chastel, *Art et humanisme,* pp. 426, 435.

49. McMahon, 579; Ludwig, 547. The term "spirituality" does not necessarily have metaphysical connotations, as light had in medieval theology. Leonardo's defini ion of power as a "spiritual and materially invisible . . . force" (MacCurdy, I, pp. 233 ff.) shows this clearly. (For Leonardo's concept of the spirituality of force see Fumagalli, p. 58, note 3, and more generally Olschki, *Literatur der Technik,* I, pp. 293, 348 ff., 353). In Florentine Neoplatonism, however, the relation between spirituality and light, on the one hand, and between matter and darkness, on the other, certainly carried a metaphysical meaning. For a brief summary, see N. Robb, *Neoplatonism of the Italian Renaissance* (London, 1935), pp. 65 ff.

50. McMahon, 577; Ludwig, 549.

51. The distinction between *lux* and *lumen,* of course, goes together with the view that the latter is derived from, and is a reflection of, the former. For the Middle Ages cf. Baeumker's work (see note 1 of the previous chapter), passim, and B. de Bruyne, *Etudes d'esthétique médiévale* (Brugge, 1946), III, p. 26. For the Renaissance period cf. A. Chastel, *Marsile Ficin et l'art* (1954), pp. 103 f. For one

characteristic Renaissance example cf. Ficino, *Convivium,* 11, 5, where the emitted ray of the sun is called *lumen,* while the light inherent in the sun is termed *lux.* Such examples can easily be multiplied.

52. In addition to the text quoted above, note 35, one should also consider the long passage which Leonardo probably intended to use as an introduction to his discussion of light (Richter, 111). Here shadow is an obstruction of *luce* and would thus seem to include what in ordinary visual experience appears as light, a view consistent with Leonardo's general concepts. And cf. also Richter, 121, where shadow is a diminution of *lucie* and (absolute) *tenebre.* I should stress again that the distinction between *luce* and *lume* in Leonardo's theory is not based only on his use of terms (which is never consistent) but on some of his ideas.

53. On eyeopenings as *luce,* see MacCurdy, I, p. 259. Windows are sometimes (Richter, 117) considered as having similar qualities to sources of light.

54. Fumagalli, pp. 68 f; MacCurdy, I, pp. 259 f.

55. Bayer, *Leonardo da Vinci; La Grace,* p. 133.

56. An identity of the sun and its rays is implied in several notes of Leonardo. See, for example, MacCurdy, I, p. 304. And cf. also Richter, 885, where Leonardo tries to prove that the heat inherent in the solar rays is the heat of the sun itself. The identity of the whole sun and the single solar rays was, of course, regarded as one of the most powerful symbols of the incarnation of the Logos. See, for instance, Tertullian, who says: "When a ray is projected from the sun it is a portion of the whole sun ... the substance of the sun is not separated but extended, as light is kindled from light. . . . So from spirit comes spirit . . ." (*Apologeticum,* XXI, 12-13). Needless to say, in the late fifteenth century one did not have to take such phrases directly from their original formulations, since they were widely known.

57. Fumagalli, pp. 68 f.; MacCurdy, I, p. 292.

58. Richter, 118. Cf. also McMahon, 598; Ludwig, 663.

59. McMahon, 139; Ludwig, 91. The idea that trees should be represented half illumined and half in shadow recalls similar advice given by Alberti for the representation of figures.

60. McMahon, 142; Ludwig, 94. Cf. also McMahon, 50, 682, 684, 836; Ludwig, 42, 681, 682, 661, where the relation of the universal light to landscape painting is stressed. On the peculiar, bright shadows caused by the universal light, he says: "When the light falls from in front of faces placed between dark side walls, this gives the faces great relief, especially when this light is also above the face. This relief occurs because the nearer side of the face is illumined by the general light of

the air before it, so that this side in the light has shadows that are almost imperceptible." McMahon, 138; Ludwig, 155. See also McMahon, 861; Ludwig, 812.

61. *Le vite,* iv, p. 49.

62. Cennini, *Il libro dell'arte,* ed. Thompson, pp. 17 ff., 94.

63. Richter, 514. The exact formulation is: "A broad light [*lume grande*] high up and not too strong will render the details of objects very agreeable." In such a light, one understands, the details will be subdued. This is precisely the opposite of the result brought about by "specific light," as we shall immediately see.

64. Richter, 520.

65. Richter, 516. "Moderate light" *(mediocre lume)* is identical with "universal light" and is not a different type of illumination. "Moderate light" can be seen on cloudy days and in the evening, which, as we have seen, are Leonardo's typical examples of "universal light." It also has the same expressive effects as *lume universale:* it renders everything "tender and graceful."

66. CF. Séailles, *Léonard de Vinci: L'artiste et le savant,* p. 472.

67. Richter, 127. "How there are two different kinds of light: one being called diffused, the other restricted. The diffused is that which freely illuminates objects. The restricted is that which being admitted through an opening or window illuminates them on that side only." Cf. also Richter, 118.

68. "Specific light is the cause of giving better relief to shadowed bodies than is universal light. This is shown by the comparison of one part of the countryside illuminated by the sun with one shadowed by a cloud and illuminated only by the universal light of the air." McMahon, 855; Ludwig, 790. See also Richter, 516: "An object will display the greatest difference of light, and shade when it is seen in the strongest light, as by sunlight, or ... by the light of a fire." Again, sunlight and light of an open fire are the usual examples for direct light.

69. McMahon, 849; Ludwig, 784. "Of those lights, which should give a true perception of the shape of the muscles, the universal ones are not good, but specific lights are perfect, and the more so the smaller in shape these lights are."

70. In the description of dramatic scenes Leonardo emphasizes the movements and gestures of the figures, of which he, like his contemporaries, conceived as the main means of expression; in this context he devotes only marginal attention to light. Moreover, the desire to be faithful to nature often prevents the application of direct light. In a battle scene, for example, the dust filling the air is an element of reality and should therefore be portrayed by the artist (Richter, 601-603). In some

dramatic scenes, however, Leonardo suggests strong contrasts between light and darkness, which have an affinity to the expressive character of direct light. In a blaze at night the figures near the fire "will all be illuminated by the ruddy light against a dark background"–a perfect description of "direct light."

71. McMahon, 764; Ludwig, 711. Cf. also Richter, 516.

72. Leonardo, of course, did not think of a real fusion of these two types of illumination, which would have invalidated the characteristics of both universal and specific lights; rather, he thinks of scenes in which these types of light appear simultaneously. See McMahon, 866; Ludwig, 754: "One should pay great attention to the lights adjusted to objects illuminated by them, for in the same narrative painting there may be parts that are in the open country under the universal light of the air and others that are under porticoes, where individual and universal lights are mingled, and others under specific lights, that is, rooms that receive light from a single window." In this description Leonardo anticipates not only the pictorial effects of sixteenth-century painting but also many discussions and descriptions of the theory of art in the Cinquecento. Both Venetian and Milanese art theory were attracted by the problems arising from an interplay between different sources of light in the same picture.

73. The placing of emphasis by means of a strong and concentrated light could also have a hidden iconographic meaning. In the *Virgin of the Rocks,* for example, the strongest, direct light falls on those parts of the picture which are most significant for iconography, e.g., the heads of Christ and the Virgin Mary. Cf. Heydenreich, *Leonardo da Vinci,* p. 35. Shearman, "Leonardo's Color and Chiaroscuro," p. 26, discussing the London version of the *Virgin of the Rocks,* correctly speaks of "selective light seeking out the compositionally and iconographically significant forms and ignoring the rest"; but he does not relate his observations to Leonardo's theoretical categories. Another example is *St. John the Baptist* in the Louvre, which has evoked so much discussion among scholars. The whole picture is painted in very soft transitions (it has, in fact, often been adduced as an example of *sfumato*), but on the raised index finger there falls a powerful, direct light.

74. ". . . in the sixth book I will investigate the many and various diversities of these rays . . .," Richter, 111.

75. Richter, 893; McCurdy, I, pp. 299 f.

76. Werner, p. 136.

77. Cf. Werner, pp. 123 ff., for an investigation of Leonardo's observations of reflections on curved surfaces, probably taken over from Euclid.

78. Werner, pp. 134 ff.

79. Alberti, ed. Spencer, p. 51.

80. McMahon, 163; Ludwig, 159.

81. Richter, 205. See also McMahon, 158; Ludwig, 157.

82. McMahon, 714; Ludwig, 579.

83. McMahon, 165; Ludwig, 163.

84. McMahon, 162; Ludwig, 171, 694e.

85. See above, p. 20, and note 67.

86. I give only a few references: McMahon, 167-172, 174-175, 196-203; Ludwig, 158, 165-166, 168-169, 216-217, 162, 170, 203, 209, 192, 239, 250.

87. McMahon, 797; Ludwig, 645.

88. McMahon, 800; Ludwig, 703.

89. McMahon, 803; Ludwig, 703.

90. McMahon, 169; Ludwig, 165.

91. McMahon, 168; Ludwig, 166. "Very rarely are reflected lights of the same color as the body where they merge with it. Let the sphere D F G E be yellow, and the object which reflects upon it be B C, which is blue. I say that the side of the sphere which is struck by such a reflection will be tinged with the color green." See also McMahon, 169; Ludwig, 165. ". . . I say that this mixed reflection of yellow and blue will strike the sphere with a concurrence of colors. If the sphere is white, the color green will result, because it is proved that yellow and blue mixed together compose a very beautiful green." The formulations show how much Leonardo was aware of the purely phenomenal character of these colors. From these passages it also clearly emerges that, according to Leonardo, the system of "local colors," which was generally accepted by Italian painters of the fifteenth century, could never lead to a true representation of visual experience.

92. McMahon, 161; Ludwig, 164.

93. Richter, 207, 478. Leonardo was aware that it is the changing position of the beholder's eye that determines the deviation of the reflected image from the real object. Although the crucial importance of the beholder's eye has been implied in any theory of perspective, usually it has not been explicitly stressed. Most Renaissance theories of perspective assume the eye as a fixed point. Leonardo's emphasizing of the moving, shifting eye is brought out even more clearly in his observations of luster. This, again, leads to a conception that has an affinity with an impressionistic outlook.

94. The term *simulacro* appears in different contexts in Leonardo's writings. Thus he speaks of a *simulacro* of the sun in the moon (Richter, 895) and of the sun in water (Richter, 875), and of the endless number of *similitudini* that emanate from every body and wander about in the air (Fumagalli, pp. 73 ff.; MacCurdy, II, p. 359). Cf. Heydenreich, *Leonardo da Vinci,* pp. 27, 34 f., 51, 99. Leonardo's most important source seems to me to be Lucretius. Cf. *De rerum naturae,* IV, esp. 26-128, where the same view is set forth in detail, and the word *simulacrum* is used in this specific terminological sense. For *simulacrum* in medieval language, see Du Cange, *Glossarium,* VII, pp. 491 f; and for the late Middle Ages cf. Eustace Deschamps as quoted by J. Huizinga, *Der Herbst des Mittelalters* (Munich, 1924), p. 233. For Leonardo, *simulacro* also has the meaning of the painted image. See McMahon, 507; Ludwig, 473: "... ancora to farai il simile nel tuo simulacro." McMahon translates, correctly as far as meaning is concerned, by "... show this in your reproduction."

95. In reading the many notes dealing with reflections one gains the impression that no particular aesthetic value is attached to them. Leonardo's attitude is, however, made clear in his advice (McMahon, 163; Ludwig, 159) that the painter represent in his picture the causes of reflection in order to avoid being "entirely blamed. . . ." See also above, note 80.

96. This has been formulated quite clearly by Leonardo. See McMahon, 795; Ludwig, 767: "You should have great regard for the objects surrounding those bodies which you wish to represent, according to the first proposition of the fourth book, which proves that the surface of every shadowed body takes on the color of the object opposite. But you should arrange deliberately to have green subjects such as meadows and other suitable things opposite the shadows of green bodies, so that the shadows that take on the color of such an object may not degenerate and seem the shadow of a body other than green. This comes about because, if you put illuminated red facing a shadow which is green, this reddish shadow will cause the shadow to become a color that will be most ugly and will be very different from the true shadow of green. What is said of this color is meant for all others." In this single fragment we are able to observe the interplay of two motives, which characterize, in fact, the essence of Leonardo's thought: on the one hand, the attempt to be faithful to nature, i.e., to show the shadow of a green object as green; on the other hand, however, the purely aesthetic consideration of avoiding the "ugly" color.

97. V. P. Zubov, in a study (in Russian) on the history of the discovery of light diffraction, has collected an impressive bibliography on the subject (see *Priroda,* [1940], no. 7).

98. Richter, 225. See also ibid., 295-296 and 130.

99. See J. Shearman, "Leonardo's Color and Chiaroscuro," passim, esp. p. 13.

100. See above, pp. 29 ff.

101. For Leonardo's technical precepts cf. Richter, 612-650. I give two examples of a similarity between the technical advices of Leonardo and Cennini. Both Leonardo (Richter, 623) and Cennini (chap. 67, p. 45) recommend *terra verde* for shadows. Leonardo says that verdigris in a certain mixture may turn black (Richter, 626); Cennini believes that this color, which is "manufactured by alchemy," may "not last" (chap. 66, p. 33). These quite detailed similarities are not close enough to lead us to the assumption that Leonardo had the text of Cennini's *Libro* in front of him while making these notes, but they are close enough to show that both obviously drew from related workshop experiences.

102. MacCurdy, II, p. 297; McMahon, 949; Ludwig, 886.

103. For the first quotation see MacCurdy, II, p. 297; for the second quotation cf. Richter, 295, where Leonardo says that the wall of a near building should be represented in "suo colore," i.e., in its "true" color.

104. MacCurdy, I, p. 258.

105. MacCurdy, II, p. 296.

106. MacCurdy, II, pp. 273 f.

107. McMahon, 518; Ludwig, 454. *"Of blue, which distant landscapes appear to be.* Of objects far from the eye, of whatever color you wish, that will appear to be bluest in color, which is the darkest, either naturally or accidentally, That object is naturally dark which is dark in itself and that one is accidentally so which is darkened by shadow cast by other objects."

108. McMahon, 108; Ludwig, 253. This view has been repeatedly stated in Renaissance theory of art.

109. "Red also will seem most vivid when set against a yellow background and so in like manner will all the colors when set against those which present the sharpest contrasts." MacCurdy, II, p. 295.

110. McMahon, 182; Ludwig, 253.

111. In medieval painting there are, of course, some well known cases where the application of brilliant materials fulfills a certain mimetic function. The best-known example is the halo covered with gold or other glittering materials. But even in medieval art this particular application of gold is only one part of the use of glittering, radiant materials. For the Renaissance painter, who covered the whole

surface of his picture with varnish regardless of what was represented in it, brilliance of this type had lost any mimetic value whatsoever.

112. Richter, 132: "Of the difference between light and luster; and that luster is not included among colors but is a sensation (?) of whiteness. . . ." That white is not a color, Leonardo said many times. See, e.g., Richter, 556.

113. Richter, 135, 893.

114. Richter, 134. Cf. also 133; McMahon, 796-782; and Ludwig, 664, 675-677, 746, 770-779.

115. See above, pp. 22 ff.

116. McMahon, 769; Ludwig, 664.

117. "If the figure you portray is in a dark house and you see it from outside, the shadows of that figure will be dark and smoky [*oscure sfumate*]. . . . Such a figure is graceful and does honor to him who represents it because its soft and smoky shadows [*ombri dolce e sfumose*] give it great relief. . . ." McMahon, 140; Ludwig, 86. The term *sfumato* seems to have been used more frequently by Venetian writers of the sixteenth century. See, for instance, Dolce, *L'Aretino,* ed. Barrocchi, I, p. 197.

118. *Libro dell'arte,* chap. xxxi; ed. Thompson, p. 18. And see above, pp. 5 ff.

119. Cf. H. Ruhemann, "Leonardo's use of *sfumato,*" *British Journal of Aesthetics,* I (1960-1961), 231 ff., esp. 234. See also E. H. Gombrich, "Controversial Methods and Methods of Controversy," *Burlington Magazine* (1963), pp. 90 ff., and O. Kurz, "Time the Painter," ibid., pp. 94 ff.

120. McMahon, 218; Ludwig, 128. The Italian text reads: "un finito fumoso."

121. Richter, 492.

122. *Opere di Filippo Baldinucci* (Florence, 1809), III, p. 144.

123. Dupuy de Grèz, *Traité sur la peinture* (Toulouse, 1699), p. 227. Cf. E. Heuck, *Die Farbe in der französischen Kunsttheorie des XVII. Jahrhunderts* (Strasbourg, 1929), p. 76.

124. Ruhemann, loc. cit., asserts that even in those parts of his paintings where Leonardo applied *sfumato* the outlines are not completely obliterated. While this may be true, it seems certain that Leonardo in such cases attributes less significance to outlines, and even tries to hide them in the soft transitions.

3

THE SCHOOL OF VENICE

I. Introduction

BOTH IN CHARACTER and development, Venetian art theory diverges from that of the other familiar Italian schools. The chronology is in itself revealing. By the late fifteenth century, Florentine theory of art was fairly complete. Alberti's and Piero della Francesca's treatises had already been composed, and Leonardo was in the process of building up a systematic "science of painting." In these fundamental works the main themes and attitudes of Florentine artistic thought were definitively formulated, whereas at this stage Venice had practically no theory of art. The philosophic and scientific interests of the artists and writers that constituted the basis of Florentine art theory do not seem to have appealed to the Venetians, and the great early-sixteenth-century transformation of Venetian painting was not accompanied by any significant theoretical discussions. By the middle of the sixteenth century, however, the situation radically changed. The great Florentine theoretical works enjoyed a position of authority, already supported by tradition, and in Florence itself something of a historical distance seems to have been reached regarding the art of the High Renaissance and its theoretical foundations. At the same time, Venice experienced a sudden flourishing of art theory, many critical or theoretical treatises appearing within the short span of about twenty years. Some of these are today numbered among the most important documents of Italian theory of art, while others, quite undeservedly, remain neglected.

Venetian literature on art started with Michiel's little book. This is more a collection of short descriptions of pictures than a treatise on the theory of art, but seen in the light of later developments, even this text seems to foretell the crystallization of certain specifically Venetian attitudes.[1] Pietro

Aretino, one of the most influential figures in the articulation of a Venetian attitude to art, was also no "theoretician" in the strict sense of the word. He was perhaps the first European writer to look at pictures mainly for their expressive mood, and not to base his evaluations upon time-honored theories. Although he did not deal systematically with light and color, his writings are an important source for our study. He gave perhaps clearest expression to the spirit of Venetian painting; and his sketchy, suggestive descriptions of Venice reveal how in his time coloristic charms were observed and evaluated, and enraptured the eyes.[2]

In 1545 a period of intensive productivity in the writing of art theory began in Venice. Among the most significant treatises of this period that deal in some way with problems of light and color is Fulvio Pellegrino Morati's book on the symbolic meaning of colors, published in 1545. Shortly afterward appeared Pino's *Dialogue on Painting* (1548), Doni's *Disegno* (1549), and Biondo's *On the Noble Art of Painting* (1549). Dolce's *L'Aretino,* a famous work of Venetian art theory, appeared in 1557, and some years later the same author published a voluminous *Dialogo nel quale si ragiona della qualità, diversità e proprietà dei colori* (1565), which, although not dealing with painting, is a source for the study of Venetian concepts of color. In the same year a late medieval French treatise on the symbolism of color, especially in heraldry, was translated into Italian and published in Venice. Cristoforo Sorte's little book, *Observations on Painting* (1580), is a late product of this short period of art theoretical activity. Even some writings of the seventeenth century, like Marco Boschini's *Le ricche minere della pittura* (the author was a pupil of the younger Palma and drew on the still living tradition of sixteenth-century Venetian painting), belong in some respects to the flourishing of Venetian art theory of the Cinquecento and reflect the concepts and attitudes crystallized in the early period.[3]

The treatises composed or published in Venice in the middle of the sixteenth century are not uniform in content and character; they do not constitute a "system" even in that vague and general sense in which we may speak of a Florentine system of art theory. Some of the authors of "Venetian" treatises were not Venetians,[4] while the Venetians themselves were deeply influenced by concepts which originated in, and were characteristic for, Florence, and to a lesser degree northern Europe. Some of the treatises published in Venice in the middle of the sixteenth century are influenced by medieval sources; others deal in a very free and modern spirit with the most recent achievements of Venetian painting. Yet in spite of this great variety one can detect some general trend of thought and orientations of interest that display common typical features. The chronological proximity of the Venetian writings on art is not only a symptom of the newly aroused interest in theoretical problems; it also confers on the diverse writings a certain, though very general, unity. Through the emphasis on specific elements and the frequent analysis of the works of contemporary Venetian painters, a common attitude, or intellectual climate, is, to some extent crystallized. It may be difficult to define this attitude exactly; it appears, however, as the focus of a more or less unified tradition. In this tradition, the discussion of light and color plays an important part.

II. Characteristics of Venetian Art Theory

Before starting our analysis of the Venetian concepts of light and color it may be useful to outline the relationship of Venetian theory to Florentine attitudes and doctrines. It is difficult to describe this relationship briefly, as it had many facets and many, often contradictory, tendencies. One may say, however, that it was essentially ambivalent. On the one hand, Venetian concepts of art relied to a very large degree on central Italian, and specifically Florentine, theory. The whole art literature of Venice would, in fact, be unthinkable without Alberti and the first edition of Vasari's Lives. Pino mentions Alberti and Dürer as theoreticians of art [5] (Dürer's affinity to Florentine theory was probably perceived in Venice); [6] Pino also has a very interesting remark on Vasari which would suggest that he might have read (in 1547) a draft of the Lives before it was printed.[7] Dolce advises painters to study Alberti's Della pittura and devotes an interesting passage to Dürer; he also refers to Vasari,[8] whose work had by now appeared in print. Dolce's "borrowings" from Vasari include not only biographical details but also conceptual frameworks and evaluations of artists and styles.[9] Printed books were not, however, the only source of the Florentine influence on Venetian thought. A lively interchange of ideas was mediated by the frequent visits of Venetian artists to Tuscany and Rome, and of central Italian artists to Venice. The significance of this interchange, although more difficult to trace exactly,[10] may have been no less important than that of the printed books.

These few facts, which could easily be multiplied, show that Florentine theory of art was not only well known in Venice but that it actually formed the basis of Venetian artistic thought.

On the other hand, a critical attitude toward Florentine concepts can be detected in most Venetian writings. As Venetian theory of art often resembles an eclectic amalgam rather than an original system, it is very difficult to define with precision its prevailing attitude. However, in comparing Venetian art literature with the famous Florentine treatises, one often perceives a significant difference in tone and atmosphere. In Florence, the tendency to base art upon scientific principles and to build up a systematic *scienza della pittura* predominated. A different approach is manifested in Venice. One also finds an attempt to formulate the practical experience of the workshops, and contrarily, to describe the expressive values of painting and the sensual pleasure to be found in color and in original brushwork, often conceived from the point of view of a nonprofessional beholder. In this respect Venetian art literature is of a more modern character than Florentine speculations. This difference is suggested by the actual literary form of the works. While Florentine treatises are usually composed according to a systematic form, in Venice the much looser shape of the dialogue is preferred.[11] One also finds here, as a type of exposition, loosely connected "observations" which do not pretend to be a system.

The difference in the literary form of exposition points to a deeper divergence. Some of the themes and concepts which are of crucial importance for Florentine theory are rather neglected in Venice, and have only a marginal significance. It is, for example, characteristic that most of the important Venetian treatises do not deal to a large extent with anatomy, or with the optical and geometrical foundations of perspective. The concept of the "rule" *(regola),* which is probably the very focus of Florentine theory, is also largely neglected in Venice.[12] When it is referred to, it is given a very general, unspecified meaning.

The relationship with Florentine concept of art was, however, not restricted to differences of tendency and emphasis; many passages show that the Venetian authors were aware of their specific position and explicitly argued against Florentine doctrines. Pino, in the preface to his *Dialogue,* says: "Leon Battista Alberti, not the least of painters, wrote a treatise on

93

painting in Latin, which is more on mathematics than on painting though it promises the contrary." [13] He criticizes Alberti's "veil," which in Florence had been regarded as a means for the "true" representation of nature, and for this very reason appealed also to Dürer. But Pino thinks that "it is still less useful to work with a veil or squaring off, discovered by Leon Battista, a trifling thing and of little practical use." [14] Aretino's invectives against pedantism in art are also perhaps directed against Florentine teachings.[15]

It is difficult to define precisely the values that, in Venetian culture, occupy the place of the concepts central to Florentine thought. The difficulty lies above all in the fact that these are not new, original values, unknown in Florence or in the other Italian schools. The difference between the two traditions of looking at art is due more to an emphasis on different elements and aspects of a basically common approach (i.e., the Renaissance approach to art) than to a confrontation of completely disparate values. Another difficulty is that in Venice terms, concepts and whole literary formulations were very often taken over from the Florentine writings without retaining exactly the same shade of meaning and the same degree of significance as in their original context. Thus, the specific tendencies of the Venetian approach to art cannot easily be illustrated by isolated quotations. One has to rely on more general tendencies and qualities; these, however, are often clearly perceptible.

Among the qualities characterizing the Venetian approach there is undoubtedly greater emphasis on direct visual perception than on the construction of bodies. In Venetian literature, and especially in the writings of Pietro Aretino, one finds many descriptions of visual, coloristic experiences which are significant indications of the general character of that city's culture. In art this tendency is reflected in the predilection for lustrous and shining surfaces and in the concern with textures.[16] Another characteristic element of Venetian literature is the great importance imputed to the psychological type of the artist and to his creative gift, which, as is often stressed, "cannot be taught." The emphasis placed on this particular aspect is common both to the intellectual life of Venice in general and to its theory of art. Dolce, for example, departs from Alberti and Vasari, his Florentine sources of inspiration, by a more extensive adaptation of Horatian principles, and he did this probably under the influence of the literary circles of Castiglione, Bembo, and Pietro Aretino.[17] The concept of *giudizio naturale,* implying the idea that an artist is born and cannot be "produced" by training was largely promoted by Bembo and Castiglione,[18] but it was also stressed by Pino and by other authors of art theoretical writings.[19] Needless to say, the theory of the artist's divine *mania* and of his "melancholic" nature pertains to different parts of Europe.[20] But Florentine humanists of the late fifteenth century did not usually stress the connection between these characteristic features of the artist's personality with the stylistic qualities of his work. In Venice, the *terribilità* of Michelangelo and the *grazia* of Raphael are not only compared, but an attempt is also made to detect these qualities in their works, and in the technical methods applied in the process of creation. The attitudes and movements of Tintoretto's figures, for example, are explained by his psychological type, and even his brushwork is interpreted as a reflection of his personality.[21] Thus the temperament—or the astrological type—of the artist becomes a more significant and a more concrete factor in the interpretation of his work.

These differences between Florence and Venice—not more than differences in shade—should be borne in mind when we analyze the Venetian concepts of light and color.

III. Pino's System

Although the Venetian authors did not show a decided inclination toward the systematic tendencies of Florentine art theory, a "system" of painting nevertheless underlies most of their works. This system is not an original creation of Venice; it is taken over mainly from Florence, or, through the mediation of Florentine humanists, from classical sources. Painting is usually divided into drawing, invention, and color. Sometimes this scheme is made the starting point of a description of pictures which are analyzed according to each element of the system; sometimes it is simply stated with no great bearing on the actual content of the treatises or on the analysis of the works of art. In Venice this system is most clearly expressed by Pino, who, as the first Venetian theoretician of art, is still hesitant in questioning the validity of Florentine principles.[22] His scheme, which may serve as the starting point of our discussion, subdivides the first part *(disegno)* into judgment *(giuditio)*, outline *(circumscrittione)*, and practice and composition; the last part, called by the traditional name of *receptione de' lumi*, is subdivided into *proprietà, prontezza,* and *lume*.[23]

Pino's rigid distinctions show many overlappings and inconsistencies that have been pointed out in modern research [24] and need not be further elaborated. The distinctions do not reveal much of the actual state of painting in Venice in middle of the sixteenth century and do not reflect the specific artistic problems of the period. The last part of Pino's system, however, is of interest for our study, as it suggests certain elements of the Venetian attitude to light and color. Two points are important:

(1) The differentiation of color into three distinct strata. This differentiation reveals a concern with the problem of color which we do not find to the same degree in most of the other schools of Italian art theory.

(2) The explicit inclusion of light in the concept of color. This suggests one of the major Venetian contributions to Renaissance theory of art.

The first element (i.e., the differentiation of color into *proprietà, prontezza* and *lume*) is perhaps nothing else than the explicit formulation of an idea that had been implicitly present ever since the beginnings of Renaissance art theory. But the fact that this idea was not explicitly formulated is, of course, of great significance, as the discussion was raised to a new and higher level and the concepts were made more articulate. As we shall presently see, the three parts of *colorire* represent three different aspects of color and of its handling by the painter. Although each of these aspects has a certain autonomy, their connection is not merely verbal.

The meaning of the three terms is somewhat ambiguous. As each of them is applied to many concepts and is used in different contexts, perhaps they cannot be defined. Exactly this ambiguity can partly be explained by a lack of precision in the formulation of the ideas, which is a characteristic feature of Venetian art theory. To a larger extent, however, the ambiguity is rooted in the very contents of the terms. In Pino's *Dialogo* we observe the Venetian color concepts in the early stages of their emergence, before they have taken on a definite shape. Their ambiguity may thus be understood as a reflection of Pino's historical position as the first art theoretician of Venice.

The concept of *proprietà*, closely related to the traditional notion of *decorum*, is the widest in scope, as Pino himself knew. He stresses the "infinite" multitude of "things belonging to coloring, which it is impossible to explain in words." [25] *Proprietà* is, however, mainly a symbolic, iconographic concept. Its principal function is to reveal the character, age, and complexion of the represented figure, or the material nature of the represented object (i.e., its texture). It is significant that Pino does not draw a clear dividing line between these two poles of the concept.[26] The "iconographic" meaning of *proprietà* should, therefore, be understood in a representational as well as in a symbolic sense. The latter, moreover, is not a conventional symbolism, attaching well-defined meanings to clearly identified colors. Rather, Pino seems to have in mind an expressive quality of coloring in painting, immediately deluding the beholder or intuitively interpreted by him. It is characteristic for his approach that he does not refer to single, isolated colors, as did the writers on color symbolism; rather, he means the relationship between colors, their "composition." The multitude of aspects in coloring, he says, cannot be explained in words "because each color, by itself or by its composition, can produce different effects, and no [single] color is capable, by its own property, of producing even a minimum of natural effects, but [it needs] the intelligence and practice of the good master." [27] Thus it is true that *proprietà* is closely related to the symbolic aspect of color, but this relationship should be understood in a specifically "modern" sense. Pino's idea presupposes both a naturalistic style of painting, to which he refers, and the conception of a master gifted and experienced in the "composition" of colors. Both elements do not occur in, and are even opposed to, conventional color symbolism.

The scope of *proprietà* is further enlarged by applying the term to the handling of color materials. Such a handling is correct or "appropriate" when it takes into account the given properties of color material. Contrary to medieval habits, Pino does not give actual precepts; he only mentions "Pliny and others" as well-known sources.[28] However, the application of the term *proprietà* to the handling of color materials clearly shows that this concept is not restricted to the symbolic or even the stylistic aspects.

The other concept, *prontezza,* is also ambiguous in meaning, or, at the least, is applied to widely different ideas. According to Pino, it denotes the expressive movements and dramatic gestures of the represented figures, especially in extreme and sharp foreshortenings,[29] as well as the painter's "sureness of hand and the grace granted to him by nature." [30] *Prontezza* is thus understood both as an objective quality of the work of art and as a characteristic feature of the creative process itself, indicating the virtuosity and the temperament of the artist. In our present context it is the latter aspect especially that becomes of importance. Needless to say, in the middle of the sixteenth century the concept of the artist's virtuosity is neither new nor restricted to Venice. It was a universal element in Renaissance conceptions of the artist, an often-quoted reason for admiring him, and always present, if not always articulate from the beginning of the period. In Venice, however, it seems to have been regarded as more closely connected with the innate gifts of the artist than in the other centers of artistic thought in Italy. Moreover, it was more organically embedded in the framework of the general culture, and therefore may be said to reflect a typical Venetian attitude.

Facilità, a concept similar to *prontezza* but not connected with art, was developed as an ideal of behavior. Both Castiglione and Bembo speak of the quality of *facilità* as related to the "natural judgment" and as opposed to the labored acquisition of proficiency.[31] Possibly influenced by Florentine theories, Pino admits that *prontezza* may also be acquired by experience, but he opposes this quality to the scientific approaches and the mechanical aids that dominated Florence. In doing so he is paving the way for a typological juxtaposition of the artist who creates his works by the force of his natural gifts and the educated artist-scientist. This particular meaning of *prontezza* was further developed in later Venetian theory. Cristoforo Sorte, in 1580, related it to *giudizio,* while *giudizio* itself was connected with "sureness of hand,"[32] thus granting to virtuosity a significance transcending that of a "science" or of an acquired skill. Sorte believes, as has already been mentioned, that *giudizio* and "sureness of hand" enable the character and temperament of the artist to be detected even in his brushwork. Marco Boschini's statement that Titian sometimes painted with his fingers rather than with brushes because he wanted to imitate God in his creation[33] may also have an affinity with the broader meaning of this concept. This famous statement suggests a belief that in the process of shaping a work of art the artist's creative force, not constricted by established and rational rules that can be learned, becomes manifest. While this belief is not new, it remains a remarkable fact that it appears in a discussion of color only in Venice, where color becomes the specific realm for the manifestation of *prontezza.*

In turning to the last part of *colore,* that is *lume,* we reach the central theme of this chapter, the tendency toward a fusion of light and color. Pino does not discuss this problem at any length, nor are his comments always clear or consistent. Nevertheless, the tendency toward such a fusion is implied in his approach. In order to evaluate his remarks, a more general issue should be borne in mind. In spite of the fact that Pino adopts the Florentine scheme of art theory, he fluctuates between a systematic approach, based on more abstract "science," and an empirical approach, based on accumulated practical experience expressed in the form of technical devices. This holds true also for his discussion of light and color. Here he wavers between the formulation of broad concepts generalizing the stylistic and expressive aspects of color, and traditional concrete workshop precepts that are of a limited and predominantly practical nature. On the one hand, he defines light as the "soul of color," but on the other, he immediately goes on to describe the appropriate conditions of illumination and the proper position of the windows in the painter's workshop.[34] In Renaissance theory of art these two types of approach usually belonged to different general conceptions of the relationship between light and color. The generalizing approach, being promoted to a large extent by *letterati* who were less concerned with the practical problems of the painter in his work, tended more toward a fusion of light and color. The workshop approach, less concerned with philosophical and literary questions but intimately acquainted with the actual work of the artist, usually tended toward dealing with light and color separately.[35] The attempt to synthesize the two streams was bound to lead to a certain obscurity and even to produce contradictions. However, Pino, like Leonardo, seems to have been aware of certain connections between the practical precept and the stylistic concept. The window in the painter's workshop, he says, should be high and facing east, since there "the air is more temperate." Seen in such a light, the represented objects and figures will have more relief and "more graceful manner."[36] These connections between the general stylistic concepts and the technical precepts, although not fully articulate and systematically developed, point to the direction of a fusion of light and color. Many formulations by contemporary or later Venetian writers, to which I shall shortly return, show the impact of this tendency more clearly.

Within the traditional framework of Renaissance art theory, this tendency toward fusion was of a revolutionary character, bound to upset some of the central assumptions and generally accepted norms of evaluation. As we have seen in the preceding chapters, light and color were frequently divided and differently evaluated in Florentine artistic thought. It is true that Alberti—who in this respect, as in many others, was in advance of his time—seems to have assumed some links between the conditions of light and the nature and appearance of color.[37] This part of his doctrine, however, remained rather isolated in the fifteenth and early sixteenth centuries. Light and color were dealt with as two different realms, although their mutual influence was sometimes observed. Leonardo, for example, was aware of the many intimate connections between light and color. He carefully studied reflections which, according to his own conceptions, are nothing but colored light. His characteristic technical invention, the *sfumato* modeling, is also partly based upon a fusion of color and light. But when it came to explicit theoretical statements and evaluations, even Leonardo made a division between *lume* and *colore,* and, as we have seen, had a very different evaluation of each of them. The modeling in light and shade, he says, is a "marvel of painting" and should be carefully studied, while beautiful colors are not the merit of the painter but of the one who manufactures them.[38] Although in Venice the distinction between light and color is not altogether obliterated, the difference grows weaker and loses sharpness, in the actual painting as well as in the theoretical reasoning. Many examples from Venetian writings, especially descriptions of paintings, can be cited as testimony to this attitude. The early Michiel speaks of highlights and halftones *(meze tente)* when he is referring to light, as well as to color.[39] Pietro Aretino, in a description of a painting by Moretto, speaks of "the natural union of colors spreading out in the lights and shadows [done] with a wonderful judgment of a gracious style." [40] He describes Titian's pictures in a way that suggests both light and color, and he praises the artist for "l'unione del vostro colorire." [41] Pino, as we have seen, defines light as "the soul of color." Dolce thinks that the foremost element of coloring is contrast. "It produces light along with shadow and is the source for a means of unifying the two opposites and making the figures appear round and more or less distant (as the need arises)." [42] Marco Boschini says that "coloring spreads into different conditions and pecularities"; he speaks of the union of colors together with the nuances of light and shade.[43]

These scattered remarks should not be overestimated. They indicate, however suggestively, only a tendency. In the Renaissance, ideas on the fusion of light and color never crystallized in a fully articulate theoretical statement, and in Venetian literature one can easily find statements implying an opposite view. Moreover, *lume* and *ombra* were to some extent traditional components of the concept of *colore* and are mentioned in this particular context by Florentine authors as well.[44] Nevertheless, it seems fairly clear that the tendency toward a fusion of light and color played a significant role in Venetian theory. This can be seen most clearly in those passages which are less influenced by time-honored notions. When Venetian authors speak of the art of their own time, or when they develop their own concepts, the distinction between light and color is often almost imperceptible. In these contexts they also discuss some problems that are actually based on a large degree of fusion between light and color. The tendency toward this particular conception of *colore* may, therefore, be regarded chiefly as a Venetian phenomenon.

We shall probably not go wrong in assuming that this direction in Venetian theory is to a large extent influenced by stylistic developments in actual Venetian paintings of the sixteenth century. It is remarkable that some of the most important discussions of this problem occur in connection with the various writers' attempts to describe, and to clarify the principles and the specific trends, of the painting of their time and region. Most of the Venetian writers were also aware of the fact that the particular style of painting which tends to fuse light and color is specifically "modern" and represents a revolution in art. They often oppose the purely chromatic coloring of the quattrocento (in their writings sometimes represented by Bellini) to the tonal painting of Giorgione and the cinquecento. Dolce, for example, opens his *L'Aretino* with a comparison of Venetian painting in the fifteenth and sixteenth centuries, stressing the "maniera di colorito morbidissimo" of the latter.[45] Pino criticizes Giovanni Bellini for his distinction between light and color in the process of painting.[46] The emergence of Giorgione's tonal painting even led to the crystallization of a historiographic scheme, most clearly formulated by Boschini. Bellini, he says, brought painting to light; Giorgione gave her a jewel; to drawing and symmetry he added grace and finish, and "in coloring he invented the *impasto* of the soft brush." This invention was regarded as so important that

Giorgione is compared with Gutenberg.[47] Where Boschini speaks of the *colorito veneziano,* he obviously means the representation of atmospheric effects derived from a fusion of light and color.

The tendency toward a fusion of light and color crystallized in some more defined problems and concepts to which I shall now turn.

IV. "Tone" and "Value"

A significant outcome of this tendency is the concept which we now call the "tone" or "value" of color. Most of the Venetian authors attempted to clarify this concept, or the whole complex of meanings which we denote by these terms. It is, I think, a characteristic feature of the Venetian discussions of tone that one immediately detects in them the influence of the workshop, while the humanistic associations, mainly derived from classical literature, play a rather marginal part.

The notion of "tone" in painting is certainly one of the most complex terms in our vocabulary. Since it has been used in widely different contexts, and often rather loosely, it has lost its precise meaning; a few words of explanation may therefore be useful. By the term "tone" we usually mean the degree of brightness or darkness of a color or of the whole picture.[48] However, if we use this term in a historical context, we have to distinguish between two distinct, and sometimes even opposite, possible meanings which are the characteristic features of two different tendencies of style. On the one hand, the term designates the degree of brightness and darkness within one, a single color (or within each isolated color); on the other, it designates the degree of brightness and darkness of the picture as a whole, and the way in which this degree of relative luminosity is achieved in relation to the other aspects of color.

The first meaning of tone was already well known in the early Renaissance, both in actual painting and in the theory of art. Its most typical formulation is the well-known workshop precept advising the painter who intends to represent a nude figure to prepare a certain number (usually six) of flesh-color shades, some for the illumined parts of the body and some for those covered by shadows. By following this advice the painter is expected to achieve the modeling of the body without breaking the chromatic character of its color. This advice, which recurs in theoretical treatises from Cennini to Armenini and Lomazzo,[49] clearly displays an intention of preserving the coloristic identity of the single figure or object represented (its *Lokalfarbe*) at the expense of the coloristic unity of the picture as a whole.

In this chapter we are mainly concerned with the second meaning of tone, the overall tonal effect of the whole picture, which was a new concept in Renaissance art theory. The overall tonal effect of a picture represents the—very complex—result of a fusion of light and colors. It entails several consequences, some of which are of importance in our context. (1) In this type of painting, tone values are not merely modifications of the local colors or of isolated color planes. In a picture, overall tonality reduces the intensity and may even obscure the very identity of pure chromatic color. It is thus, at least potentially, opposed to that specific quality which was called the *bellezza* of a color in the sense of its own inherent brilliance. What the "tonal" picture loses in the brilliance of isolated colors, it gains, however, in the continuity of coloring, in a general and unified coloristic attitude that pervades the whole painting. (2) Overall tonality tends to eliminate the linear values of pictorial representation. While the modeling by light and shade within each isolated color tends to emphasize linearity (as Shearman has correctly pointed out), the overall tonal effect of a picture necessarily impedes this linearity. "Not only is there no break of tone at the junction of color-planes, but in many cases, where the junction is lost in shadow, the break will even be invisible chromatically." [50] (3) Most important in our context is the fact that in paintings executed in the style of an overall tonality, the basic element will necessarily be the halftone, that is, a slight shadow or an obscured pure color tempered and "broken" by such a shadow. At least in some Venetian paintings executed in this style there is a symptomatic predilection for subject matter that, in its natural form, suggests halftones and tempered colors, like cloud-covered skies or brownish and grayish walls. It is further significant that in such paintings the artists tended to introduce new hues which are typical products of the blending and tempering of colors.[51] In these paintings pure colors are usually not applied; where they do appear, they represent no more than one tone in a whole scale. In other words, even where pure colors are used, they lose their specific character qua pure colors and acquire a new meaning qua tones.

After this short description of the concept of tone, based mainly on modern research, we now return to the Renaissance.

The sixteenth century did not possess, as far as I know, a special and generally accepted term for tone, but it would be wrong to assume that the concept itself was unknown to artists and writers. We shall see rather that it stood in the focus of interest of Venetian theory and was frequently discussed, although certain overlappings and the lack of sufficiently precise definition are sometimes characteristic of these discussions. Several terms frequently used by Venetian writers seem to have been connected with the concept of tone in painting, although these terms may also have had other meanings.

Pino speaks of a *"diversità di tinte in un corpo solo,"* and this has been interpreted by modern scholars, probably correctly, as referring to the tones in painting.[52] Dolce, in his *L'Aretino,* has several times described tonal painting and analyzed its most important values. "The blending of the colors," he says, "needs to be diffused and unified in such a way that it is naturalistic, and that nothing offends the gaze such as contour lines, which should be avoided (since nature does not produce them), and blackness, a term I use for harsh and unintegrated shadows." [53] Raphael's colors are *sfumate et unite,* [54] and Giorgione's colors "have such a degree of *sfumate* that shadows are not discernible." [55] The principal part of coloring, Dolce says, is the relationship between light and shadow which produces "a middle" *(un mezzo),* uniting the opposite poles. This "middle" is, of course, also the principal means for modeling and for the representation of volume. Dolce was aware that a good mixture implies a limitation of the intensity of light as well as of pure colors. He considers such a limitation an aesthetic value. A "brownish color" is to be preferred to an extremely bright one. Dolce also wants to avoid glaring colors, like reds on cheeks and lips. The main difficulty of coloring, he says, consists in the representation of the variety of tones *(tinte)* and of the softness of flesh.[56] Before the end of the sixteenth century, Lomazzo, perhaps influenced by Venetian treatises on art which he knew, compares Titian with Appelles, who was "the first inventor of tones" *("il quale fu il primo inventore dei tuoni").*[57]

The concept of a "middle" tone was further elaborated by Marco Boschini. To him, *meze tinte* is a principal category in the art of painting. He relates that the old Titian used *terra rossa* as a middle tone into which he carefully put the lights and shadows. His finish consisted mainly in "rubbing with the fingers whereby he gradually united the highest lights, drew them nearer to the half-tones, and united one tone with the other." [58]

In the seventeenth century, definitions of tone were also given by French authors who were, however, influenced by the Venetian tradition.[59] As far as the concepts of tone and tonal painting are concerned, French theory of art does not go beyond what was established in Venice and articulated in the Venetian treatises.

The definitions and descriptions quoted above show, I think, that the problem of tone and tonal painting was well known in Renaissance Italy, and especially in Venice. Moreover, it follows that the overall tonality of painting was considered as a significant artistic achievement. Why was tonal painting so highly evaluated? In what precisely did the Venetian authors see the characteristics of tonal painting? And how did they relate these characteristics to the other aspects of color? In order to answer these questions we shall first analyze their attitude toward pure color.

In Renaissance theory of art, each of the different elements of painting (i.e., invention, drawing, and color) was assigned, so to speak, a particular social status, according to the groups of people to whom these specific elements were supposed to appeal. The different "parts" of painting are usually arranged in a hierarchic scale of values. Invention ranks highest in this scale, since it appeals particularly to the educated, and recalls classical literature with which only the learned are familiar. Pure glaring colors, on the other hand, occupied the lowest rank of the ladder, as it was habitually connected with the taste of the ignorant and people who lack refined judgment. A few examples will suffice to illustrate this point. In 1546 Benedetto Varchi, in preparation for two lectures published three years later, invited a number of artists to state their opinions on the relative merits of painting and sculpture. The answers deal largely also with the value of color. Pure color is almost unanimously denied higher value. The sculptor Benvenuto Cellini praises "the able Bronzino" because he employs carefully studied methods of sculpture. "I see the others," he continues, "drowned among nosegays, and employing themselves with many varicolored compositions which can only cheat the simple." [60] A generation later Armenini writes that the more glaring colors are, the more they attract the eyes of the uneducated.[61]

The assumption of a sociological, so to speak, connection between bright colors and the taste of ignorant peasants is also to be found in Venetian art literature. Pino says that "beautiful colors" (i.e., pure, glaring colors) are destined for the ignorant. Some painters apply such "beautiful colors" only in order to earn money.[62] Dolce, in a letter to Gasparo Bellini, says that the ignorant appreciate a certain childish variegation of colors more than art. A man of low taste, like Pope Sixtus, whose judgment Dolce criticizes, is impressed by "such colors which gorge the eyes." The "wealth of colors" employed by certain contemporary painters is, according to Dolce, intended only to afford pleasure to the ignorant, [63] and a generation later Sorte says that "the wealth and charm of colors" appeal ónly to the uneducated.[64]

Besides the "sociological" context there is also another, specifically artistic, reason for the low evaluation of pure colors. Here, too, Venetian authors accepted the traditional Florentine views and formulations. We have already mentioned Leonardo's opinion that pure colors are not the merit of the painter but of the one who manufactures them. In the sixteenth century this became a formula frequently used in the treatises on art. I shall quote only a few Venetian examples. Beautiful colors, Pino says, are beautiful also in their containers.[65] Dolce comes back to the same motif. And let no one think that what gives coloring its effectiveness is the choice of a beautiful palette, such as fine lakes, fine azures, fine greens, and so on; for these colors are just as beautiful without their being put to work." [66] Beautiful colors without good drawing are sometimes compared with beautiful words without thought.

From this low evaluation of pure color in general Dolce turns to a more specific problem of painting which was being discussed at the time, namely, the method of representing nature in clearly outlined planes of pure local color. He criticizes this method both from an aesthetic and from a naturalistic point of view. "Seldom, perhaps never, does one see people together who look according to a certain division, some wearing scarlet-red garments, other yellows and others again, dark-violet ones, these azure, the others copper-green." [67] This carpetlike arrangement of pure colors, which was suggested by Alberti, [68] is here criticized because it impedes the possibility of creating a convincing illusion of nature. By inference one may conclude (although Dolce doesn't say it in this context) that such an illusion can be created only by tonal painting.

In sum, pure colors are denied higher value because they appeal to the ignorant; because they do not show the workmanship of the artist; and because they offend the truth of optically perceived nature.

This contempt for pure color, as well as its sociological and artistic justification, is not a specifically Venetian phenomenon; it can also be found in Florence and in the other important centers of Renaissance art theory. But different conclusions were drawn from this common evaluation in Florence and in Venice, and this difference reflects the basic tendencies of these two great traditions or "schools" of art theory. In Florence the contempt for pure color leads mainly to the placing of further emphasis on drawing. Together with pure colors, color in general, at least to some degree, is denied higher value. There are of course exceptions, and as an example it will suffice to recall Leonardo. Yet speaking in broader terms, one may safely say that in Florentine theory, which did not arrive at a basic distinction between pure colors and color in general, the low evaluation of pure colors necessarily influenced the situation of color in general. In Venice a different conclusion was drawn. Here, too, pure and glaring colors are not appreciated, but this does not lead to a denial of the value of color in general. Since the Venetian writers distinguished between pure and tonal color, they could reject the application of pure color in painting and yet highly esteem coloristic values in general. Venetian writers even tried to associate refined colors, which are the result of blending and of artistic creation, with the learned, and thus to establish, so to speak, an honorable social basis for the appreciation of tonal color. Sorte clearly states this program by saying "that with colors one should try to satisfy the taste of vulgar people." [69]

The concept of tone, in painting, even if only vaguely defined, thus had an important impact on the appreciation of color.

What were the origins of the concept? Although it was not clearly formulated or crystallized in a specific term, its expression in Venetian theory can be analyzed in relation to influences from various sources. Ancient literature provided certain suggestions. Pliny, for example, in Book 35 of his *Natural History*, gives a brief but suggestive description of tone in painting which he regarded as an important achievement of art.[70] Such a passage could not have been overlooked in humanistic circles or by the writers on art who belonged to them. Another source, contemporary with Venetian theory of art, was perhaps the theory of music which played a significant role in Venetian culture of the late sixteenth century. In this period of music theory the comparison between musical tones and color tones was a familiar theme. Gioseffe Zarlino, for example, the important Venetian music theorist, says that pure white and black, are less agreeable to the eye than mixed and blended colors. Among musical tones, the *acuto* and *grave* correspond to white and black, while the "soft" musical tones correspond to what we call in painting the "middle hues." [71] This comparison was also formulated in music theory outside Italy, and it is sometimes invested with metaphysical significance. To Père Marin Mersenne, an early-seventeenth-century French music theorist who was deeply influenced by Italian humanism, this comparison suggests a deeper meaning. He compares "Unison" with the simplicity of the First Cause, and says that "it is white like the whiteness of an angel's robes or the garments of the Saviour at the Transfiguration." Those who prefer blended colors to white, he believes, are those whose eyes cannot endure the light, "and who receive more contentment from speculation of particular truths than from contemplation of the universal truth . . ." [72] A generation earlier, another French humanist, Amadis Jamyn, believed that the Egyptians painted the robes of Osiris, who is the First Cause, in pure white while the garments of Isis, the goddess of the material world, were represented in different shades and in mixed colors.[73] From all these texts two main characteristics of tone emerge: (1) it is more agreeable to the eye than pure colors, and especially than pure white and black; (2) it is more appropriate for the perception and representation of the material world. Both characteristics are in general accordance with the actual application of tones in painting.

In spite of these literary reminiscences and half-articulated religious symbolism, the main foundation for the discussions of tone in Venetian theory seems to be the painter's workshop, and his experiences and problems in his actual work. This emerges perhaps most clearly from the contexts in which the concept of tone appears in Venetian treatises. The problems of tones are often discussed in immediate connection with the work of particular painters, and the concept is exemplified either by the style of famous Venetian artists or by the analysis of particular works of art. The precepts laid down for the representation of particular themes offer another occasion for this type of discussion.[74] The close connection of the concept of tone with the artist's work and procedures may also be seen in a negative way, that is, in the fact that this concept does not occur in the discussion of color in nonartistic spheres. In some treatments of color that

are not connected with art it is even explicitly rejected. At the beginning of
this chapter I remarked that problems of color were extensively discussed in
Venetian writings of heraldry and color symbolism. In this literature the
reader is often expressly warned of the danger inherent in the mixtures and
blendings of colors. Fulvio Pellegrino Morato, the author of an important
treatise on color symbolism, difines the blending of colors as a "corrup-
tion." [75] Lodovico Dolce in his volume on color symbolism also calls
mixtures of color corrupt,[76] yet the same Dolce in his book on painting,
L'Aretino, praises the value of color blending as showing the ability and
achievement of the artist. The reason for this distinction is obvious. For
conventional symbolism the clear identity of color, and consequently its
readability, is, of course, essential; this identity can only be obscured by
mixtures and blendings. The painter, however, seeks values other than clear
readability of single isolated colors; his particular values are realized by
mixtures and blendings. The obvious distinction between the symbolic
approach (which is intimately connected with literary and emblematic
traditions) and the approach of the painter is, I think, an additional proof
for the decisive influence of the atelier in the discussions of tone in the
theory of art.

We may conclude by saying that in the discussion of tone Venetian
theory not only formulated new and important theoretical concepts of color
but also sharpened one of the main foci of actual Venetian painting. Here
the theory of art reflects, and at the same time helps to clarify, the actual
tendencies of contemporary art.

I have emphasized the Venetian origins of the concept of tone. However,
it would be a mistake to assume that it emerged and was known in Venice
only. In fact, it was also familiar to artists and writers on art in other
centers. Again I shall mention only a few examples. Some scattered remarks
by Raffaelo Borghini, Vasari's most important follower in Florence, attest to
his acquaintance with tone in painting. He distinguished, for example,
between several kinds of white, "like [the white] of snow, of pure plaster, of
milk, of pearls, of ivory and the color similar to the skin of a white woman;
and while the white [color]. of snow and of plaster disturbs the eye . . . the
white [color] of milk and of pearls and of similar objects delights it, and if
it [the white color] is provided with a certain whitish brilliance it endows
charm; and that [i.e., the pleasure of the eye] follows from the fact that this

white contains a hidden reddish mixture [*un'occulta mescolanza san-guigna*]." [77] This suggestive description certainly shows that Borghini was familiar with the concept of tone.

Another instance is Armenini, who stood midway between the Florentine-Roman and the north Italian (Venetian and Lombardic) traditions. He emphasized the importance of light and color as against the Tuscan's concentration on *disegno*, but he did not go as far as the Venetians in his evaluation of coloristic effects. Armenini studied the different schools of Italian painting and was well aware of their stylistic differences; he also accepted (perhaps influenced by Lomazzo, whose *Trattato* appeared several years before Armenini's book) the existence of different styles of light. He divided painters into two groups: the artists of the one group represent "a fiery, broad and large light," while those belonging to the other group paint "a slight, weak, shadowed and dim" light. In his discussion of the second type, which displays "more science" than the first, Armenini describes the typical effects of tonal painting. The painters of this group represent, instead of the bright, the half bright, and, instead of deep darkness, the "sweet shadows." The main merit of the dim light, however, is good visibility; in it the *minutezze* of the represented body are better perceived.[78] While Armenini was acquainted with the effects of tonal painting, he conceived of it not as an autonomous artistic value but as a means for a clearer perception of objects. In this respect he obviously differs from the main Venetian current of thought.

These examples, to which some others could be added, show that the concept of tone was known to writers on art also outside Venice. Yet it should be borne in mind that discussions of "tone" outside Venice postdate the appearance in print of the important Venetian art treatises; and one can, therefore, assume that these discussions were, at least in part, influenced by the formulations presented in those works. Further, neither in Florence nor in Rome (nor even in Milan, which in other respects was influenced by Venetian theory) did "tone" constitute one of the major problems of art theory. Only in Venice was it a focal point of discussions on painting.

This can be seen, not only in the frequent use which Venetian writers made of such descriptive formulas as "soft shadows," "graceful light," "sweet transitions," and the like, but also in the themes which they recommended to the painter for representation. These themes show an affinity to the particular values and characteristics of tonal painting. Pino praises painting because it is able to represent a sunrise, the blush of dawn, and the mood of a rainy day.[79] Sorte points out the particular potentialities of painting by enumerating scenes which again suggest the specific values of tonal painting. Particularly interesting are his descriptions of the seasons as themes for pictorial representation. The spring shows a great wealth of different shades of green; the summer is characterized by a certain "whitish ripeness"; autumn reveals a wealth of colors as the leaves tend to reddish and yellowish hues; the winter shows a special charm of color as nature is covered by fog. The painter, Sorte concludes, should therefore be careful in the blending of colors.[80] Such an elaboration of scenes which would tend to lead the artist to tonal painting is, as far as I know, not to be found in the other Italian Renaissance traditions of art theory. The singling-out of these themes, therefore, indicates specifically Venetian tendencies. Venetian writers were also attracted by the expressive qualities of tonal painting. In a later part of this chapter we shall come back to this aspect.

We may then summarize our analysis of Venetian discussions of tone as follows: (1) there was no term for tone, but the authors were clearly aware of the characteristics of tonal painting; (2) this concept emerged in Venetian theory of art, although its influence was not restricted to Venice; (3) in the literary discussions it is usually connected with, and mainly derived from, actual Venetian painting; (4) it is regarded as an aesthetic and artistic value; and (5) it indicates a new evaluation of color in general or the evaluation of a new aspect of color.

V. Texture

Another problem which attracted the attention of Venetian painters and writers to a more than ordinary degree was the imitation of different materials in painting, that is, to what we now call "texture."

For several reasons, the convincing representation of textures was considered in Venice a great artistic achievement. First of all, it was regarded as a significant amplification of the representation of nature, as it introduces into the realm of pictorial imitation the whole range of material qualities which form an important aspect of reality itself and of our visual experience. Second, the representation of textures provided the painter with an opportunity to show his skill and the subtlety of his execution. The deep sensibility of Venetian culture to sensual experiences and values, which is so often expressed in literature, is perhaps an additional reason for the high appreciation of the representation of textures in painting. For all these reasons Venetian writers frequently discuss the rendering of textures in painting.

By texture we understand, as is well known, the peculiar material quality of objects, or of their surfaces. For the painter who represents these objects in his work, texture is intimately connected with light. The optical impression of a given texture is evoked by the specific reaction of a particular object to light. According to their specific material qualities objects either absorb light or reflect it in different ways, and with differing degrees of intensity. The painter creates an impression of textures by portraying these various reactions of objects to light. There is thus a clear connection between the rendering of light and the representation of textures. Needless to say, this holds true, and is practically perceived, even if the painters are not aware of the more scientific aspects of this connection, as happened in Venice. It is in any case a significant fact that the Venetian authors discussed the problem of texture in connection with color while they seem to have completely disregarded the scientific, optical aspects and theories that may have been related to it.

Before we discuss the Venetian concepts of the representation of texture it may be useful to summarize the history of this problem. The creation of a convincing pictorial illusion of the material qualities found in nature is an old and well-known theme in art literature, already expressed in antiquity.[81] Cennini's *Libro* demonstrates that early Renaissance painters were aware of this problem, while his comments reveal an ambiguity deriving from the various tendencies prevailing in the art of his time. The very fact that Cennini is aware of the problem of rendering differentiated materials is, on the one hand, important evidence for the emergence of realistic tendencies. On the other hand, Cennini does not envisage the creation of an illusion of textures, achieved by the peculiar means of the painter, that is, by representing reactions to light. He rather advised the painter actually to duplicate the portrayed texture in the picture. Thus the effect of woolen texture should be achieved, according to Cennini, by actually roughening the picture's surface.[82] This approach, as has been said in a former chapter, is very close to the thought of the medieval artist who, in order to achieve the brilliance of gold, put actual gold on the surface of the picture.

It is an interesting fact that, as the naturalistic and scientific tendencies of quattrocento painting deepened and gained ground, concern with the representation of textures seems to have faded out. The emphasis placed on the correct representation of space and the high evaluation of the *rilieuo* effect suppressed the urge to evoke an illusion of the material qualities of objects. It is true that the problem of textures in painting was not altogether forgotten. Alberti, for example, said that a baby's body in pictorial representation should be not only "round" but also "soft in touch," while that of an aged man should be "rugged and edged." The painter should not use pure gold, but he should represent the brilliance of gold by the skillful application of colors.[83] However, these remarks of Alberti remained more or less marginal, and the idea expressed in them cannot be counted among the dominant motifs in quattrocento painting and theory of art. Speaking in broad terms, one can say that the scientific theory of painting, as it was developed in the fifteenth century, constituted in this respect a certain regression compared with the earlier traditions of the artistic workshops mirrored in Cennini's *Libro.*

Leonardo attached greater importance to the problems of texture, but he did not place them in the context of light and color. Besides the observations on highlights, which we discussed in an earlier chapter, he also mentioned reflections in water and discussed at some length the forms of folds in different materials, such as linen, wool, and silk. But although he observed these phenomena, he dealt with them mainly as questions of linear form and of iconographic appropriateness.[84] He did not look at textures primarily from the point of view of the specific reactions of different materials to light.

In the sixteenth century artists and writers paid greater attention to textures. Reading the treatises of this period, especially those composed in Venice, one sometimes has the impression that the painter's eyes were fascinated by the sudden discovery of the material qualities of nature and the possibility of representing these qualities in painting. The new concern with textures is, of course, not restricted to Venice. Vasari often attests it in his descriptions of paintings. [85] Yet it seems that the full articulation of the artistic concepts for texture, and especially their close connection to light and color, is to be found mainly in Venetian art literature. Here again this literature reflects the actual tendencies of Venetian painting.

As in the case of "tone" Italian theory of art did not possess a special term of texture. But an attempt to define the realm of texture by a single word may be found in Pino's *proprietà*. As we recall, *proprietà* refers to symbolic as well as to representational criteria in the application of color. The latter meaning is suggested by the examples which Pino gives in discussing *proprietà*. The suitability (*proprietà*) of colors "should be reduced to the similarity with real objects, like the variations of the flesh colors according to age and complexion . . . , to the distinction between a linen garment, or a woollen, or [one] of silk, between gold and copper, between brilliant iron and silver . . . between water and air." [86]

The Venetian authors emphasized the specific artistic value of texture representation. Interesting in this respect are Pino's comparisons of painting and sculpture. He introduces a somewhat new motif into this famous and much-discussed topic by basing the superiority of painting over sculpture on the ability of the former to represent textures. "We [painters] . . . make an armor recognizable, a garment of silk or of linen." The sentences following this quotation clearly show that Pino was aware of some connection between the representation of textures and the specific problems of the application of color. " . . . and if you will say, [these the representations of textures] are the effect of colors, I shall reply: no, because the green [color] represents all green things, but it does not represent the peculiarities of velvet or of a garment of linen, since colors cannot produce such effects if the master does not add to them his art. The sculptors are imperfect since they do not possess the ability to represent an object in his peculiarity, but only in its contours." [87]

This interesting passage indicates one of the central tendencies in Venetian theory of art. The representation of textures, which is expressly connected with color, is here explicitly conceived as the very foundation of the superiority of painting over sculpture. Implicitly, however, the validity of Pino's statement is not restricted to sculpture. The specific element that here stands for sculpture—that is, contour, outline—is in fact common to all works of art which lack color, and may even designate a linear style in painting in which coloristic effects are suppressed. The appreciation of texture, therefore, is an appreciation of the value of color in general. The attitude behind this statement can be even more closely defined. The representation of textures is not achieved by the application of pure colors. Pino does not say what precisely is the "art" which the master adds to pure colors in order to evoke the illusion of velvet or linen, but we shall probably not go wrong in assuming that this "art" is connected to tone, that is, to the modification of colors by light. Such a modification seems to be the main difference between a pure green and one which creates the impression of a green velvet or linen or silk. If this interpretation is correct, the problem of textures leads back to the central problem of Venetian color theory, namely, to the fusion of light and color, and to its consequences for the whole art of painting.

The intimate connection between the representation of textures and the application of colors, especially in the style of tonal painting, was never explicitly stated and systematically developed in Venetian theory. But such a connection is suggested—though sometimes only vaguely—in most Venetian treatises. A typical example is Dolce's discussion of the problem. He sees the main difficulty of applying color in the imitation of flesh, which consists, he says, in representing the softness of the body and the variety of its tones *(tinte)*. This difficulty is linked to the other problems of rendering textures, like the representation of wool, silk, gold, and the brilliance of weapons. Dolce relates these specific texture problems to the common themes of tonal painting (the brightness of the day, the hues of water, earth, etc.). It is, moreover, characteristic that this whole discussion is contained in a passage which opens with the demand that in a picture the colors be toned down and united so as to represent nature.[88] From this passage, as from others that could be adduced, it emerges that the representation of texture was conceived of as belonging to tonal painting.

As I said at the beginning of this section, the Venetians esteemed the representation of texture so highly because it widened the realm of *imitazione* and added to painting a dimension of reality hitherto neglected in Renaissance art and art theory. The Venetian authors seem to have believed that a painting fulfills all the conditions for creating a convincing illusion of reality when, in addition to the formerly applied criteria (correctness in anatomy, perspective, modeling, etc.), it also faithfully renders the textures of the objects. Marco Boschini concludes a long passage dealing with Titian's ability to represent textures with a statement that the artist was a "mirror reflecting truth." [89] The concept of "life in painting," which in Renaissance literature is the formula used to designate the climax of naturalism, is connected with the rendering of textures. "When the painter," Dolce says, "produces a good imitation of the tones and softness of flesh and rightful characteristics of any object there may be, he makes his paintings seem alive, to the point where breath is the only thing missing in them." [90]

The representation of texture is bound up with the conception of color as a noble value, that is, with tonal painting; moreover, the evaluation of texture seems to ascribe a new function to color. In Renaissance thought the representation of texture may have something to do with the cognitive function of painting, and especially of color. In representing a woolen cloth differently from a silken garment, the body of a baby differently from that of an old man, the painter visually articulates differences in nature. Painting becomes the medium in which an additional aspect of nature is made recognizable by a specific use of colors. It cannot be conclusively proved that this idea was consistently thought through by Renaissance authors, but several passages would seem to suggest it. Sorte's remark that in coloring the painter should try to satisfy those "who have knowledge and seek the truth," rather than give pleasure to the ignorant, may be interpreted in this sense.[91] Lomazzo's assertion, which we shall discuss in the next chapter, that by means of color one can distinguish between different kinds of stone [92] would also seem to refer to the representation of textures, and therefore to the use of color, as a medium of recognizing nature. We can summarize the views on this problem in three main points:

(1) The representation of textures is highly appreciated as a means of creating the illusion of reality.

(2) These representations are intimately connected with light and color and are conceived as a particular application of tonal painting.

(3) They may have had some connection with the cognitive function of color.

It should be said finally that literary traditions and sources played a very limited part in considerations of the representation of texture in painting. Whatever observations the Venetian authors made on the problem seem to have been based on actual paintings and perhaps on workshop discussions, which may indeed be the reason for the vagueness in the verbal formulation of these observations. Thus the whole problem of textures in Venetian theory of art is a reflection of a central trend in contemporary Venetian painting. It is one of the points where the theory comes closest to the actual art.

VI. Oil Colors

The problems presented by sixteenth-century Venetian painting and discussed in the contemporary treatises necessarily involved matters of technique as well as concepts of expression. Among the technical themes, the evaluation of oil painting plays an important part.

It is characteristic of Venetian art theory that painting in oil colors is more appreciated than painting in any other technique. This is clearly expressed in Pino's *Dialoga*, the first important Venetian treatise. Pino says that an artist can excel in all techniques of painting, but he adds that "painting with oil colors is the most perfect way and the true practice." [93] In opposition to the generally accepted opinion that oil painting was "invented" in Flanders, or that it was "German" (i.e., northern) tradition, Pino maintains that it was invented in Italy.[94] In most of the other Venetian treatises the superiority of oil painting is not explicitly stated but is implied by the praise of painters like Titian whose works are executed in oil colors.

Italian workshops of the fourteenth century were acquainted with oil painting, although they knew it in a rudimentary and undeveloped form. It was sometimes referred to, in theoretical statements, but mainly as a means of lending durability to a decoration or perhaps to a painting.[95] The Venetian authors of the sixteenth century radically departed from this traditional view. They discussed painting in oil colors as a medium which was particularly suitable for the realization of certain pictorial values. In other words, it was considered and appreciated not as a purely technical means but as having an affinity to a certain style.

The high esteem in which oil painting was held is clearly opposed to the tendencies which dominated in the fifteenth century and still prevailed in Florence in the middle of the sixteenth. In Florentine theory *fresco* was the technique most highly valued. Vasari's introduction to the *vite* is a document that enables us to perceive this difference between Florence and

Venice. Vasari was well acquainted with the specific properties of oil painting, but he asserts that "of all the methods that painters employ, painting on the wall is the most masterly and beautiful." [96] The reasons for the assumed superiority of *fresco* painting are, on the one hand, the fact that this technique requires great skill and virtuosity (the necessity of working fast and impossibility of correcting mistakes) and, on the other, the belief that ancient painting (which was much admired but not well known) was primarily wall painting. Pino also knew ancient painting and, like his contemporaries, thought of it as wall painting.[97] Nevertheless, he believed in the excellence of oil painting and explicitly stated its superiority over the technique of *fresco*. Why did the Venetians believe in this predominance of oil painting?

As I have already said, Venetian authors did not discuss their ideas systematically, and therefore the evidence for their views is often only "circumstantial evidence." Yet, in reading Venetian observations on the nobility of oil painting one clearly gets the impression that their judgment was not determined by a consideration of the purely technical advantages of this method but by their awareness of the fact that oil painting was especially suitable for the production of tonal color; in other words, that it was capable of embodying in painting precisely those artistic values which were highly appreciated in Venice.

The suitability of oil painting for producing tonal effects was well known in all sixteenth-century schools. Vasari, for example, described this property of oil colors:

> This manner of painting kindles the pigments and nothing else is needed save diligence and devotion, because the oil itself softens and sweetens the colors and renders them more delicate and more easily blended than do the other mediums. . . . In short, by this method [i.e., by painting with oil colors] the artist imparts wonderful grace and vivacity and vigor to these figures.[98]

Although Vasari was well aware of the stylistic potentialities of oil painting, he preferred the technique of *fresco,* which lacks these properties. For Pino, however, these very properties constitute the basis for the superiority of oil painting. Oil colors, he says, "give a greater perfection and a better union of one hue [tinte] with the other." [99]

An important source, although not always an altogether reliable one, is the description of pictures painted in oil colors. The early Michiel described the tonal effects of oil paintings by Italian masters (especially by Giorgione) as well as by Flemish artists, stressing their brilliance as well as the unification of tones.[100] Aretino admired the coloring in oil paintings because it was "sweet and *isfumata*." [101] Dolce praises the colors in Raphael's mural paintings which overshadow the coloring "of many good masters in oil, and they are tonally diffused and unified, to the accompaniment of projection of its finest kind and everything that art can achieve" [102]–a clear testimony to the fact that *sfumare* and unifying the colors were regarded as characteristic properties of oil painting. He stresses the softly united and yet lively colors in Giogione's oil paintings.[103] Of Titian, whose works were, of course, executed in oil colors, he says that he avoided superfluous virtuosity; in his coloring there is "no crudity [crudezza] but the mellowness and softness of nature." [104] Sorte seems to regard oil painting as particularly appropriate for the rendering of atmospheric effects in which he saw a supreme instance of the whole art of painting.[105]

All these passages suggest that the Venetian authors were aware of a particular connection between the technique of oil painting and stylistic trend of tonal painting. One may, therefore, assume that their belief in the superiority of oil colors emerges from their belief in the value inherent in this type of painting.

VII. The Expression of Colors

We have considered the main focal points in the development of Venetian art theory, and seen that literary movements and workshop experiences merged more fully there than anywhere else in Renaissance theory. Did a doctrine of the expressive qualities of color arise from this particular historical constellation? It is difficult to answer this question, and the difficulty in itself illuminates the nature and the specific character of this theory. Expression in art was appreciated by Venetian writers. Dolce summarizes what seems to him to be the very essence of art by saying that "paintings need to move the spectator, and . . . that the painter is born that way." [106] The appreciation of expression, together with the deep interest in color, could have led to the formulation of a doctrine of the expressive qualities of colors. But observations on the expressive meanings of colors, although extant and sometimes even prominent, are implied rather than explicitly stated in Venetian literature. The nontheoretical character and the loose literary formulation of the treatises, as well as their intimate connection with the artist's actual working experience, probably impeded the development of a systematic and articulate doctrine of the expressiveness of color.

As far as we can speak of the existence of theoretical statements about the stirring of emotions in Venetian art literature, the authors repeat the usual humanistic formulas, which are well known, especially from Florentine sources. The attitudes and movements of the figures, their physiognomy and some characteristic details of the scene represented (like wind-blown garments) are regarded as the main means of expression. However, besides these widely known *topoi*, color also was regarded as imbued with a certain emotional quality and, therefore, capable of evoking feeling. The authors often speak of the "sweetness" of colors and transitions, and the "softness" of shades. The well-known formula that color endows the painting with life is also sometimes used. All this, however, is vague and attests only to a general feeling for color expressiveness. Venetian authors did not formulate a classification of the expressive value of colors, and consequently they did not give any detailed advice on how to achieve varied expressive effects by the appropriate application of different hues. The descriptions of paintings clearly reveal that the authors perceived an evocative, expressive quality in colors and lights. But as far as this quality is concerned, the descriptions remained rather general, using time and again the same stereotyped literary formulas. The reference to the expressive character of color is only an overtone of these descriptions. Dolce's letter to Alessandro Contarini, largely consisting of a description of Titian's *Adonis,* is an interesting document. Although suggesting the expressive effect of the coloring, it remains vague and general in its statements.[107] By the end of the sixteenth century we find, in Sorte's *Osservazioni* a somewhat more detailed discussion of this aspect. In his description of a fire (which may have been influenced by a Flemish painting) greater emphasis is placed on the expressive character of colors and types of light, and some indications are given of how to achieve these effects in painting.[108] In his discussion of the function of color in religious paintings the expressive character is more strongly stressed. The invisible God, Sorte says, should not be represented by conventional bodily colors "but by sweet and soft [colors] that are suited to show a superhuman substance and a pure and simple divinity." All divine appearances should be surrounded by a "sweet brilliance that does not terrify but permeates man with astonishment and adoration." [109] But even these descriptions and suggestions, although more elaborate than those of the former authors, do not constitute a theoretical doctrine of color expression.

Some scattered passages in Venetian literature on color symbolism may also have a bearing on our problem. Although this literature deals with the conventional meanings of colors, it sometimes refers to the emotions evoked by the specific hues. It will suffice here to mention one example, taken from Dolce's volume on color symbolism. A certain gray *(cesio)*, he says, expresses cruelty. Its emotional character is exemplified not only by many quotations from ancient literature but also by the mention of contemporary works of art. Thus, Michelangelo painted the eyes of Charon in this specific shade in order to express the cruel nature of this figure.[110] Such examples show that even in the literature on symbolism color was perceived as having some emotional quality. But as I have already said, this literature was not concerned with the emotional character and the evocative power of color. Therefore, the suggestions of the expressive character of color, occurring in treatises on symbolism, could not constitute a doctrine of the expressive value of color in art. It was only in the last stage of Renaissance theory of art, in Milan, that an articulate theory of color expression was developed.

Notes

1. Marcantonio Michiel, *Notizia d'opere di disegno* (ed. Th. V. Frimmel in *Quellen-schriften für Kunstgeschichte*. Neue Folge, I [Vienna, 1888]. See, for instance, p. 80 on the harmony on tones *(convenienza delle tinte)*, highlights, and halftones *(meze tinte)*; p. 98 on soft shadows. His description of Giorgione's *Three Philosophers* (pp. 86 ff.) also suggests a deep concern with the play of light and color which is characteristic for the Venetian treatises after Pino. Venetian theory of art has been studied several times. Cf. S. Ortolani, "Le origini della critica d'arte a Venezia," *L'Arte,* XXIV (1923,) 3 ff.; M. Pittaluga, "Eugene Fromentin e le origini della moderna critica d'arte," *L'Arte,* XX (1917), 240-258 (on color). R. Palluchini, *La critica d'arte a Venezia nel Cinquecento* (Venice, 1943). And see Mark W. Roskill's introduction to *Dolce's "Aretino" and Venetian Art Theory of the Cinquecento* (New York, 1968), esp. pp. 14 ff.

2. Cf., e.g., Aretino's letter to Domenico Bolani from October 27, 1537 (in the Paris edition of Aretino's letters [1609], I, 169v ff.), containing vivid descriptions of the Venetian cityscape. Venice, Pietro Aretino says, is full of "delizie visive." Cf. also Ortolani, "Le origini," pp. 11 ff.

3. See the bibliography of sources at the end of this book.

4. It might be useful to give here some brief information about the authors of the principal Venetian treatises. The question of Pino's origin has caused some discussion. Schlosser *(Die Kunstliteratur* [Vienna, 1924], p. 210) assumed that Pino might have been of Sicilian origin and was perhaps identical with the "Pino da Messina" of whom Francesco Sansovino talks in his *Venezia descritta* (1581), p. 49, Ridolfo and Anna Palluchini, in the introduction to their edition of Pino's *Dialogo di Pittura* (Venice, 1946), pp. 12 ff., have, however, convincingly shown that he was of Venetian origin. Pietro Aretino's life need not be discussed here. Lodovico Dolce (1509-1568), a prolific writer, was born in Venice, studied in Padua, and was then a proofreader in the Venetian press of Giovanni and Gabriele Giolitto where the *editio princeps* of his *L'Aretino* appeared in 1557. The fullest account of Lodovico

Dolce's life may be found in E. A. Cicogna, "Memorie intorno la vita e gli scritti de Messer Lodovico Dolce," *Memorie dell' I.R. Istituto Veneto,* XI (1862), 93-113. See also Eitelberger's introduction to his German translation of Dolce's treatise (in *Quellenschriften für Kunstgeschichte,* II [Vienna, 1871]; Giuseppe Toffanin, *Il Cinquecento,* 3 ed. (Milan, 1945), p. 114; and the interesting discussion of Dolce's contribution to Italian style and grammar in Ciro Trabalza, *Storia della grammatica Italiana* (Milan, 1908), pp. 127 ff. Recently Roskill in his *Dolce's "Aretino,"* pp. 5 ff., has summarized Dolce's life story. See also J. Schulz, "Cristoforo Sorte and the Ducal Palace in Venice," *Mitteilungen des kunsthistorischen Instituts in Florenz,* X (1962), pp. 123 ff.

5. *Dialogo,* ed. Barocchi, pp. 96, 135; ed. Palluchini, pp. 63, 148.

6. Perhaps because of the mathematical method of Dürer's theory of art Pino mentions him together with Alberti. Of Dürer's treatise Pino says (Barocchi, p. 135; Palluchini, p. 148) that it is written in his native tongue "but deserves to be written in Latin." With Pino this advice might have a certain ironical meaning. Cf. the introduction to the *Dialogo* where he says that Alberti's treatise is composed "in the Latin tongue and has more of mathematics than of painting."

7. *Dialogo,* ed. Barocchi, p. 135; ed. Palluchini, p. 148. (For a number of studies in which this question is discussed see Barocchi, p. 43, note 10.)

8. *L'Aretino,* ed. Barocchi, p. 187. Dolce refers to the Italian translation of Alberti's *Della pittura,* and, of course, to the first edition of Vasari's *Lives.* Dürer is referred to as a painter on pp. 165 ff.

9. Dolce's borrowings from Vasari have been studied in detail by Roskill, pp. 14 ff.

10. It suffices to mention the best known visits and journeys. In 1500 Leonardo paid a short visit to Venice (perhaps not longer than a month). In 1509 Lotto worked in Rome, in 1511 Sebastiano del Piombo settled in Rome, but later visited Venice (in 1528). Rosso Florentino came in 1530 to Venice; in 1540 Giovanni da Udine worked there; in 1545-1546 Titian paid his famous visit to Rome. This list could be considerably enlarged (cf. Roskill, pp. 75 ff.).

11. Cf. Creighton E. Gilbert, "Antique Frameworks for Renaissance Art Theory: Alberti and Pino," *Marsyas,* III (1943-1945), p. 93. See also Roskill, *Dolce's L'Aretino,"* pp. 9 ff. In Renaissance literature the dialogue was more frequently used in the vernacular than in Latin, and it was a typical form of prose discussion. Cf. Ch. S. Baldwin (ed. by D. L. Clark), *Renaissance Literary Theory and Practice* (Gloucester, Mass., 1959), pp. 42 f. The mood of lighthearted conversation is often

emphasized in the opening sentences of the Venetian dialogues on art. Pino begins his work with the praise of Venetian woman; Dolce opens his dialogue by recalling a visit to a beautiful church.

12. The Venetians' neglection of "rules" may have something in common with the important trend in late sixteenth-century criticism which passionately rejected mathematics as the basis of art. (See the famous sentences of Zuccari in his *Idea*, II, [Turin, 1607], pp. 29 ff.). There is, however, a significant difference between these approaches. While Zuccari rejects mathematics in favor of an elaborate metaphysical conception of the artist, Pino rejects *scienza,* especially mathematics (see ed. Barocchi, p. 96) in favor of a vague concept of "nature," which may include the gifts bestowed upon the artist by nature, as well as *delizie visive* of reality.

13. Ed. Barocchi, p. 96; ed. Palluchini, p. 62.

14. Ed. Barocchi, p. 116; ed. Palluchini, p. 106.

15. See Pietro Aretino's letter of June 29, 1537, to Girolamo de Correggio (Paris edition, I, fols. 124v ff.) where the critical attitude toward pedantism is implied rather than explicitly stated, and his letter to the cardinal of Ravenna, written on August 27 in the same year (I, fols. 142v ff.). Cf. Ortolani, op. cit., pp. 7 ff., and A. Semmerau, *Pietro Aretino: Ein Bild aus der Renaissance* (Vienna, 1925), pp. 174 ff., who gives a useful collection of Aretino's statements against pedantism in literature and life, unfortunately without any bibliographical references. Pietro Aretino also ridiculed the–specifically Florentine?–"Neoplatonic parlance" *(Il Filosofo,* especially V, 4) and the literary fashion of frequently quoting from Dante and Petrarch. Cf. E. Panofsky, *Studies in Iconology,* p. 148, note 68.

16. For suggestive descriptions of visual experiences see, in addition to Aretino's letters quoted in note 2, his letter of March 1544 (Paris edition, III, fols. 48v ff.). For his views as representing the Venetian concepts of art cf. L. M. Gengaro, *Orientamenti della Critica d'Arte nel Rinascimento Cinquecentesco* (Milan-Messina, 1941), p. 135, and the brief remarks of Lionello Venturi, "Pierre Aretin, Paul Pino, Louis Dolce ou la critique d'art à Venise au XVIe siècle," *Gazette des beaux-arts,* 66e année (1924), pp. 39 ff. See also K. Vossler, "Pietro Aretinos künstlerisches Bekenntnis," *Neue Heidelberger Jahrbücher,* X (1900), 38 ff. The frequent characterization of Venetian taste as tending toward lustrous surfaces can be corroborated by many texts from the Renaissance period. Marcantonio Michiel, for instance, speaks of paintings which are "very lively and perfect, and resplendent as if they were oil paintings." Cf. Anonimo Morelliano, *Notizie d'Opere del Disegno,* p. 80. One may assume that one of the reasons for the acceptance of oil painting in Venice was the fact that a picture executed in this medium has a lustrous surface that appealed to Venetian taste.

17. Dolce himself made a translation of Horace's *Ars poetica* which he dedicated to Pietro Aretino (appeared in Venice, 1535). In his dialogue *L'Aretino* he quotes the famous Horatian phrase, "Si vis me flere" (p. 186) and refers frequently to Horace (pp. 147, 167 ff., 180). For a recent detailed discussion of the Horatian tradition in Renaissance literary theory cf. B. Weinberg, *A History of Literary Criticism in the Italian Renaissance* (Chicago, 1969) PP. 71-249. Dolce himself applied the principles of Horatian poetics to a contemporary poet, Ariosto. See Weinberg, p. 174.

18. For a discussion of the concept of *giudizio naturale* in Renaissance aesthetic thought see R. Klein, "*Giudizio* et *gusto* dans la théorie de l'art au Cinquecento," *Rinascimento,* 2d series, I, pp. 105-116.

19. Pino, ed. Palluchini, pp. 141-142.

20. Klibansky, Saxl and Panofsky, *Saturn and Melancholy* (London, 1964), pp. 241 ff.

21. Sorte, *Osservazioni,* p. 300. See also my study in *Arte Lombarda,* X, 253 ff.

22. Pino's acceptance of Florentine patterns has been noticed several times. See R. Palluchini, *La critica d'arte a Venezia nel Cinquecento* (Venice, 1943), p. 15: "Il Pino accettà principi teoretici dell'umanesimo toscano, ma li stempera, li corregge in base alla sua stessa esperienza figurativa, ciòe al gusto veneziano." See also the observations of Paola Barocchi in the critical notes to her edition, I, pp. 312 ff.

23. Pino, ed. Barocchi, pp. 113 ff.; ed. Palluchini, pp. 100 ff.

24. Cf. C. Gilbert, "Antique Frameworks," Marsyas, 1941, pp. 94 f. Pino's scheme is, of course, derived from the Tuscan division of painting into outline, composition, and reception of lights. Cf. Gilbert, pp. 95 ff.; ed. Barocchi's note, I, p. 314, and Palluchini in the introduction to Pino's *Dialogo,* pp. 37 ff.

25. Pino, ed. Barocchi, p. 117; ed. Palluchini, p. 109. Here, one should also recall a related concept that coloring cannot be taught, which appears in Venetian theory of art. Cf. Sorte, p. 273 (". . . li modi del colorire nelle opere della pittura non si possano terminatamente insegnare"); p. 292 (in the context of a discussion of color, ". . . perciò che questi e cosi fatti sono soggetti tanto particolari e proprii del giudicio e della mano del pittore, che non si penne ne esprimere, a meno insegnare. . . .)".

26. " . . . la proprietà delli colori et intender bene le composizioni loro, cioè redurli alla similitudine delle cose proprie, come il variar delle carni corrispondenti all'età, alla complessione et al grado di quel che si figne, distinguere un panno di lino da quel di lana o di seta, far discernere l'oro dal rame . . .", ed. Barocchi, pp. 116 f.; ed. Palluchini, p. 109.

27. " ... e niun colore vale per sua proprietà a fare un minimo dell'effetti del naturale, però se gli conviene l'Intelligenzia e pratica de buon maestro," ed. Barocchi, p. 117; ed. Palluchini, p. 109.

28. Ed. Barocchi, p. 117; ed. Palluchini, p. 110. The fact that Pino does not give any practical precepts is a characteristic feature of his "literary," humanistic approach to the problem of painting.

29. " ... le prontezze degli atti [of the represented figures], come negli scurci, dove alcune parte fuggono dal vedere," ed. Barocchi, p. 99; ed. Palluchini, pp. 69 f. " ... perchè ciascun maestro si debbe acuir nella prontezza degli atti moventi e pronti, dove le figure in più parti fuggano, scurzano o diminuiscano," ed. Barocchi, p. 103; ed. Palluchini, p. 78.

30. Ed. Barocchi, p. 118; ed. Palluchini, p. 110. Barocchi, in her comments to Pino (I, pp. 414 f.), suggests that the roots of this concept may be found in Alberti, who interprets *prontezza* (which had not yet acquired a terminologic character) as the result of *ingegno* and *esercizio*. In *Della pittura* (ed. Mallè, p. 110; ed. Spencer, p. 95), Alberti says "your mind moved and warmed by exercise gives itself with greater promptness [*pronto*] and dispatch to the work; and that hand will proceed most rapidly which is well guided by a certain rule of the mind."

31. The idea—and ideal—of *facilità* pervades the whole work of Castiglione (a concise formulation in *Il Corteggiano*, I, 36) and most of Bembo's writings. Although conceived mainly as an ideal of social behavior, it had well-known implications on the conception of the artist and his work. See A. Blunt, *Artistic Theory in Italy 1450-1600*, pp. 94 ff., and the article by S. Monk, "A Grace Beyond the Reach of Art," *Journal of the History of Ideas*, V (1944) 131 ff.

32. Sorte, pp. 299 ff. (description of Tintoretto's procedures); p. 277 (a discussion of the "power of judgment"). For the spiritual nature of *prontezza* see, for instance, Francesco Sansovino's treatise, *Tutte le cose notabili e bene che sono in Venezia*, which appeared under the pseudonym Anselmo Giusconi, p. 18, in which Tintoretto is characterized as "tutto spirito, tutto prontezza." See Palluchini, *Critica*, p. 23. The use of *giudizio* as a term denoting an expressive or creative faculty seems to have been specific for Venice. Ortolani, *Le origini*, p. 10, notices this use of the term in Pietro Aretino's writings. See also R. Klein, *Giudizio et gusto*, p. 112.

33. "Ed il Palma mi attestaua per verità, che ne i finimenti dipingeua più con le dita, che con pennelli. E veramente [chi ben ci pensa] egli con ragione così operò: perchè, volendo imitare l'operazione del Sommo Creatore, faceua di bisogno osseruare, che egli pure nel formar questo corpo humano lo formò di terra con le mani." *Breve instruzione*, no pagination (p. 18 from the beginning of the text of the

Breve instrvzione). Cf. Erwin Panofsky, *Problems in Titian* (New York, 1969), pp. 16 ff., and note 23.

34. Pino, ed. Barocchi, p. 118.

35. Pietro Aretino may be regarded as a representation of the first type and Armenini of the second. For Aretino's tendency to fuse light and color see the texts mentioned in notes 40, 41. For Armenini's differentiation between light and color see his *De veri precetti della pittura* in which he discusses light and shade (mainly pp. 80-85) and color (mainly pp. 105-134) under different headings and without any significant intrinsic relationship between them, except for the adding of white and black to colors in order to make them brighter or darker.

36. Pino, ed. Barocchi, p. 118; "Le cose [seen and painted in such a light] ... si scuoprano meglio e con più graziatio modo." In Leonardo's *Treatise on Painting* (ed. McMahon, 134, p. 70), one finds a very similar precept with a similar expressive connotation. "If you have a courtyard that you can cover when you wish with a linen awning, this light is good. ... In the streets at twilight note the faces of men and women when the weather is bad, how much attractiveness and softness [*gratia e dolcezza*] is seen in them."

37. See above, pp. 20 ff., 29 ff.

38. See above, pp. 46 ff.

39. Michiel, *Notizie d'opere* (see note 1), 80, 86 ff., 98.

40. " ... la naturale unione de i colori distesi ne i lumi e nelle ombre con mirabile giudizio di gratiosa maniera" (Paris edition, III, p. 59).

41. See his letter to Titian from November 19, 1537 (Paris edition, I, fol. 180r).

42. Dolce, *L'Aretino,* ed. Barocchi, p. 183; Roskill, *Dolce's "Aretino,"* p. 153.

43. "Diro adunque, che si come il Dissegno ha molti membri così anco il Colorito si dilata in varie circonstanze, a particolarita." In this manner is formed "il Colorita alla Veneziana" which refers mainly to the representation of the body. See Marco Boschini, *Breve instruzione,* the chapter on *Colorito.*

44. See, e.g., Dolce's description of Polidoro da Caravaggio (ed. Barocchi, p. 199) whose chiaroscuro frescoes are praised but of whom it is said that he failed as a colorist.

45. Dolce, ed. Barocchi, p. 145.

46. Pino, ed. Barocchi, p. 116; This observation of Pino has been noticed and discussed by serveral art historians. Ortolani, *Le origini,* pp. 13 ff., considers it as one of the original observations in Pino's treatise; Schlosser, *La letteratura artistica,* p.

241, sees it as connected with other expressions of Venetian sixteenth-century authors who criticize the former generations. Dolce also regarded Giovanni Bellini's works as "dead and cold" (ed. Barocchi, p. 202); he was a "good and diligent master," according to his "age" (*età*) but was surpassed by Giogione (p. 145). Gengaro, *Orientamenti della critica*, pp. 137 f., holds that Dolce characterizes the tension between the painting in the Quattrocento and the Cinquecento by opposing the Bellinis to Giorgione and Titian.

47. "E veramento se Gio Bellino (come habbiamo detto) leuò la Pittura dalle tenebre, e Giorgione le ha postò in fronto vn Diamante così purgato, e risplendente. . . . Nel colorito trouò poi quell'impasto di pennello così morbido . . . e ben si può credere, che Giorgione sià stato nella Pittura un'altro Gio Guthembergo inuentore de Caratteri di Stampe." *Breve instruzione,* chapter on Giorgione. I have changed somewhat the sequence of the quoted passages.

48. An extensive discussion of tone, from a modern point of view, may be found in A. Pope, *An Introduction to the Language of Drawing and Painting* (Cambridge, Mass.), I *The Painter's Terms* (1929), pp. 11-30, 93-100; II, *The Painter's Modes of Expression* (1931), pp. 63-106.

49. I give only a few examples. See Cennini, *Il Libro dell'Arte,* p. 46; Armenini, *De veri precetti della pittura,* p. 108; Lomazzo, *Trattato,* II, pp. 109 f.

50. J. Shearman, *Andrea del Sarto* (Oxford, 1965), I, p. 133.

51. Th. Hetzer, *Tizian: Geschichte seiner Farbe,* 2d ed. (Frankfurt, 1948), pp. 133 ff., notices that in the forties Titian employed colors that cannot be found in the former stages of Venetian painting, like different hues of gray, olive tints (greenish and brownish), and blackish or reddish velvet hues. Tints of this type, which are the product of blending different chromatic colors (that is, not only brightening or darkening a color by the addition of white and black), have of course the tendency to reinforce the overall tonal effect of the painting.

52. Pino, ed. Barocchi, p. 117. Ortolani, *Le Origini,* pp. 13 ff., sees here the "ideal of pure Giorgioneism." Gengaro, *Orientamenti della critica,* p. 130, also interprets this sentence of Pino as suggesting tonality. Palluchini, in the edition of Pino's *Dialogo,* p. 109, note 1, rightly stresses that this is a "confused definition of tone." The confusion, I think, is that the overall tonality, to which here Pino apparently refers, is limited to one single body. Barocchi's reference (*Trattati d'arte,* I, p. 414, note 7) to Alberti's concept of "friendship of colors" is, in this context, misleading. Alberti means the "friendship" between pure and clearly distinguished colors,

whereas Pino here means the tones which restrict the autonomy of plain colors.

53. Dolce, p. 184; Roskill, *Dolce's "Aretino,"* p. 155.

54. Dolce, p. 197: ". . . e sono sfumate et unite con bellissimo rilevo e con tutto quello che puo far l'arte." And see Dolce's letter to Casparo Bellini, written in 1544 (Bottari-Ticozzi, *Raccolta de lettere sulla Pittura, Sculture ed Architettura* [Milan, 1822-1825], V, pp. 166-176, esp. p. 172). An English translation in Roskill, *Dolce's "Aretino,"* pp. 200 ff. In the first edition of the *Lives,* Vasari praised Raphael's coloring in similar terms: " . . . con quella concordanzia et unione di colorito l'une con l'altra, che non si può non che fare" (Vasari, *Le vite . . . ,* ed. by C. Ricci, Rome, [1927], pp. 663).

55. Dolce's, pp. 198 f.: ". . . Giorgio di Castelfranco, di cui si veggono alcune cose à olio vivacissime e sfumate tanto, che non si scrogono ombre." Cf. Roskill, Dolce's "Aretino," p. 181.

56. Dolce, p. 183.

57. Lomazzo, *Idea,* chap. 13.

58. ". . . Ma il condimento de gli ultimi ritocchi era andar di quando, in quando unendo con sfregazzi della dita ne gli estremi di chari, auicinandosi alla meze tinte, et unerdo una tinta con l'altra. . . ." *Breve instruzione,* p. 17, from beginning of text.

59. See, e.g., B. Dupuy de Gréz, *Traité sur la peinture* (Toulouse), p. 197. The author draws largely from Italian theory of art, especially from Lomazzo. In his color theory, however, he is mainly influenced by Venetian treatises. In his appreciation of individual painters he also seems to follow Venetian models. Titian, he says, is the best painter because of his mastery of colors (p. 204). Dupuy de Grèz also has an interesting chapter on Veronese (p. 206). Cf. also Roger de Piles, *Dialogue sur le coloris* (Paris, 1699).

60. All the letters are reprinted in Barocchi, *Trattati d'arte,* I, pp. 59-82, the passage quoted on p. 80. This quote is from Elizabeth Holt's English translation.

61. Armenini, *De veri precetti della pittura,* p. 118; cf. also p. 106.

62. Pino, ed. Barocchi, pp. 108, 118.

63. In the letter to Bellini. See above, note 54. See Roskill, *Dolce's "Aretino,"* p. 207; cf. also p. 209.

64. Sorte, pp. 295 ff.

65. Pino, ed. Barocchi, p. 118;

66. Dolce, pp. 185 ff.

67. Bottari-Ticozzi, V, p. 175.

68. See above, pp. 30 ff.

69. Sorte, p. 296. "Ma a me parrebbe che converrebbono più tosto sadisfare a colore che sono di cognizione et intendono la verità, che a questi altri, e seguir più tosto la poca che la volgar gente." See also Armenini, p. 106.

70. Pliny, *Natural History,* XXXV, xi, 29 (in the Loeb edition, iv, pp. 282-283): "Then came the final adjunct of shine, quite a different thing from light. The opposition between shine and light on the one hand and shade on the other was called contrast, while the juxtaposition of colors and their passage one into another was termed attunement [... commisuras vero colorum et transitus harmogen]." For a discussion of this passage see W. Seibt, *Helldunkel.* Pliny, though not this particular passage, is, of course, frequently mentioned by Venetian writers.

71. See *Sopplimenti musicali del Rev. M. Gioseffo Zarlino da Chioggia* (Venice, 1588), pp. 75, 166, 174 ff. Zarlino's authorities for the parallelism between musical tones and colors are the ancients (see esp. p. 111). The relationship between Venetian theory of art and theory of music (which flourished here in the second half of the sixteenth century) deserves more attention than it has received so far, and would probably yield interesting results. For the art historian Venetian theory of music is significant both as a parallel expression of the tendencies dominating Venetian culture of that time and as a possible source for direct influences. It is also remarkable that Venetian writers on painting often mention music and musicians. Cf. Pino, ed. Barocchi, p. 107, for a comparison between painting (with special emphasis on colors) and music; for painters who were also musicians, see ed. Barocchi, p. 135, and Dolce, p. 153. Both Pino and Dolce refer to Silvestro (Ganassi), who wrote treatises on the teaching of music (see Palluchini's edition, p. 149, note 3, and Barocchi, I, p. 430, note 11). As a background, dealing with an earlier period, see A. Chastel, *Art et Humanisme à Florence au temps de Laurent le Magnifique* (Paris, 1961), pp. 189 ff.

72. Quoted after F. A. Yates, *The French Academies of the Sixteenth Century (Studies of the Warburg Institute,* XV (London, 1947), p. 290. In the original edition of Mersenne's *Harmonie universelle,* pp. 13 ff.

73. Quoted after Yates, p. 147. F. Yates, loc. cit., note 2, suggests that A. Jamyn might have drawn either from Pierio Valeriano's *Hieroglyphics* or from Plutarch, *De Iside et Osiride.*

74. The theme most frequently mentioned in this connection is the nude (the "softness of flesh"). Cf. Pino, ed. Barocchi, p. 118, and Dolce, p. 183. For the discussion of tone in the works of individual painters see the texts quoted in notes 54, 55, 57, 58.

75. Fulvio Pellegrino Morato, *Del Significato de Colori e de Mazzoli,* 2d. ed. (Venice, 1545) (no pagination, pp. 44 ff. from beginning of the text), chapter called *Il Mischio mostra bizzaria di testa.* Although *mischio* here probably means an undefinable color, this short chapter is illuminating for the concept and evaluation of color blending in general. It reads: "Misto, cioè mescolato, significa corrotto. Greci chiamano bizzarri; che habbiano la mente di molte contrarietà corrotta; in tal colori sono molti fiocchi quasi atomi di diuerse specie varij. ... Adunque (qui vsaremo il verso di Dante) qual è colui che disuol cio che uolle. Vuole, e non uuole, & seco insieme contrarie cose mischia, & è nell uolere di diuerse uoglie, addobbarassi di tal colore sendo vno & molti."

76 *Dialogo di M. Lodovico Dolce nal quale si ragiona della qualità, diversità, e proprietà de i colori.* (Venice, 1565), fols. 33r ff., closely following the text quoted in the former note. See also the beginning of this *Dialogo* (fol. 6r) where Dolce emphasizes that "il uedere ogni cosa distinta col suo proprio coloro."

77. "Ma è da avvertire, che sono più sorte di bianchi, come quello della neve, del gesso purgato, del latte, delle perle, dell' avario, del marmo fine, e delle carni di bianca donna; e sebbene il bianco delle neve e del gesso disuniscono la vista, non fanno tale effetto i bianchi del latte, delle perle, e gli altri detti; anzi con un certo lustro biancheggiante danno vaghezza e diletto: e ciò adiviene, perche tal bianchezza porta seco un' occulta mescolanza sanguigna." Raffaello Borghini, *Il Riposo* (Florence, 1730), p. 185 (original edition, p. 234).

78. ". . . che molti vsano questo lume diuersamente, perchè lo uni lo danno fiero, spatioso, grande, & molto aperto, altri l'usano poco, debole, ombroso, & quasi che abbacinato, e in questo vltimo vi e più scienza destrezza, & auertimento, che nel primo, percio che nel picciol lume il rilieuo, et il naturale, dimostra più le minutezze de i loro muscoli, quantunque siano dolci, che non si fà nel chiaro. . . ." *Le veri precetti,* p. 82.

79. Pino, ed. Barocchi, p. 128; ed. Cf. also p. 106. For an interesting example of a similar effect in actual painting, preceding the theory of art in Venice, see M. Meiss, *Giovanni Bellini's St. Francis in the Frick Collection* (Princeton, 1964), passim, esp., pp. 14, 32 ff. Here it should also be mentioned that Pino, who knew Flemish landscapes, found Italian representations superior, and in their description

emphasized atmospheric effects: "... pur io ho veduto di mano di Tiziano paesi miracolosi, e molto più graziosi che li fiandresi non sono. Messer Gierolamo bresciano in questa parte era dottissimo, della cui mano vidi già alcune aurore con rifletti del sole, certe oscurità con mille discrizzioni ingeniosissime e rare, le qual cose hanno più vera imagino del proprio che li fiamenghi." Pino, ed. Barocchi, p. 134.

80. Sorte, pp. 288 ff.

81. See the texts mentioned in note 118 of the previous chapter, especially Pausanias' description of a crystal cup.

82. Cennini, *Il libro dell'arte,* pp. 89 ff.

83. Alberti, ed. Spencer, p. 85; ed. Janitschek, p. 137.

84. See *Treatise on Painting,* p. 85; ed. McMahon, 559-574 (pp. 203-208). It is characteristic that Leonardo emphasizes that "garments should be diversified with different kinds of folds" but proposes only different linear types of folds, more angular or more curved (562), or the adaptation to age and decorum (574). When he mentions a specific material (wool) he says only that the folds should be made "accordingly" (572), while in the discussion of other materials he has the linear forms of the folds in mind (564).

85. For a few examples, chosen at random, see Vasari, *Le vite,* IV, p. 40 (on Leonardo); p. 98 (on Giorgione); and VII, p. 657, on Vasari's own attempts to represent the luster on armor.

86. Pino, ed. Barocchi, pp. 116 ff.

87. Pino, ed. Barocchi, p. 128.

88. Dolce, pp. 184 f. Cf. also p. 197, "Ma Raffaello ha saputo col mezzo dei colori contrafar mirabilmente qualunque cosa, e carni e panni e paesi. ...." It is also interesting that Dolce (p. 173), like Alberti, criticizes the painter who uses actual gold in his work instead of imitating the brilliance of gold.

89. *Breve instruzione,* chapter on Titian.

90. "E certo il colorito è di tanta importanza e forza che, quando il pittore va imitando bene le tinte e le morbidezze delle carni e la proprietà di qualunque cosa, fa parer le sue pitture vive e tali che lor non manchi altro che'l fiato." Dolce, p. 183; Roskill, *Dolce's "Aretino,"* p. 153. This seems to be one of the rather rare cases where the formula of the lifelike picture that lacks only breath is used in connection with the representations of textures.

91. Sorte, p. 296. The example given by Sorte immediately after this sentence does, however, not belong to the textures of nature but to a theological sphere.

92 Lomazzo, *Idea,* chap. 21.

93. Pino, ed. Barocchi, p. 120. Schlosser, *La letterature artistica* (1864), p. 240, interprets the preference given to oil painting as a specific Venetian phenomenon. Similarly Palluchini in the edition of Pino's text, p. 116, note 1.

94. Pino, ed. Barocchi, p. 124; Pino's source might have been Vitruvius, VII, 9 (see Barocchi, p. 420), but he certainly intended to claim the merit of inventing oil painting for Italy in a more modern sense. Although he does not mention the northerners in this context, he says earlier (ed. Barocchi, p. 121): "Il modo a colorire a guazzo è imperfetto e più fragile, onde lasciamolo all'oltramontani–quali dono privi della vera via."

95. E. Panofsky, *Early Netherlandish Painting* (Cambridge, Mass., 1953, pp. 151 ff.

96. Vasari, *Le Vite...*, ed. Milanesi, I, p. 181.

97. Pino, ed. Barocchi, p. 121.

98. Vasari, *Le Vite ...* ed. Milanesi, I, pp. 185 ff.

99. "Io tengo che la dipingere à oglio sia la più perfetta via ... laonde se li puo dar maggior perfezzione e meglio unir una tinta con l'altra," ed. Barocchi, p. 120.

100. Michiel, ed. cit., pp. 80, 86 ff., 98 ff.

101. In a letter to Jacope de Giallo written March 23, 1537. See the Paris edition, I, fol. 103r.

102. "... Raffaello avanzato il colorito di molti buoni maestri a olio, e sono sfumate et unite con bellissimo rilevo e con tutto quelle che puo far l'arte." Dolce, p. 197; Roskill, *Dolce's "Aretino,"* p. 179. In the *Vita* of Raphael, in the first edition of Vasari's work, the *Disputa* is described in similar words: "... con quella concordanzia et unione di colorite l'una con l'altra, che non si puo imaginare che fare," ed. Ricci, p. 663.

103. Dolce, pp. 198 f. Quoted in note 55 of this chapter.

104. Dolce, p. 200.

105. Sorte, p. 288.

106. Dolce, p. 187.

107. Bottari-Ticozzi, *Raccolta di lettere;* Roskill, *Dolce's "Aretino,"* pp. 212 ff.

108. Sorte, p. 290. Cf. E. H. Gombrich, "Renaissance Artistic Theory and the Development of Landscape Painting," *Gazette des beaux arts* (1953), pp. 335 ff.

109. Sorte, p. 294.

110. Dolce, *Dialogo . . . nel quale si ragiona . . .*, fols. 10v ff. "Ora essendo il color Cesio solamente de gli occhi, e da vedere, se questo perauentura fosse quello, que da Aristotele e chiamato Caropon. Perciocchè egli cosi chiama il Leone per la crudelta e fierezza, ch'esso dimestra ne gli occhi. . . . Il che espresse mirabilmente anco Michel Agnolo nel Caronte, che egli dipinse nel giudicio. . . ." Dolce's work on color symbolism is largely dependent on Telesio's little book on color.

4

LOMAZZO:

THE MILANESE THEORY OF ART

I. Background

TURNING FROM VENICE to the other important center of art theory in northern Italy to Milan, we evidently find similarities in ideas and themes. But there are also significant differences, since in Milanese art theory, problems and attitudes crystallized which we do not encounter in the other schools. As we shall see in the following section, authors of the Lombard school (in particular, Lomazzo) drew on sources unknown in earlier periods: Some of the problems that were emphasized in their treatises were hardly articulated in the other schools of artistic thought. These problems and attitudes are characteristic of the last stages of the Renaissance (we should remember that all the Lombard art treatises were composed in the last two decades of the sixteenth century); they reveal the impact of the Counter Reformation, and they sometimes foreshadow baroque motifs. One also discerns in these treatises the effect of the artistic and cultural development of Lombardy and of the specific position of this region, situated between central Italy, Venice, and northern Europe. The following observations are not intended as a comprehensive survey; I shall only indicate some trends in Lombard art and culture which may be of some help in illuminating Lomazzo's concepts of light and color.

In contrast to Florence, Rome, and especially Venice, Milanese theory of art did not emerge from, and develop in close contact with, an important artistic tradition. It is true that Leonardo founded a tradition which maintained some degree of influence for many decades after he left Milan in 1499,[1] and exercised a remarkable impact on Lomazzo (1538-1600), but it seems to have remained rather isolated. Lombard art of the sixteenth century was more deeply influenced by Gothic style than was the art of any other region of Italy, and the general influence of the north was more significant there than anywhere else in the peninsula. The relatively "conservative" character of Lombard art may also be seen in the fact that folk art acquired more significance there than in any other center of artistic creation.[2] In the last decades of the sixteenth century, that is, in the period when its great theory of art crystallized, the artistic production of Milan was overshadowed by the art of other centers and was influenced even by minor schools (especially that of Cremona). One should also note the mark left on Milanese art by the visits of foreign artists from the important schools of Renaissance painting. (The Venetian Savoldo worked in Milan and in nearby Brescia in the early sixteenth century, and late in that century the Campi family from Cremona lived and worked in Milan.) Toward the end of the century Milan produced Arcimboldo and was, for a short while, the home of Caravaggio, but, as is well known, both did not stay there very long; Arcimboldo traveled to northern Europe, and Caravaggio soon left for Rome. Taking all this into account, it is not surprising that Milanese art tended to be eclectic and that it formed a suitable background for the emergence of an eclectic approach in Milanese ethical discussions. Milanese art theory is indeed poor in observation of nature, in independent judgment, and in vivid descriptions of paintings; it lacks the sensitivity for color composition and brushstrokes which is so prominent in Venetian writings. A theoretical spirit and a scholarly style of writing, often overloaded with antiquarian erudition, permeates Lombard treatises and gives them a scholastic character, detached from actual art. Given these conditions, however, Milanese art literature developed certain particular features and made a substantial contribution to Renaissance theory of art.

It has sometimes been said that the intellectual and artistic tendencies of the Renaissance acquired different shades of meaning in the different countries of Europe, and even in the different regions of Italy. In a sweeping generalization one may say with Panofsky that, while philosophic and aesthetic tendencies dominated Florence, antiquarian and philologic interests were more prominent in northern Italy.[3] This seems to be true also for the theory of art. One of the products of the "northern" spirit, emblem literature, originated in this region, and had a considerable influence on the art theory of Lombardy. It is also remarkable that some of the intellectual circles of northern Italy were ready, perhaps more than in other regions, to accept forms of intricate religious symbolism and to absorb esoteric doctrines that were reaching Italy from northern Europe. Here it will suffice to recall that a north European scholar, deeply devoted to magic and to obscure types of religious symbolism, Agrippa of Nettesheim 1486?-1535), was well known in northern Italy and exercised an important influence on Milanese theory of art, especially in its conception of light and color. [4]

The impact of emblem literature on Lombard theory of art is remarkable. In the late sixteenth century emblem books were recommended to artists as an immediate and direct source of inspiration and instruction. Lomazzo advises artists to study Cartari's *Imagine,* and in fact his elaborate iconographic system is based on Cartari's book.[5] He also mentions other authors of treatises on emblematics and hieroglyphics, like Giraldi and Pierio Valerian.[6] These tendencies and influences constitute a significant dimension in Lombard theory of art. Some of the intellectual sources of Renaissance art and culture—in themselves not new—are here discussed extensively for the first time in connection with art, and thus confer on Milanese theory a specific character differentiating it from the types of art theory that we have so far analyzed.

Milanese theory of art developed late enough in the century to be affected by the tendencies of the Counter Reformation, Milan being an important center of that movement. Venetian art literature, largely contemporary with the beginnings of the Counter Reformation, does not reflect the influence of the new ideas to any considerable extent. The one generation that lay between the middle and the end of the sixteenth century was enough lapse of time for the Counter Reformation to make its impact on art theory.

We need not discuss here the specific conceptions of art that emerged in the Counter Reformation. As we know, these conceptions were focused on the function to be fulfilled by art. It was believed that the main aim of a picture was to move the beholder and to evoke his emotional response. In other words, the expressive quality of the work of art was considered one of its main values.[7] Parallel to this attitude of the Counter Reformation, we find a deep concern with expression in art theoretical treatises of the late sixteenth century. Francesco Bocchi, for example, a Florentine scholar, dealt extensively with expression, and even coined a term for it. He reminds us of Counter Reformation language when he says that the work of art "elevates the soul to piety and arouses the love of God." [8] In Lombardy the impact of these tendencies seems to have been particularly strong. Valerio Angelini wrote to Lomazzo that the visual arts should be an effective tool for "guiding to the cognition of the great God, the Creator of all things." [9] Another north Italian writer, G. B. Paggi, believed that the stirring of a religious experience is the particular task of painting. "While the other arts," he wrote, "are in the service of man, this art [i.e., painting] serves God and the Holy Men, painting their holy countenances and evoking piety in the heart of men." [10] In some treatises the influence of the Counter Reformation led to the main emphasis being placed on the religious value and function of art (as in the writings of Carlo Borromeo on ecclesiastical architecture, and in Cardinal Comanini's book on painting), while in other writings (as in Lomazzo's works) it underlies the significance ascribed to expression in general.

Apart from the general heritage of art and art theory, these two particular sources—the northern and north Italian tradition of symbolism, and the significance given to expression in the Counter Reformation—were probably the most important factors in shaping the Lombard concepts of art. They were also important in the emergence of new concepts of color and light.

Venetian theory of art, as we have seen, was the collective achievement of a whole generation of artists and critics, based upon a rich artistic tradition. The treatises are not anonymous; we know the names of the authors, and sometimes have quite an extensive knowledge of their lives and experiences. However, each individual contribution is rather limited, nor can it be said that a single treatise holds a dominating position in Venice, overshadowing all other works.[11] In Milan the situation is different. Lombard theory of art, especially of painting, is to a large extent dominated by a single figure, Giovanni Paolo Lomazzo. It is true that Lomazzo was not an isolated figure. Other Milanese authors of art theoretical treatises, however, came from such different backgrounds and evinced such different interests that they can hardly be taken as sources for our study. Carlo Borromeo, the author of a book on ecclesiastical architecture, was a cleric of austere spirit who wrote in Latin, discussing chiefly symbolic ideas and the exigencies of ritual.[12] The other important Lombard author, Gregorio Comanini, a man of great humanistic learning, associated his treatise with the name of a painter, but in fact he neither had an intimate knowledge of painting nor was he concerned with the specific problems of this art; he was mainly interested in the philosophical discussions of the then fashionable question of how painting compares with the other arts.[13] It is not surprising, therefore, that these authors do not make any substantial contribution to the problems of light and color in painting. Lomazzo, on the other hand, was trained and worked as a painter before he went blind at the age of thirty-three. He not only had an intimate knowledge of many works of art and of the artistic traditions of both Italy and northern Europe, but he also knew the different aspects, technical as well as psychological, of the painter's work. It is, of course, true that he was deeply influenced by the broad philosophical trends of the period, but he was never completely detached from the artistic work. We shall try to show that when Lomazzo discusses general philosophic problems or presents a symbolism that prima facie has nothing to do with art, his awareness of the artist's needs and interests can often be sensed. This is not to say that he achieved a full and well-balanced synthesis between general cultural sources and trends and the painter's specific needs. However, in spite of many shortcomings and inconsistencies, Lomazzo's work constitutes the single extensive attempt to be undertaken in late sixteenth-century Milan to assimilate new cultural sources and trends for incorporation in his theory of art.[14]

In recent discussions of the structure of Lomazzo's literary works it has been shown that his main treatise, the *Trattato dell' arte della pittura, scultura ed architettura,* consists of several drafts, composed from different points of view dealing with different aspects of the arts, and only haphazardly combined in the printed edition. As a result of this procedure, many overlappings and contradictions face the reader. As far as our study is concerned, the literary vices of Lomazzo also have their virtues. The pieces, written from different points of view (humanistic, technical, astrological, stylistic), represent the wide range of problems involved in a discussion of art in the late sixteenth century, while the very absence of literary unification shows that the different sources and traditions had not merged organically in that period.[15]

II. Light

(1)

Light and color play a significant part in Lomazzo's overall system of art. They are only two of the seven "parts" of his theory of painting (the others being proportion, emotions [*moti*], perspective, "practice" and iconography [*forma*], but he seems to have considered them as the "most specific" elements of painting.[16] He discussed light and color at greater length and probably gave them more value than they had received before. In ascribing such significance to *lume* and *colore* he comes close to accepting the scale of pictorial values that had been evolved in Venetian theory. But when we compare his concepts with those of the Venetian authors, an important difference—and perhaps even an essentially different approach—instantly becomes clear. While most of the Venetian writers tended to merge light and color, Lombazzo strictly distinguished them from each other, dealing with them in two separate "books" of the *Trattato,* and in distinct chapters of the *Idea.* There are but few cross-references from the third "book" of the *Trattato* (dealing with color) to the fourth "book" (dealing with light) and vice versa, and these cross-references do not concern any essential points. Moreover, Lomazzo explicitly states the mutual independence of the two elements. In a polemical remark directed against the *filosofi peripatetici* who believe in the unity of light and color, he says that the rays of the sun or of any other light "do not produce or generate the colors" but merely illumine, and thereby reveal, the colors already existent in the bodies.[17] This division is made not only in "scientific" contexts but also in discussing light in art and in dealing with the actual problems encountered by the painter in his work. In describing the stages of the production of a painting he says that "the picture is already proportioned, it has movement, it has color," and now it only has to be illumined.[18]

Lomazzo's separation of light and color is hardly accidental or merely the vestige of a traditional approach. He was acquainted with Venetian theory of art and thus was certainly aware of the tendency to discuss light and color as a single, though complex, phenomenon. The breaking up of the discussion of *lume-colore* into two independent parts, therefore, must be considered as a purposeful procedure; it also indicates Lomazzo's particular position in the development of the theory of art. In this section we shall follow his division and deal with light and color separately.

(2)

The *Trattato,* in its printed version, follows a more or less consistent pattern. Almost all the "books" of the *Trattato* with chapters on the *virtù* and necessity of the specific "part" of painting dealt with in the "book," give a definition of that aspect, and then go on to a more detailed discussion. Accordingly, the "Book of Lights" (the fourth book) opens with chapters on the "virtue" and necessity of light and then gives a definition of *lume.* The first two chapters (which probably belong to the first draft of the *Trattato)* [19] remind us, with their flowery style and commonplace *topoi,* of rhetorical literature, which Lomazzo has used extensively, and they contain hardly any original ideas.

Good illumination, Lomazzo says, is a necessary condition for good painting. Well-placed lights reveal the excellence of drawing and modulation and create the impression of relief which he, together with his many predecessors, conceived as a central value of painting.[20] Without good illumination one cannot know whether a body is round or square and, therefore, *a regolata disposizione dei lumi* is recommended. When the lights are applied "without reason and art" and shadows become visible where lights are expected, good drawing will not achieve its full effect. Moreover, introducing a Neoplatonic formula into the theory of art, he says that if the lights are beautifully distributed even over a badly drawn body they will evoke in the beholder a "certain desire" to see more.[21] Lomazzo stresses that light should be studied, by which he apparently means that it should be mastered theoretically, according to "reason and art." The artist should have an understanding *(cognition)* of light and he should not be content with "simply imitating" the illumination observed in his models.[22] In the proper command of light one may see "so to speak, the aim [*fine*] of art; because without it there are no orders, no forms, no proportions, no composition." [23]

These chapters, as we have said, do not contain any original ideas or contributions; they are made up of an almost continuous series of well-known formulas and motifs, taken over from traditional art theory and from the fields of science, theology, and literature. Perhaps, because of the very lack of originality, the two opening chapters of the fourth book of the *Trattato* clearly set out the main aspects of Lomazzo's theory of light.

The first chapters of the "Book of Lights" suggest what we have called a "functional" concept of light. In them emphasis is placed on the "necessity" of light, its conception as a condition for making visible the other elements of painting, the high esteem in which "rational" illumination is held, that is, an illumination according to the rules, and the stressing of the importance of theoretical comprehension; all these are typical features of the "functional" approach. In this respect, Lomazzo depends on the concepts and views formulated in the art theory of previous generations.

In the course of his discussion Lomazzo instances several painters as paragons in the representation of light, and when these names are put together another aspect of his theory of light emerges. The names that appear most frequently in this context are Leonardo, Titian, Tintoretto, Federico Barocci, Veronese, and the Bassani. The highest praise for the rendering of light is bestowed upon Correggio, described as a painter whom nobody equals in the representation of light and in the use of color. Lomazzo refers to two paintings by Correggio which he saw in the house of Leone Aretino, a *Juno and Jupiter on a Cloud* and a *Danae and Jupiter with a Cupid*.[24] Correggio's *Nativity* (a painting that made a deep impression on sixteenth-century critics and to which we shall return later) is "tra le opere di pittura una delle singolari che siano al mondo." [25] The rendering of light in the works of these painters, and especially those by Correggio, cannot be called "functional"; it may, in fact, be classified as opposed to the functional approach. A modern scholar has rightly observed that the names of the artists selected by Lomazzo constitute a program.[26] Lomazzo was certainly aware of the specific character of these works, and would have known that for these masters light was not only a neutral condition for good visibility, but rather had an expressive, and sometimes symbolic, meaning of its own; the free, often irrational distribution of lights in the works of these painters sometimes even obscures the shapes and outlines of the figures represented. That Lomazzo was indeed aware of these characteristics can be sensed in some of his *Rime,* especially in the eulogistic sonnet devoted to individual painters.[27] Moreover, his own painting, though inferior in quality, also attests to his understanding and admiration of the expressive, nonfunctional style of light of some masters of the late sixteenth century.[28] It is because of this obvious discrepancy between the theoretical formulation and the pictorial examples, I think, that one can see in Lomazzo's selection of painters and in his discussions of their works a separate aspect of his theory of light, in addition to, and distinguished from, that presented in his theoretical formulations.

A third aspect of Lomazzo's theory of light is revealed in the long and confused chapter in which he undertakes to define light. I give the first part of this rather obscure definition in a literal translation.

> This word "light" has different modes and meanings. First, and foremost, it signifies the image of the divine mind, which is the Son of God, and his unique splendor whom the ancients called the image of the divine mind. It signifies, further, the ardour of the Holy Spirit. It is perceived by means of a divine virtue, diffused among creatures, which in the rational [creature] is his divine grace, and among all the creatures together it is the preserving and defending virtue, as, according to Dionysius, is that of the Seraphims. With the angels it becomes then specifically intelligence and a pleasure exceeding all our thoughts, but it is differently perceived according to the nature of the intelligence which perceives it and in which, as Ficino says of Plato, it is reflected. Descending afterwards from the celestial bodies, where it becomes a copy of life, it is an efficient propagation and a visible splendor in the fire, and a certain vigour and accidence proceeding from its nature. Men, finally, perceive it by the active intelligence which illumines the existing or the possible; and in sum, [it is perceived] by a lucid discourse of reason, and a cognition of divine things. It is perceived ultimately by a quality proceeding from the sun or from fire which reveals color.[29]

It is difficult to imagine what a painter could have done with this exalted and bewildering description, although to an Italian artist of the late sixteenth century it may have said somewhat more than to a modern reader. For the historian, however, this passage has the value of clearly indicating an additional aspect of Lomazzo's thought; the permeation of the theory of art by the Neoplatonic metaphysics of light. The symbolic meanings of light (cosmological, astrological, and theological) which played such an important role in the thought and imagery of the Middle Ages were always present in the background of Renaissance thought; but in art theory these meanings were usually neglected, or only briefly and vaguely suggested. The authors of art theoretical treatises, in spite of their awareness of the different symbolic meanings, conceived of light essentially as of a practical problem facing the painter in his actual work; they therefore never explicitly discussed these meanings. Lomazzo is the first author who introduced a lengthy discussion of the symbolic significance of light into a treatise on art, and tried to connect these occult meanings with the painter's practical problems. He thereby not only articulated a revolutionary turn in the development of the theory of art but also, more specifically, showed that light had lost its clearly limited and precise meaning in art.

We may now summarize our remarks. In the first chapters of the "Book of Lights" three main aspects appear: (1) the functional approach, where a certain norm of illumination (a "regular light") is formulated; (2) an "artistic" aspect consisting of names of artists and short descriptions of paintings, and revealing an altogether different approach in which the expressive meaning of light is stressed, even at the expense of a simple good visibility; and (3) the assimilation, and often the undigested taking over, of symbolic ideas and images from the literary and theological tradition. These ideas are later partly reformulated so as to bring them into connection with the painter's work, and, as we shall see, they eventually develop into an iconography of light.

(3)

The sources of Lomazzo's theory of art are as diversified as are its aspects. In the case of a humanistic author of the late sixteenth century it is often difficult, and perhaps even senseless, to try to establish a single source for a certain concept or literary formula, particularly if the theme is so common as was the notion of light. Certain symbolic interpretations, scientific concepts, and descriptive formulas belonged to the common heritage; they were, so to speak, "in the art," and could have reached the author in a variety of ways. We shall try, therefore, to establish the main groups of sources from which Lomazzo drew, in the expectation that this may help to define more exactly his place in the development of art theory and enable us to evaluate his own contribution more precisely.

At the end of the third chapter of the "Book of Lights," Lomazzo himself suggests his sources. "And this theory," he says, "... has been carved largely from Aristotle, from Vitello, and from St. Thomas Aquinas and, to conclude, from the most excellent philosophers and theologians." [30] Although this list is certainly not complete, and in one case it is even purposely misleading, [31] it does suggest some of his most important sources. There are, I think, three principal groups of sources from which Lomazzo drew his theory of light.

Probably the largest group consists of scientific manuals and workshop treatises. This group is, of course, of a very wide range, reaching from purely optical investigation to the practical workshop treatise. But, as is well known, [32] in the late sixteenth century workshop practice was permeated by scientific or technical knowledge, and the gap between the theoretical and the practical, so wide in the early fifteenth century, had been bridged.

In the late sixteenth century much attention and careful philological study was devoted to ancient and medieval treatises on light. Aristotle's *De anima* (containing an important chapter on light) and the pseudo-Aristotelian *De coloribus* were edited several times during that period. [33] Vitello's *Perspectiva* and other medieval scientific treatises on light were frequently read and quoted. [34] The contents of these famous works were accessible to more than a small group of scholars; many popularizations were available. It will suffice to recall the *Margarita philosophica,* that often reprinted encyclopaedia, written by a German author and in the sixteenth century also translated into Italian, which sums up the main contents of optical science clearly and comprehensively. [35] Lomazzo may have known some of his sources in their original version, but the optical concepts could have reached him through other channels as well.

Art theory itself may have been a channel for the transmission of scientific concepts. Art theory treatises of the fifteenth and sixteenth centuries summarized and popularized certain optical concepts. Lomazzo knew Alberti [36] and had probably read Leonardo's observations on light which were still in manuscript, [37] and we may assume that he was acquainted with Venetian theory of art. [38] From the theory of art Lomazzo could have derived not only a general knowledge of some basic optical terms but also the actual idea of "functional light."

Another important group of Lomazzo's sources are philosophical and astrological treatises. The single short description of light given in the fourth book of the *Trattato* ("Light is a bodiless quality") seems to have been copied from Ficino's *Symposium*.[39] However, in his theory of light Lomazzo was particularly dependent on another single source which he does not quote by name (and perhaps even tried to hide); namely, Cornelius Agrippa's *De occulta philosophia*. The exalted cosmological definition of light which we have quoted above is almost literally transcribed from the famous and controversial book of the German humanist, who seems also in other respects to have exerted a deep influence on him.[40]

There is little doubt that Lomazzo drew also from other "philosophical and theological" sources, although it may not always be easy to detect them. These sources may have included some of the sixteenth-century works of emblematics. As has already been remarked, Lomazzo mentions Cartari and Pierio Valeriano,[41] and it seems likely that he also knew some of the other important works of this literature. The spirit of emblematic literature was an important factor in his intellectual world, and it may even have influenced his judgments of works of art.[42] In emblematic literature of the sixteenth century the symbolism of light played a conspicuous role, and it would indeed not be too difficult to find passages in the great works on emblematics which call to mind Lomazzo's formulations.[43] This, of course, does not necessarily mean that he took them directly from the original works. In the late sixteenth century emblematics were very much in fashion, and the ideas expressed in this literature could have reached him in many ways. Even without going into closer comparisons we may therefore assume that Lomazzo drew on what may be called an "esoteric" tradition of the late Cinquecento.

In trying to identify Lomazzo's sources and the principles of selecting painters and describing their works, we are on much less certain ground. His descriptions, though sometimes suggestive, are too short to enable us to establish a clear relationship to recognizable literary sources. He knew Vasari's *Lives*, of course, and some of his phrases seem to be foreshadowed by Vasari's descriptions. But these were general formulas, used also in other writings. In the few cases where Lomazzo's descriptions of paintings are somewhat more elaborate, a relationship to the *Vite* cannot be denied. Thus his description of Correggio's *Nativity* closely resembles Vasari's wording.[44] Two paintings by Titian which Lomazzo mentions in this context are also described by Vasari.[45] But Lomazzo's own impressions and judgments are not completely obscured by these borrowings. The two mythological paintings by Correggio which he saw himself are not mentioned by Vasari. Lomazzo's list of painters, as far as I know, has no precise parallel in sixteenth-century art literature. It would therefore seem that in giving pictorial examples of his theory of light he is less dependent on established literary traditions than he is in the other aspects of his theory.

In summarizing we may now say that Lomazzo drew from a very wide range of literary sources. Besides these one could expect (mainly art theoretical treatises and scientific works), he also relied on sources which had not been used before by writers on painting, like Agrippa's *De occulta philosophia*. Lomazzo's selection of pictorial examples (paintings that either had not been described at all by other authors, or not in the particular context of light) also indicates a certain originality. We may thus say that Lomazzo, while relying on the full range of theoretical discussions of art, broadens the horizon of art theory by drawing from new sources. As we shall see later, the contexts of these sources vary greatly, and some of them have no immediate connection with art. Did Lomazzo attempt, and achieve, a synthesis of these divergent tendencies? In the limited number of studies devoted to Lomazzo, it has become usual to stress his lack of systematization, and the haphazard arrangement of the *Trattato*.[46] While this lack of order is undoubtedly true, it has not been noticed that, as far as the subject of our analysis is concerned, he at least attempted a synthesis of some of these dissimilar sources and tendencies.

(4)

The categorization of light, as we have seen several times in earlier chapters, was a traditional feature of Renaissance art theory. It is, therefore, not surprising that Lomazzo, too, divides light into several categories. What is new, however, is that he has two different systems of light, which do not merge with each other but are presented side by side. Here one can see that Lomazzo has absorbed two different concepts of light, two different traditional approaches to the same complex phenomenon.

The first system is called "primary and secondary light." "By primary light," Lomazzo says, "one means the light that touches these parts of the illumined body which are directly opposed to the illuminating body and which are reached by straight rays. . . . That [light] which is born from the primary light is called secondary light." [47] Primary light itself is further divided into first, second, and third primary light (the first being full sunlight; the second, the light of a clouded day as well as "divine light"; the third, artificial light). The second system consists of three different categories—direct, reflected, and refracted light. Direct light is created when the rays emanating from the illuminating body reach the illuminated one directly; reflected light, defined by its name, emerges from the reflection of rays; refracted light denotes a diffused light.

Obviously the two systems largely overlap. Primary light, in its three subdivisions, is identical with direct light, since in all cases the rays reach the illumined body directly. Secondary light, by its definition, is identical with reflected light. This being obvious, one is bound to ask: Why did Lomazzo formulate two sets of categories? The assertion that the final version of the *Trattato* was carelessly edited does not explain this fact completely. A closer investigation, I hope, will indeed reveal some subtle differences between the two systems, which may be almost nonexistent for the optical scientist but are of considerable significance to the painter. In the more detailed analysis of Lomazzo's categories of light, to which I shall now turn, I shall stress this difference.

The "first primary light," also called *lume naturale*,[48] is mainly plain, unobscured sunlight, although it may also occur indoors when it directly penetrates a window.[49] Lomazzo does not deal extensively with this type of light, perhaps because, being the most obvious and widespread kind of illumination in Renaissance painting, it had frequently been formulated in art theory and in workshop practices. What he does say about it is in complete agreement with the traditional views. He seems to regard it as the "regular light," that is, both as the most common in nature and as the most easily rendered according to rules in painting. He recommends that in painting the light should come from above, "because in this way the figures are of a perfect relief and appear round." The ancients used to illumine their temples from above in order to render their "false idols" more beautiful; some of the "good moderns" follow their example.[50] This light should, however, not be placed perpendicularly to the figures, since in that case the faces will be covered by shadows and their features will become indiscernible.[51]

Lomazzo's concept of the first primary light betrays the influence of traditional workshop precepts and of certain trends in sixteenth-century painting. The advice just mentioned (not to place the lights perpendicularly to the figures) seems to have been known in the workshops, and it can be found also in other treatises on painting.[52] Lomazzo also revived an old and rather artificial workshop precept by advising painters to illumine their figures in the middle, the intensity of light then diminishing toward the sides.[53] When he refers to contemporary art in this particular context, the same conservative tendency becomes apparent. Seemingly with some manneristic trends in mind, he criticized artists who illumine their figures from below ("di sotto in sù") or who impede the progression of the rays by various obstacles. Such a "wrongly distributed light," he says, creates "false" and "confusing" impressions.[54] These forms are significant because they indicate that Lomazzo conceived of the first primary light as rational light par excellence, or, as he says, as the light of "natural order." Its specific function is to reveal the figures clearly and distinctly, without itself appearing as a factor in the painting. In short, it is the functional light.

The next category in this system is the "second primary light." The description of this type seems, at a first glance, rather puzzling. It includes, on the one hand, the natural light of a clouded day (similar to Leonardo's "diffuse light"); but, on the other, it denotes the splendor surrounding angels and holy figures; it is, therefore, also called *lume divino.*[55] Lomazzo gives no definition of this type of light but indicates its nature by a series of pictorial examples, the most important being Titian's *Divinità;* Correggio's *Nativity;* the *Pentecost,* "which has been very well expressed in a painting by Gaudenzio in Vigevano"; and Raphael's *Transfiguration.*[56] Besides the actual paintings, Lomazzo also gives a long list of themes whose representation requires the "second primary light." The list consists of religious themes only, both from the Old and the New Testament, and particular emphasis is placed on the Apocalypse.[57]

The paintings and themes mentioned by Lomazzo help us to understand the particular nature of the "second primary light." In all the paintings referred to, light is not "functional"; its chief aim is not the revealing of the forms and structures of the represented figures and bodies while not being perceptible as a factor in its own right; on the contrary, it has both an iconographic meaning and glowing brightness of vision that dissolves the forms of bodies and makes of light itself a dominant value. As I have said, other sixteenth-century descriptions of these particular paintings would seem to indicate that such an interpretation was not uncommon at the time. Lomazzo's selection of biblical themes also suggests that he had in mind a nonrational, radiant light.[58] The consistent accordance between the illumination in the actual paintings described in the *Trattato* and the illumination required in the biblical themes clearly indicates the meaning and character of this light, although no proper definition is given.

Although Lomazzo was, as far as I know, the only Renaissance author who formulated the "second primary light" as a special category, this type of light was not unknown in north Italian painting of the sixteenth century; it also appeared in the art literature of the second half of the century. A few years before Lomazzo's *Trattato* appeared in print, the "divine light" had been described in nearby Venice. Cristoforo Sorte, in his *Observazioni nella pittura,* remarked that the "graceful light which surrounds the divine things" dissolves "fixed colors" and shadows.[59] We have no proof that Lomazzo was acquainted with Sorte's little book, but since Sorte refers to Giulio Campo, the Lombard painter and Lomazzo's friend, as "an excellent painter and my great friend," [60] it would not seem improbable that Lomazzo had some knowledge of the Venetian painter's treatise.

The specific position of "Divine Light" in Lomazzo's system may perhaps indicate that it was derived from pictorial rather than from literary sources. One asks, of course, how can divine light be placed together with the natural light of a cloudy day in the same category? The arrangement of first, second, and third primary light is a hierarchical one, the criterion of the hierarchy being the brilliance and intensity of each particular type. Now, the light of religious visions, being nonrational, cannot be measured. In medieval and Renaissance metaphysics, *lume divino* would not be compared with the light of an ordinary cloudy day, nor would its brilliance be measured; it would certainly not be found inferior to regular sunlight; thus religious and symbolic literature could not have provided Lomazzo's sources. Only in actual paintings could he have observed the particular degree of brightness of "divine light" and compared it with the intensity of other types; hence it seems probable that he adduced this specific category from looking at paintings. This is admittedly a conjecture, but I think it helps explain the rather surprising placing of the *lume divino* in Lomazzo's scale.

The last category of the primary light (the "third primary light") is the "artificial light," that is, the light produced by open fires, burning torches, candles, and so on. In its earliest stages Renaissance theory of art had already observed this type of light,[61] but closer attention was paid to it only in the second half of the sixteenth century, probably under the influence of manneristic painting, which was fascinated by the surprising and dramatic effects of burning torches, open altar fires, and so on. Lomazzo's comments on artificial light do not contain any original contributions, but the length of his discussion is remarkable. Artificial light, like the two prior categories, fulfills a function of "showing": it reveals both the nature of the "burning matter" and the material quality of the illumined object (specific mention is made of the effects of this light on metal objects). Lomazzo further stresses that artificial light can never be as intense as the former categories, thus placing it in the established scale of measurable light intensities. However, he is not concerned primarily with optics but with the expressive values of artificial light in art, stressing the irregular propagation of its rays and the inconsistent, unstable illumination resulting from it.[62] As with "divine light," the character of artificial light is illustrated by reference to works of art, the main example being Titian's *Martyrdom of St. Lawrence*. It is clear that Lomazzo deals with artificial light as a specific problem of painting. He notices, for instance, that artificial light looks different in the daytime and at night. This obvious observation would be of no consequence for a study in scientific optics, but it is, of course, of great significance for a painter who represents a fire on an altar in a daytime scene, or in a night scene lit by burning torches. It is, therefore, not surprising that in this context Lomazzo refers to the sixth book of the *Trattato,* which deals with the "practice" of the painter.[63]

The main context of artificial light, however, is iconography. Again Lomazzo gives a long list of themes (including both religious scenes and mythological *istorie)*, the rendering of which requires the representation of artificial light. As there is a great variety in the possible applications of this light, the painter is advised to study the meaning of the scenes in order to represent the artificial light properly. Of his examples Lomazzo says, "I believe [them] to suffice in order to demonstrate how carefully these lights should be applied at night and in the daytime, according to the effects on all things; one should always look at the *istoria* which shows us the painting as it should be." [64]

In a very short chapter (consisting only of a few lines) Lomazzo then discusses "secondary light." Being a "derived light," this can never be as bright as the three former types.

We can now consider Lomazzo's first system of light as a whole and summarize its characteristic features.

First, one observes thematic connotations of the different types of light belonging to this system. This is obvious in the case of the "second primary light," the *lume divino,* but it also emerges from the analysis of the other categories. The thematic connections are, of course, largely based on literary sources, and reformulate well-known theological, astrological, and philo- sophical ideas. It is, however, important to notice that these ideas are not formulated as abstracted meanings of light but are rather implied in, and form the basis of, discussions of pictorial representations.

Second, Lomazzo largely depends on actual paintings in order to illustrate the specific nature of each category of light. This can be seen both in the paintings which he describes favorably and in the artists and styles which he criticizes and rejects. Compared with earlier stages of art theory— for instance, with Leonardo—Lomazzo is poor in independent observation of nature. But he gives a conceptualization of some important pictorial trends and problems of the sixteenth century.[65] The notion of a "style of light," to which we shall return at the end of this chapter, is the final result of this tendency.

Third, the very criterion of Lomazzo's scale has to be considered. As I have pointed out, he arranges the different types of light according to their specific degrees of brightness, starting with the most shining and concluding with the dimmest. The brightness of some of the lights, such as that of the *lume divino,* cannot be experimentally measured, nor is it likely to have been derived from literary sources, a fact that reinforces our conclusion that the system of "primary and secondary light" is closely connected with actual painting.

The second system, consisting of direct, reflected, and refracted light, is discussed schematically and very briefly (hardly a page and a half in the *Trattato*).[66] The criterion of this system is not the brightness of light, that is, not a visual quality, but the direction in which the rays are propagated; in other words, here a scientific criterion is employed. In direct light the rays move in a straight line; in reflected light they are thrown back by the directly illumined bodies on the others; in refracted light they are scattered and diffused. In the sixteenth century this division is a commonplace which could be found in almost any manual of optics. In reading the short chapters in which Lomazzo sets forth this system one notices that no painters, no pictures, and no themes for representation are mentioned. On the other hand, Lomazzo twice claims the *fisiologici* as his source, [67] thus disclosing, I think, the true nature of this system. It constitutes a short and schematic summary of the principal categories of light in optical science, with no effort to adapt them to the painter's work.

In spite of the fact that the two systems largely overlap, they have different aims and are concerned with problems belonging to different realms. The first system is intimately related to painting; the second belongs to science. This becomes particularly clear in a comparison of "primary" and "direct" light. The identity of these two types of light is obvious, since in both cases the rays emanating from the illuminating body reach the illumined body directly, without being reflected by another object or scattered by a dense medium (like water or air). To optical science it does not matter whether the rays emerge from the sun, from a divine appearance, or from a burning torch as long as they reach the illumined objects directly and in a straight line. For the painter, however, the iconographic meaning of the light and the specific mood it conveys may become of decisive importance. It is, I think, this difference which accounts for the establishing of two different systems of which the subject matter is one and the same. The greater attention Lomazzo pays to the system of primary and secondary light obviously shows that he was mainly concerned with the problem of light in painting. Purely scientific traditions and concepts had only marginal significance for him. Despite its theoretical character, Lomazzo's thought is focused on actual painting.

(5)

These two systems indicate the central problem discussed in Lomazzo's theory of light. There are, however, other aspects, added to, rather than merging with, the former, which deserve our attention, the more important among those being the introduction of an astrological scheme in the theory of light. This scheme is manifested both in the differentiation of several styles of the depiction of light and in some practical precepts for painters concerning the reception of lights by different bodies. We shall return later to the first broad aspect of astrological influence; now we turn to the second.

In the chapters discussed so far, Lomazzo dealt with light per se, disregarding the actual illumination of figures and objects, that is, the question of how light is "received" by different bodies and materials. The term *ricepzione dei lumi* had frequently been employed since the beginnings of Renaissance theory of art, its meaning being simply illumination or coloring.[68] This term was now given a new interpretation by its introduction in a new context.

According to Lomazzo, the reception of lights is determined by the *composizione* and *disposizione* of the illumined body. By *disposizione* he means the form of the body and its spatial relation to the source of light. This is dealt with in a few sentences, mainly calling the painter's attention to the fact that the shape of the object may determine the effect that light produces on it; an angular object will show sharp, a concave object mild, light.[69] This observation remains within the traditional framework of the Renaissance workshop.

Composizione, also called *qualità delle materie*,[70] is given a more original treatment. Stated simply, the term *composizione* as used here means that the effects of light seen on any object or figure are, at least partly, determined by the material properties and nature of these figures or objects. The term is thus an abstract formulation of the idea of texture, but in Lomazzo's *Trattato* this notion was derived from a source which in the Renaissance workshop had so far not been brought into connection with the representation of texture, namely, astrology. What we call "texture" Lomazzo believes to be determined by this mixture, and "sympathy of the planets, signs, and elements [of which] all bodies are composed." [71] He therefore opens his extensive discussion of *composizione* by summarizing some of the central astrological concepts. Any one element is capable of receiving more or less light than any other element, while the nature of light and its "reception" are further determined by the cosmic region in which the illumined figure is situated. Lomazzo adduces the traditional hierarchic division of the universe into a supercelestial, a celestial, and a terrestrial world, each with its specific corresponding light.[72] Here he takes up some of the ideas and motifs of that bewildering definition of light (copied, as I have remarked) from Agrippa of Nettesheim quoted earlier in this chapter, and tries to relate these abstract ideas to the work of the painter. Although he is certainly not always successful in this attempt, the tendency toward this goal remains a central theme of his thought and constitutes an original contribution to the theory of art.

The hierarchy of light, as taught by "the Platonists," is, says Lomazzo, "also confirmed by the Holy Scripture, and we wish to imitate and observe it in paintings." Closely following Sorte's formulation, Lomazzo says that many painters "do not want to represent God the Father if He is not veiled by certain transparent lights so that His form remains dazzling." [73] The brilliant lights which Moses and St. Paul saw in their visions attest to the splendor of God. But in summing up the hierarchy of light, Lomazzo again refers to actual art. "In such works [of art]," he says, "we have observed that light is given first to God, secondly to the angels, thirdly to the skies, fourthly to us, and fifthly to hell." The painter is advised always to consider his figures according to the quality of their metaphysical aptitude to receive more or less light. The following characterization of different lights is a summary both of well-known theological symbols and of pictorial images: ". . . God is the source of light, in the angels it is resplendence and in hell it is, so to speak, matter, and a scum of light to which are referred all the greasiness and foams of things. And this is the basis of art about this faculty of the lights [to be received] by the substance of imagined and visible bodies." [74] Here, I think, we can clearly see Lomazzo's intention to blend astrological and theological symbolic imagery with actual representations in painting. He obviously assumes that a painting can show, so to speak, the

metaphysical nature of light and the different degrees of its emanation
much in the same way as, a few generations earlier, it was assumed that a
work of art can show the actual structure of the human body.

The concrete discussion of the reception of light according to *composizione*
centers around two questions: How does the prevalence of a certain element
in any object determine its reception of lights? And how does the human
body receive light at different ages? These problems are, needless to say,
perennial, but Lomazzo gives them a new significance, and a new meaning
for painting.

The discussion of the reception of lights by the four elements (or by
bodies consisting of them) constitutes a strange mixture of astrological
beliefs, observations on broad problems of style, and actual workshop
practices. Lomazzo is clearly dealing with texture, but, as I have said, he is
not content with simple observation of nature; rather, he bases his attitudes
on the "science" of the four elements. As far as a guiding principle can be
discerned in these chapters, it seems to be the view that the harder and more
condensed a body, the sharper will be the light seen on it and the more
reflections will it generate. This, Lomazzo says, is a *sicura regola* for the
depicition of light effects on different bodies,[75] and he arranges the four
elements in a sequence or scale according to this rule, starting with the
hardest, earth; going on to water and then to air; and concluding with the
most spiritual element, fire. Even within each element he often follows the
same principle, making interesting observations about specific problems of
representation and thereby again revealing his close acquaintance with
procedures in Renaissance workshops.

For example, in discussing the reception of light by the earth element he
places great emphasis on the difference between a stone or plaster cast, on
the one hand, and flesh on the other. The former, being of extreme
hardness, shows sharp lights and produces many reflections; the latter, being
of a softer quality, shows "soft and sweet shadows with only a few
reflections." Seen from a distance, the shadows, especially of very soft bodies
like those of babies, almost disappear. Painters who neglect these
distinctions are severely criticized. For "not considering such a multitude
[of textures], many painters who have represented in their youth figures
after such plaster casts and marbles with crude, fiery and sharp lights, have
maintained such a style of illuminating which, as it is caused by such bodies

[i.e., marbles and plaster casts], is appropriate for their representation only." [76] In the representation of the nude the difference between the softer and harder parts should be observed; shoulders and knees, being more bony, should not look like the fleshier parts of the body. "And this is the true manner to which one has to adhere in their [the bodies'] imitation." [77]

The treatment of the other elements is governed by the same *sicura regola*. Watery substances, for instance, include precious jewels, and these reflect more light because their watery substance is more condensed.[78] Pure water, like that of a well, will show weaker lights than the dense water of a stormy sea. The same is also true of air. While pure air is transparent, and therefore shows light per se, it is not able to "receive" light, that is, to be an illumined object. If, however, the density, that is, the "material character," of air increases, as in clouds, it will be able to catch light and even to throw some reflections.[79] In the discussion of fire Lomazzo also follows the same principle, again associating material qualities and specific position in the cosmic hierarchy. The strongest and sharpest lights will emerge either from the conflagration of solid, thick materials (like coal or wood) or they will be seen on figures of a low moral rank, like those in hell. "In infernal fire the demons and souls tormented by thick and heavy flames will have the sharpest lights of major brightness." "This rule," Lomazzo says, "should be observed in all fires." [80] The chapter on fire shows an underlying conflation of two tendencies that may be seen, though less clearly, also in the other chapters. On the one hand, there is a general Platonic trend, identifying the more material with the morally lower (coal and hell have the same kind of light); on the other hand, the inclusion of iconographic themes (like demons, and souls tormented in hell), and some vivid descriptions of color, point to the painter's work and may even refer to some actual paintings.

The same blend of astrological imagery and almost technical workshop practice also characterizes the chapter on the illumination of the human body. Here man is divided into seven ages, each age corresponding to a planet. As the body's shape and texture change in these ages, the "reception of lights" will be different in each of them. In "lunar" infancy the lights are "broad and without any sharpness"; in adolescence, governed by Venus, they are of "great sweetness . . . and charming to the eye . . . the shadows are soft and firm"; in youth, subordinated to the sun, the lights are of a major force but they tend "neither to crudeness nor to too much sweetness"; in "manhood, dominated by Mars," the lights are sharp and reveal the muscles; in old age, pertaining to Jupiter, the lights are "grave, full of majesty and greatness, as one sees in the philosophers"; finally, in decrepitude, governed by Saturn, "the body becomes angular and, therefore, the lights are sharp and contrast with deep shadows." [81] The division of man's life span into seven ages and the connection of these ages with the seven planets is, needless to say, an age-old doctrine which had never been forgotten.[82] In this tradition the changes occurring in the texture of the body had of course been noticed (the skin of the baby being soft, that of the old man being dry and angular). But so far as I am aware, no attempt had ever been made to link these changes with different types of the "reception of lights" in painting. It is true that one finds incidental observations on the texture of the human body in its successive ages; a youthful body is sometimes compared with that of an old man. [83] These observations are necessarily connected with the question of how to apply light; they had, however, never been extended to the full range of seven "ages," nor had they been brought into association with the planets. Lomazzo connected these two traditions, enunciating the astrological theory in the form of devices for the painter and thereby suggesting an expressive quality of illumination to correspond to the "essence" of each age and planet.

In sum, it is obvious that Lomazzo's theory of light was not cast into a unified shape and that its different parts and aspects were not organically welded. This in itself is an important testimony to the very complex situation of north Italian theory of art in the late sixteenth century. The concept of light had lost the comparatively simple meaning attached to it in former stages of development of artistic thought and, with Lomazzo, had entered a highly speculative phase. This speculative character is expressed not only in the introductions to the discussions, but affects also the actual contents of Lomazzo's treatise, and some of his essential attitudes to the painter's personality, methods, and work. It should, however, be stressed that his speculative tendencies and astrological sources did not remove Lomazzo's thought from the workshop and did not detach him from the concrete problems and tasks of the painter. His theory of light remains deeply rooted in the workshop, and his thought is focused on the artist's work.

III. Color

(1)

Lomazzo investigates color in the third book of the *Trattato* and in several chapters of the *Idea*. In the twenty-first chapter of *Idea* he asserts that "coloring can be said to be the root of painting and that which gives her perfection."[84] In the *Trattato* he similarly emphasizes the importance of good coloring," since without it painting cannot be accomplished, nor can it reach perfection; because this [color] is what properly expresses and, as one says, gives life to the things designed by the force of other media."[85] These statements, although repeating the well-known formulas of rhetorical literature, show that Lomazzo held color in surprisingly high esteem. In the course of this study we have frequently seen that color was regarded as a less noble element than the other parts of painting, and that it was believed to appeal mainly to peasants and the ignorant who are unable to make a more refined judgment. It is true that later in the sixteenth century, Venetian art theory paid greater attention to color than had been done before. As we have seen, Venetian authors enriched the discussion of *colore* by many vivid descriptions of paintings and even suggested some new stylistic notions of color in art, but we know that this greater concern for color did not find consistent theoretical formulation. Outside Venice, color occupied a low rank in the generally accepted scale of artistic values. Even in the late sixteenth century it was usually connected with a vulgar, "low" naturalism which lacked the nobler values of invention and design. The contexts in which notions like *colorire del naturale* now appeared (originally this term had a different meaning) clearly mirrored these beliefs. How deeply rooted these views were in that period can be inferred from Agucci's well-known criticism of Caravaggio.[86] In the late seventeenth century Bellori still echoes the typical association of color with a low-ranking naturalism.[87] Seen against this background, Lomazzo's esteem of color is remarkable and demands an explanation.

Lomazzo's discussion represents the most extensive and most systematic analysis of color in Renaissance literature on art. It constitutes also a departure from established patterns of dealing with color. Leonardo's observations of color phenomena, which did in fact influence Lomazzo,[88] are largely of an empirical, descriptive character; the comments of Venetian authors, though wider in scope, do not constitute a theoretical system. Lomazzo lacks the wealth and vividness of the immediate observation of nature that so enriches Leonardo's writings, and the evocative descriptions of color effects in painting in which Venetian art literature abounds. However, his drawing from a wider range of literary sources, his tendency toward a systematic explanation and, especially his extensive discussion of new aspects of color in art—all these make Lomazzo a turning point in the history of color concepts in the theory of art.

(2)

What does Lomazzo understand by "color"? The answer is not as obvious as one would expect. Three main aspects of color can be discerned in Lomazzo's theory, each of them being discussed in a separate and self-contained set of chapters (which probably originated in different drafts for the *Trattato*). The three aspects may be described as: (a) the scientific approach, explaining color as a property of bodies, perceived in visual experience; (b) the conception of colors as pigments, that is, both as color material to be found in nature and as the color area or color surface in painting; and (c) color as a symbol and as the bearer of expression. I shall analyze these three aspects separately.

(a) *Color as a property of bodies*. Only once did Lomazzo attempt to define color. In the third chapter of the "Book of Color" (a chapter called "What color is, what its sources are, and whence colors are taken" he says: "Color, as Aristotle says, is the outermost part [*estremità*] of a thing, or what is visible on the outermost part of an opaque body, which is potentially visible before it is illumined and, by the benefit of light, becomes actually visible." [89] This definition cannot be regarded as the basis of Lomazzo's whole color theory; it is valid for only one of its aspects. It implies, however, two important assumptions: one, that color belongs to the object (being "the outermost part of the body"); the other, that it is independent of light. At the beginning of this chapter I have already briefly discussed the second assumption. Though of great practical significance for the painter, it follows to a certain extent from the correct interpretation of the first assumption, and it is, therefore, to this that I shall now turn.

In defining color as the "border" or "skin" of objects, Lomazzo probably had Aristotle's famous definition in mind: ". . . for color exists either in the boundary or constitutes the boundary of a thing, and hence (a corroborating circumstance) the Pythagorean terminology identified the visible surface with color. This was plausible, for color exists on the boundary . . ." (De sensu, 439a).[90] The Aristotelian concept was well known and often discussed in the Renaissance. In philological and scientific literature it was either directly quoted or freely paraphrased from Aristotle.[91] It also found its way into the treatises on art.[92] Both in scientific literature and in the art treatises the presumption that color belongs to, or constitutes, the surface of objects seems to have enhanced the value of hues and tints. In many investigations the belief seems to be implied that color can be used as a criterion for the correct cognition of reality. Since it belongs to, or constitutes, the surface of things, its correct identification helps us to distinguish between different objects and thus reveals something of nature.

This specific function of color seems to have played a rather important part in sixteenth-century thought. In Venice it had already been observed that color shows the texture, or material quality, of figures and objects. But since Venetian authors conceived of color as closely connected with, and dependent on, the changing illumination, they could not turn color into a general criterion of cognition. In Tuscan, Roman, and especially Lombard art theory of the late sixteenth century, color is considered less dependent on light than in Venice. It is now color itself, detached from the conditions of a concrete and therefore necessarily changing illumination, that is regarded as having a cognitive value. Thus, the sculptor Vincenzio Danti, who has nothing to say about light, believes that color alone would enable us to discriminate between one kind of stone and another, or between some plants and others.[93] Cardano, the famous Milanese scholar, several times discussed color as a means of distinguishing different materials, without mentioning, in this context, light or even art.[94] Similarly, Lomazzo speaks of painting as demonstrating "the difference between the things by means of colors" and gives a very long list of objects and materials whose character can be discerned and portrayed by sufficiently varied colors.[95] It would, I think, be wrong to assume that these authors, and especially Lomazzo, had in mind only the visible surface of objects which is perceived in immediate visual experience, that is, "texture" in the Venetian sense. In Milan the concept of the cognitive, discriminating function of color is more deeply influenced by scientific traditions and modes of thought. Good examples are the devices given for the portraying of different temperaments. Lomazzo deals at great length with the coloristic complexions of the four temperaments. Venetian authors, too, demanded that the coloring be adapted to the different complexions, but this remains very general talk.[96] Lomazzo gives the actual quantities of the different colors that are to be used in preparing the proper hue for each temperament. From this we can infer that the choleric looks most reddish; the sanguinic also looks reddish but less than the former; the phlegmatic has a pale complexion tending toward a light, dull gray; while the complexion of the melancholic is dark and tends towards a grayish yellow.[97] The apportioning of definite coloristic requirements to the temperaments is, of course, not surprising, as Lomazzo drew here from the well-known popular and substantially uniform descriptions of the humoral system.[98] He himself indicated the scientific character of his doctrine by stressing that the painter, like the physician, recognizes the "nature" of men according to the color of their complexions.[99] His text reveals both a close acquaintance with scientific theories and an adaptation of these theories to workshop practice, the transference being indicated, for example, by the fact that, instead of giving an accurate description of the complexion, he prescribes the exact amount of specific colors to be mixed in their representation.

Lomazzo's reliance on the scientific tradition is the background, and perhaps one of the major motives, of his separation between color and light. If color per se is considered as a means for the cognition of reality, it is natural that one wants to perceive it in a, so to speak, pure state, and therefore one tries to avoid its being obscured by accidental and variable illumination. Much in the same way as the physician, in order to diagnose the "humor" of his patient, will try to see his complexion in a neutral light, the painter will try to depict his figures in a light that does not create ambiguous hues but shows the "true," that is, local colors. These colors may be brighter or darker, but their chromatic identity should never be modified by strongly colored reflections or by a light carrying hues of its own. This idea, though never expressly stated, seems to underlie Lomazzo's concept of color and may have had some bearing upon his views of the painter's handling of colors in his work.

(b) *The workshop tradition.* The second aspect of Lomazzo's theory of color, which has no essential connection with the first one, is based on the experiences of Renaissance workshops, and attempts to systematize these experiences. Here it is only the actual narrowly limited needs of the painter which determine the selection and discussion of the material. In the discussion of the other "parts of painting," Lomazzo also claims the workshop experience as his source. However, as the doctrine of color was the least systematized part of the "art of painting," it may not be pure chance that in discussing it he grants practical experience a more important role than in the other "parts." Besides the scientific (Aristotelian) and, as we shall see later, the symbol-expressive meanings, color also, of course, has for him an eminently practical and technical significance. He speaks of "l'arte e pratica del colorare," [100] the first term, *arte,* probably denoting the theoretical aspect (scientific optics as well as symbolic meanings), and *pratica* the knowledge and skills in the application of colors gained by experience.

In his discussion of technical questions two sides may be distinguished. On the one hand, he deals with color materials, their chemical properties and the places where they may be found; on the other, he discusses the application of color, that is, the coloring of paintings.[101] In the discussion of the practical aspect Lomazzo deals with many technical details that need not concern us here. We shall make only a few remarks on the indications of the general character of Lomazzo's color theory offered by his many specific precepts.

In discussing the color materials and their appropriate mixtures Lomazzo draws from experience accumulated for centuries in painters' workshops. He frequently quotes his sources. A long passage about the blending of certain colors is concluded by the sentence: "E questo è l'alchimia dei pittori veneziani." [102] A certain blending of colors is the "invention" of Pierino del Vaga.[103] He also draws from art theoretical treatises which originated in the workshops. Thus, for example, he refers to some Venetian writings which are particularly close to the workshop, and to "un copioso e diligente trattato" on colors by his friend Bernardino Campo of Cremona.[104] Within this context it is, of course, not surprising that he emphasizes the significance of the main principle of workshop practice, namely, experience. Whether a certain color can be blended with another color, he says, we can find out only by experience.[105]

Here Lomazzo's judgment of the different media and techniques of painting requires comment. He knows at least six media, but he holds oil painting in highest esteem.[106] This preference for oil painting may be considered characteristic of northern Italy and strongly contrasts with the high regard for fresco painting in Tuscany.[107] Lomazzo values oil painting because he believes that in this medium the maximum effect of naturalism and representation of texture can be achieved. Interestingly enough, he quotes in this context, besides Italian artists, mainly Flemish painters whose work he saw in Italy.[108] It is also chiefly in relation to oils that he establishes the principle of the blending of hues in what he calls "friendship and hostility" among colors.

Lomazzo's advice for applying color in painting is rather meager, and cannot be compared with the vivid and subtle descriptions in Venetian literature. But the respective chapters in the *Trattato* sometimes give some interesting insights into the workshop practice of the sixteenth century. Lomazzo did not draw from one workshop tradition alone. The eclectic character of his theory, which becomes so clear in the philosophical parts of the *Trattato* and the *Idea,* can also be observed in his discussion of the practical aspects of color application. In general Lomazzo seems to favor a style that applies large stretches of more or less uniform color, varying mainly in brightness,[109] though vividness also plays a significant part in his opinions. A typical workshop precept says that the noblest and central figures in a composition should be the most vividly colored areas in the painting.[110] He also deals extensively with transparent colors and discusses their ability to represent different textures, especially the sparkle of precious stones and other highlights (like the luster on melons and on the tips of noses).[111] Of iridescent colors, which incidentally occupy an unprecedentedly large place in Lomazzo's discussion, he says that they are particularly fitted for the representation of silk.[112] It is significant that in the chapters discussing the painter's application of color he frequently quotes Venetian and northern painters.[113] From these traditions he could indeed have learned more of the "alchemy" of colors than from the other Italian schools, but the selection of these particular schools as models also indicates a tendency of style, which goes beyond the acquisition of merely technical knowledge and skill. On the other hand, however, Lomazzo speaks with a Tuscan voice when he criticizes the Venetian painters who, in their affection for color, disguise design, and who are more devoted "to the charms of color than to the power of art." [114] The "true," that is the "local," color is so important that the painter who represents it carefully, varying the degree of brightness but not the chromatic character of the color itself, is regarded as a "true imitator of nature and eminent in his art; otherwise [i.e., if he violates this rule] he deserves being called a destroyer of nature." [115]

In his views of the artist's application of color in painting, Lomazzo thus seems to waver between different attitudes, characteristic of the important schools of sixteenth-century art, without crystallizing an attitude of his own.

(c) *The expressiveness of color.* As we have seen in the first section of this chapter, Lomazzo considered the ability of color to represent nature as one of its main values. This ability, however, is not restricted to the representation of material objects; it encompasses all possible themes of pictorial rendering, reaching from the representation of different kinds of stone to "the form of the eternal Creator of things." [116] In this wide range of content, the portraying of emotions, moods, and passions plays a particularly important part. I do not refer here to conventional color symbolism, which had been seriously studied in the Renaissance period, but to the suggestive or evocative force of hues in painting. The presentation of this particular aspect is probably the most original part of Lomazzo's doctrine of color and constitutes an important development of Renaissance theory of art in general.

The concept of the work of art as indicating mood, needless to say, was widely held in the Renaissance, and was frequently formulated in the art theory of the period.[117] But it was also widely assumed that the artistic rendering of moods and passions could be detached from the representation of the human figure. Abstract elements of art, like line or color, were usually not regarded as appropriate media for the representation of mood. It was the mimesis of the face and the attitudes and gestures of the body that were held to convey to the beholder the *movimenti d'animo* of the represented figure and, therefore, to permeate the work of art with life.

Lomazzo, who was an heir of this tradition, held, of course, similar views. But he transcends the limits of the theory of his time by considering color, as well as bodily movement, as a means of expressing moods and emotion. He believes that by a proper application of hues the painter is able to indicate specific feelings, such as terror, shame, pain, mourning, joy, and anger. A significant passage in the *Trattato,* discussing the ability of color to convey feeling and to evoke emotion, is worth quoting:

> Because all colors have a certain different quality, they produce different effects in the beholder. The black, shining, earthen, leaden, and dark colors generate, through the eyes, in the soul of the beholder their [own] quality which is nothing else but sadness, tardiness, thoughtfulness, melancholy, and the like. The black, green, sapphire hues, some reds or darks, the color of gold mixed with silver which is yellow [*flavo*] render softness and playfulness. The red, the ardent, the fiery or flaming, the violent, purples, and the colors of the hue of hot iron and of blood induce fierceness, and awaken the mind by means of the eyes not less than fire. The colors of gold, yellow, and bright purples and light [colors in general] make man attentive in looking and render grace and sweetness. Pink colors, light greens and some yellows render gracious pleasantness, cheerfulness, delight and softness. The white color generates a certain simple attention which is almost more melancholic than the others.[118]

This list, although based on traditional symbolism, is, I think, more than a merely conventional code of color symbols which lend themselves to purely technical manipulation and to a simple and clear reading. Conventional color symbolism, to recapitulate, can be characterized by two criteria in this context: each color has an unequivocal character and meaning; and the same meaning applies to all possible appearances of the same color (the application of these rules not being restricted to painting or to any other specific realm). These criteria do not hold good for Lomazzo's discussion. In the passage quoted he attributes different meanings to the same color.[119] It is also obvious that he speaks of problems specific to painting and does not refer to any other possible use of a hue in a symbolic context or function. We may, therefore, say that what Lomazzo here had in mind was the immediate, evocative effect of color in painting; in short, what we, very ambiguously, designate by the term "expression." It is on this level of intuitive experience that, by the proper application of colors, the painter can distinctly visualize a wide range of differentiated emotions and arouse specific feelings in the beholder. What is the basis of this range of color expression, and how does color affect the beholder and produce in him the appropriate emotional responses?

In the other realms of shaping expression–above all in the gestures and attitudes of the human figure–Renaissance theory of art drew mainly from literary traditions (best exemplified in the literature of rhetorics) and from observation of nature. We recall that Alberti advised the painter to read the *rhetorici* and to observe nature. Leonardo, in some of his most famous observations, urged the painter to observe arguing people who gesticulate with their hands, or the dumb who communicate by means of gestures. But he also took over some descriptions of expressive movements from literary sources.[120] The sources from which we can draw our knowledge of the expressive connotations of colors are necessarily both different and more restricted. While everyday experience shows us that the expressive movements of the human body are amazingly flexible and therefore capable of conveying a great variety of feelings, the coloristic phenomena in nature, expressive of emotional states, are more limited.[121] Moreover, Lomazzo's own observations of nature, as we have already said, were confined within very narrow limits; it is therefore not surprising that his opinions are mainly based on broad cultural traditions. When speaking of the spontaneous response of the beholder to color in painting, he is in fact relying on an impersonal cultural heritage permeating some of the traditional concepts with, so to speak, a direct, subjective immediacy, and transforming crystallized notions and images into emotional experiences.

Lomazzo discusses the meaning of color in two different contexts, as the "subjective" emotion evoked in the beholder, and in its "objective" or symbolic significance. While the subjective emotional character is most clearly stated in the passage quoted above, the objective or symbolic meanings are discussed in a set of seven chapters, each dealing with a separate color. Here Lomazzo analyzes the "meaning" or "connotation" of each color, quoting ancient authors, the Bible, and Christian writers. Though some slight differences may be observed between the subjective and objective formulations, they essentially agree. Black, for example, "means" sadness and pain, evoking sadness and melancholy; white "means" simplicity and purity, evoking a certain "simple attention which is almost more melancholic than the others"; red "signifies" *(denota)* revenge and fierceness (but it may also denote vehement love), evoking "terror, ardor, and attention in looking"; green "means" hope, evoking charm and joy.[122]

This discussion of the "objective" or representative meaning of hues strongly reminds one of color symbolism. This concept, as I have already said, experienced a revival in the Renaissance period; treatises were written on the subject, and attempts were made to apply it to the study of different fields. As far as the basic meanings of colors are concerned, there is a surprising uniformity in all these writings, which may ultimately all be traced back to a common tradition. It goes beyond the scope of this study to discuss color symbolism in European culture, or even in the Renaissance; I shall, therefore, restrict myself to pointing out some obvious relations between this tradition and the theory of art.

In a culture in which color symbolism attracted attention, it was natural that painting, and consequently the theory of art, should be affected. In sixteenth-century Italian literature on the visual arts, even before Lomazzo we find that certain colors were related to certain meanings. Raffaelo Borghini, for example, devotes several pages to the meanings of colors in his *Il Riposo* and thereby carries astrological and symbolic imagery into the theory of art. As far as I can determine, Borghini did not rely on a specific literary source but expressed ideas which were common currency in his time. He was not, however, concerned with the emotional impact of color on the beholder and did not discuss the possibilities of expression inherent in colors.[123] This is precisely what Lomazzo did.

Although Lomazzo was certainly influenced by various tendencies that prevailed in his time, in discussing the expressive qualities of color he largely relied on a single source. His description of the emotional responses of the beholder to certain colors in painting largely corresponds to Agrippa of Nettesheim's account of the relation of colors to planets,[124] and it is obvious that Lomazzo copied this passage, with only some slight changes, from *De occulta philosophia*. For a sixteenth-century author attempting to establish symbolic "meaning" of colors as well as their emotional connotations it was perhaps only natural to turn to the tradition of astrology, which at that time provided the most articulate system of color meanings. But it would be a mistake to assume that such literal "borrowings" excluded a far-reaching transformation of the ideas which were taken over and transferred into a new context. In our case it is precisely this almost literal correspondence which reveals a crucial difference. While Agrippa simply relates a specific color to a specific planet (mentioned by name), Lomazzo describes the relation of this color to a certain emotion. It is true that the specific emotion corresponds to the character of the particular planets. Thus, for example, where Agrippa says that black belongs to Saturn, Lomazzo says that it evokes sadness and melancholy; where Agrippa states that red and fiery colors belong to Mars, Lomazzo claims that they induce terror and fierceness. Sadness and melancholy were, of course, regarded as the "essence" of Saturn, and terror-provoking fierceness as the character of Mars. The change of formulation from Agrippa's to Lomazzo's text, therefore, would seem to be only slight, without any deep difference in meaning. These slight changes of formulation, however, indicate that the well-established color meanings have been transplanted from a purely and conventionally astrological to a specifically emotional and artistic frame; that color is now said to fulfill a different function and acquires a different quality. Agrippa's color list is a "code," a system of objective signs, the meanings of which are firmly established and well known; Lomazzo gives a description of immediate experiences which, though articulate, retain the direct quality of emotions. He is the first author to formulate such a translation of astrological meanings into emotional experiences in connection with art.

Lomazzo's attempt to establish a connection between the symbolic meaning of colors and their evocative power is by no means isolated in his time. This connection was variously formulated in the sixteenth century. A number of writings composed in that period discussed the expressive character of color. These writings, which have received little attention from modern scholarship, are essentially in accord with the codified symbolic interpretations, but they attempt to show that colors have an emotional meaning that can be derived from, and tested by, experience. A few examples will suffice to illustrate this tendency. Giovanni Rinaldi wrote a treatise on the meaning of colors and flowers. In his introduction he says that his manual is not addressed to philosophers or men of great learning but to simple lovers who want to convey their moods in "colorate divise e impresse." [125] Another important document of this tendency is a little book by Thylesius. The famous Renaissance scholar writes, as he himself puts it, neither as a painter nor as a philosopher, but as a philologist who investigates color terms and what they reveal about the "nature" of color.[126] Thylesius, trying to establish the "true meaning" of colors by quotations from ancient literature, stresses the emotional quality of hues. *Ater*, for example, is a "terrible color," the shade of extinct coal (that is, an almost black, dull gray) and expresses death. The author distinguishes *ater* from *nigro*, that is, a tired gray from a saturated, full, perhaps shining black, and grants the latter a different emotional quality. "In this *ater* is different from black color; while it is true that each *ater* is black, not each black is *ater*; this [i.e., *ater*] is horrible, sad, repulsive to vision, appropriate to sadness, opposed to daintiness and charm ... while we do nothing so voluptuously watch as black. . . ." [127] In this little treatise we find not only subtle distinctions between tones but also an attribution of emotional qualities to these tones.

Another significant example of the conflation of traditional symbolism and the perception of the emotional qualities of colors is provided by Ariosto. The *Orlando furioso* reflects opinions on colors, especially in the selection of cloth, held at the court of Ferrara, but it also shows some broader tendencies of the time. The color of cloth worn at different occasions is not *sensa misterio*, obviously alluding to a conventional symbolism. But Ariosto also describes some combinations of tones (like black and a yellowish green) that do not easily fit into the conventional scheme. Moreover, personal, immediate experience, far removed from traditional symbols, is mingled with conventional meanings. The hue of wilted foliage, for example, evokes sadness and even despair.[128] In this mixture of traditional symbolism and intuitive perception of the emotional character of colors, a mixture that has an affinity to the art of the period, Ariosto shows that Lomazzo's approach was not isolated in his time.

Nevertheless, Lomazzo's discussion of the expressive aspect of color remains unique. I have not been able to find in sixteenth-century literature a work to equal Lomazzo's *Trattato* in the systematic transposition of the symbolic meanings of colors into emotional experiences. Even more important is the fact that no other treatise so extensively applied this transposition to painting. Lomazzo was the first, and perhaps the only, author who attempted to do this.

IV. The Color Scale

A significant achievement of Lomazzo's theory is the formulation of a color scale. Although only a few short passages of the *Trattato* are devoted to this subject, they sum up a long development and crystallize a concept significant for painting as well as for the theory of art.

Renaissance studies of painting, which often included subtle examinations of colors and tones, revealed the complexity of the problem of formulating a comprehensive classification of colors and suggested the difficulties involved. According to Pino, colors are too multifarious to be explained in words; their composition is a "vera alchimia della pittura." [129] Theoreticians of art endeavored, therefore, to reduce this complexity to a rational system and to find a formula for some intrinsic order among colors that might prove useful to painters in their work. Sixteenth-century theory did not arrive at such a definite formula, but the attempts made in this direction deserve a careful study. One of these resulted in the creation of a system of "natural friendships and hostilities among colors, in their material nature as well as in their appearance." Another was the distinction between "natural and derived colors." And still a third attempt, based on observation, sought to arrange colors in a scale. Renaissance theory of art, in attempting to show that painting is a science based upon definite principles and governed by exact rules, was bound to raise the problem of creating a comprehensive classification in the different fields of art. In the realm of color this need for a comprehensive classification led to the formulation of a color scale.

A scale, according to the Oxford English Dictionary, is a "series of degrees, ladderlike arrangement or classification, graded system." Such a concept assumes that each of the elements in that ladderlike system has its specific and unchangeable place; in other words, a scale has a serial order. It is, therefore, more than the mere sum total of its elements. A scale confers on each of the isolated elements of which it is composed a specific meaning depending on the place it occupies in the ladder. These general determinations are also valid for the scale of colors.

To what extent did the theoreticians of the sixteenth century establish a scale of colors? What was the nature of the criteria employed in disposing colors along the scale? Was the standard based on the brightness and luminosity of the hues, their "temperature" ("warmth" or "coolness"), the degree of saturation; or was it based on their "material nature"? Writers on art in that period spoke of *composizione dei colori* and *ordine dei colori;* [130] they believed that the merit of the painter lay not in the application of beautiful, isolated colors but rather in their graceful arrangement and proportion.[131] Although they dealt with color arrangement, the authors of the *Trattati* had no definite and generally accepted concept of a color scale; but the theory of art, the philosophy, and the natural sciences of the period sought in different ways to discover a comprehensive classification of colors and to formulate criteria adopted to this end. These efforts gave rise to the idea of a color scale.

The idea of a color scale is, of course, not an invention of the sixteenth century. Even in remote antiquity we find some knowledge of an intrinsic order of hues and tones. This order could be observed in the rainbow or in the spectrum of sunlight. The most important literary formulation of the idea of a color arrangement is to be found in Aristotle's *De sensu,* a book of basic significance for medieval and Renaissance thought.

According to Aristotle, all colors are composed of light and darkness, or of white and black. "Their multipiclity is due to differences in the proportion of their composition" (439b).[132] Colors compounded in simple, commensurate proportions are pure; other are not. Seven colors are produced by mixing white and black in a calculable proportion, and these are also the pleasant hues (442b). The text of *De sensu* intimates, although vaguely, that white and black lie at the extremes of a chromatic continuum in the center of which the other tints are to be found. Aristotle does not attempt to assign to any one of these colors its exact place in the continuum or to determine its affinity to either of the extremes. But since all colors consist of mixtures of white and black in a commensurate ratio, they can, at least in principle, be arranged along a continuous line.

In his discussion of the rainbow, in the *Meteorologica,* Aristotle again refers to the idea of a color scale.

There are never more than two rainbows at one time. Each of them is three-colored; the colors are the same in both and their number is the same, but in the outer rainbow they are fainter and their position is reversed. In the inner rainbow the first and largest band is red; in the outer rainbow the band that is nearest to this one and smallest is of the same color: the other bands correspond to the same principle. These are almost the only colors which painters cannot manufacture: for these are colors which they create by mixing, but no mixing will give red, green, or purple. These are the colors of the rainbow, though between the red and the green an orange color is often seen. (372a).

The arrangement of these three colors (red, green, purple) is explained by Aristotle in another chapter as showing the strength of sight and the brightness of the hue. He observes that a cloud in the sky looks white, but when we look at the reflection of the same cloud in water it bears a trace of "rainbow coloring." This circumstance is explained by the theory that

When sight is reflected it is weakened and, as it makes dark look darker, so it makes white look less white, changing it and bringing it nearer to black. When the sight is relatively strong the change is to red; the next stage is green, and a further degree of weakness gives violet. No further change is visible, but three completes the series of colors (as we find three does in most other things), and the change into the rest is imperceptible to sense. (374b)

There are some significant differences between the scale described in *De sensu* and the one in *Meteorologica*. The former consists of seven colors, whereas the latter consist of only three; in the former each color consists of a mixture of white and black, while in the latter the hues are explained by the relative strength or weakness of sight (which is, of course, intimately related to the brightness of each color). However, a serial order prevails in both scales and is even more evident in the latter.

The classical concepts of the color scale were not forgotten in the Middle Ages; on the contrary, a great deal of information based on observation of the arrangement of color in natural phenomena had been accumulated. Natural scientists and classical scholars of that time formulated or referred to a color scale in the rainbow as well as in sprinkled drops of water.[133] In medieval theory of art, however, I find no formulation of this idea, although this theory was deeply concerned with problems of color. Despite the fact that artists and writers on art from the ninth to the thirteenth centuries evinced a fine sensitivity for color effects and were able to appreciate coloristic accomplishments for their own intrinsic value,[134] the arrangement of colors in a series was not considered. What concerns us here, however, is not the practice of the medieval artist or his theoretical reflections but rather the emergence of the color scale in Renaissance theory of art. Therefore, I shall only recall Cennini's *Libro dell 'arte* that mirrors so clearly the craft tradition in the period of transition from medieval habits to Renaissance modes of thought. "Know that there are seven natural colors, or rather four actually mineral in character, namely, black, red, yellow, and green; there are natural colors but need to be helped artificially, as lime-white, blue-ultramarine, azzurite, giallorino." [135] Cennini's color list is based upon the Aristotelian and medieval tradition that assumed seven principal hues. This list, however, is not a color scale, since it shows no serial order. It contains, it is true, white and black, but these colors are not placed at the extremes and therefore do not suggest a ladder, nor do the other five colors show any serial order.

Renaissance theory of painting begins with Alberti's *Della pittura*. In the Latin version of his book (which appeared in print only in 1540), Alberti—perhaps influenced by certain scholastic sources—came very close to formulating a color scale. The whole passage reads:

Let us omit the debate of the philosophers where the orginal source of colors is investigated, for what help is it for a painter to know in what mixture of rare and dense, warm and dry, cold and moist color exists? However, I do not despise those philosophers who thus dispute about color and establish the kinds of colors at seven. White and black [are] the two extremes of color. Another [is established] between them. Then between each extreme and the middle they place a pair of colors as though undecided about the boundary, because one philosopher allegedly knows more than the other. It is enough for the painter to know what the colors are and how to use them in painting. I do not wish to be contradicted by the experts, who, while they follow the philosophers, assert that there are only two colors in nature, white and black, and there are others created from mixtures of these two. As a painter I think thus about colors: from a mixture of colors almost infinite others are created. I speak here as a painter.[136]

It is significant that this whole passage is cast in the form of an argument with the philosophers. Although Alberti accepts the philosophers' views both in regard to the limitation of the number of colors to seven and in regard to the serial order, he gives the impression of rejecting their opinions as futile for the painter. The concluding assertion, "I speak here as a painter," can be understood only as in opposition to the philosopher. More important, however, is the fact that out of the seven colors Alberti names only two, white and black, the other five remaining anonymous. While the quoted passage shows that he was aware of the concept, or principles, of the color scale, one cannot say that he actually formulated a scale of hues for the painter.

In the Italian version of *Della pittura* (which appeared in print in 1547 but may have exerted an influence on painters in manuscript form), this whole passage is omitted. The translator, Lodovico Domenichini, had good reason for this omission. The two colors actually named in the Latin passage, white and black, are regarded by Alberti as embodiments of light and darkness; and therefore he believes that "white and black are not true colors but an alteration of other colors." [137] He explicitly repudiates the Aristotelian theory that included white and black in the color lists.[138] The exclusion of white and black eliminates the indication of a serial arrangement of colors. This is again confirmed by the practical suggestions given to the painter. "The dark colors stand among the bright ones not without the same dignity, and the bright colors are similarly enhanced by being among the dark colors." [139] Thus the colors should be distributed in the picture without continuous gradations of brightness or saturation.

In the Italian edition another passage was retained (which in the Latin edition stands together with the passage quoted above) where the number of colors is further reduced. Here Alberti, relying perhaps on Pliny, assumes the existence of only four basic colors. "I say that through the mixture of colors an infinite number of other colors is produced; but just as there are four elements, there are four true colors from which many other subtypes of colors are produced. The color of fire is red, of air, blue, of water, green, of earth, gray or ashen." [140] The criterion employed in limiting the vast variety of shades to four basic hues is not an aesthetic one; but Alberti was also aware, as we have seen earlier, of an aesthetic relationship between colors. There is a "certain friendship among colors and such colors placed side by side endow one another with consistency and grace." [141] Here the idea is suggested that a color attains its own full effect only through its position among other colors.

This idea occurs again in the practical suggestions offered to the painter. In a picture Alberti wishes to see all sorts of colors in an arrangement that is pleasant and delightful to the eye. Delight is produced when a color stands out clearly in contrast to its neighbors.[142] The aesthetic relationship among colors is thus of major significance for the practical purposes of the painter, but a serial order does not apply to it.

A significant portion of Leonardo's notes is devoted to colors. On the whole, Leonardo seems to have agreed with Alberti's concepts. He, too, was of the opinion that a color attains its maximum beauty when placed among opposite shades. "Of several colors, [which] are equally white, that will look whitest which is against the darkest background. And black will look intensest against the whitest background; and the same is the case with other colors when surrounded by their strongest contrast." [143] Like Alberti, Leonardo did not consider white and black as colors but merely as representatives of light and darkness and without a coloristic value of their own. However, when he composed a color list for the practical needs of the painter, he included white as well as black.

> The simple colors are six, of which the first is white, although some philosophers do not accept white or black in the number of colors, because one is the origin of all colors and the other is their absence. But as painters cannot do without them, we include them in the number of the others, and say that in this order white is the first among the simple and yellow is second, green is third, blue is fourth, red is fifth, and black is the sixth.[144]

This list constitutes a color scale. The idea of a serial order is here conveyed by numbering the colors as well as by referring to "this order" *(questo ordine)*.

It is, however, interesting to note that Leonardo seems to have restricted the validity of his color scale. The serial arrangement of the six colors in Leonardo's list does not rest upon theoretical foundations and makes no claim to mirror the "true" order of shades. This arrangement is valid only in the workshop of the painter and has a purely practical aim. This is again most evident in the case of black and white, which are included in Leonardo's list, not because they are basic components of all colors (as in Aristotelian tradition), but simply because the painter cannot dispense with them in his practical work.

The late sixteenth century thus did establish a color scale leading from white to black. This scale is often inconsistent and sometimes obscure, but it is not arranged for practical reasons only. Its authors believed that the serial order of this scale mirrors a cosmic structure of unlimited validity. How did this change from a merely practical scale to a theoretical one come about? What are the sources of this new concept?

The search for a color scale was not confined to the theory of art. Attempts to formulate such a scale were made in various sciences and intellectual disciplines during the Renaissance. These attempts were not directly connected with art, but they are of significance for a better understanding of the color concepts in art theory. Here I shall briefly examine a few examples taken from different fields.

The first example is to be found in a letter that Ficino wrote to his friend Cavalcanti. It is well known that Ficino draws from the Neoplatonic tradition of light metaphysics and accepts the famous symbolic connotations: light is an image of spirit; darkness is an embodiment of matter. In Neoplatonic philosophy a hierarchic ladder extends from the purely spiritual God to gross matter, that is, from supersensual brightness to deepest darkness. Thus Ficino, who believed that "color is opaque light, light is transparent color," [145] describes this ladder of light gradations as a color scale.

In light there are as many ideas of colors as there are colors in objects. At the lowest degree where it is communicable, there is the idea of black [*niger*], at the second the idea of brown [*fuscus*], at the third dark yellow [*flavus*], at the fourth dark blue and green [*caeruleus et viridis*], at the fifth sky blue and sea green [*caelestis et galucus*], at the sixth full red [*rubeus plenior*], at the seventh light red [*rubeus clarior*], at the eighth saffron yellow [*croceus*], at the ninth white [*albus*], at the tenth the transparent or the shining [*limpidus sive nitidus*], at the eleventh the brilliant [*splendidus*], and finally there is the idea of splendor [*splendor*].[146]

It is evident that here Ficino gives a consistent color scale (which, incidentally, seems to have exerted a certain influence on art theory).[147] Two aspects of this scale attract our attention. First, the circumstance that it has no practical aim, and therefore its validity is not restricted to one particular sphere of activity or to any one profession. The hierarchic structure of Ficino's color scale is not based on the needs of the painter but rather mirrors the structure of the Neoplatonic universe. This foundation had been established independently in philosophy without any artistic connotations, but it had an important bearing on art theory. Ficino's influence on the aesthetics and the art theory of the sixteenth century, particularly on Lomazzo, is well known.[148] Lomazzo's later formulation of a color list that consistently stretches from white to black and is not based upon practical and professional foundations like that of Leonardo, may partially be accounted for by Ficino's influence.

The other significant aspect of Ficino's list is that it clearly indicates the criterion employed in disposing the colors along the scale. The color scale is a scale of light values. This scale not only extends from white to black; but Ficino even distinguishes between several shades of the same basic color and arranges them according to their specific degree of luminosity. Thus, the four names and degrees of brightness which, as they appear in a color list, we are bound to interpret as degrees of white. His scale contains two shades of red: a full deep red *(rubeus plenior)* and a light red *(rubeus clarior)*. There are also two degrees of darkness: a dull grayish black or dark brown *(fuscus)* and a deep black *(niger)*. The arrangement according to luminosity is most evident in the case of yellow. Yellow appears twice in Ficino's list and the two shades are assigned to completely different places; the dark yellow *(flavus)* is the third color from the bottom and comes immediately after *fuscus,* and the light saffron yellow *(croceus)* is placed immediately before white. In another place Ficino states the criterion explicitly; ". . . if colors are, so to speak, light, then they have as many degrees."[149] Ficino's arrangement of colors is thus determined by metaphysical considerations.

The disposition of colors according to their brightness was common in the sixteenth century. I shall mention another source, Portius's commentary to the pseudo-Aristotelian *De coloribus.* This book, although ignored by art historians, is an important source for the study of sixteenth-century concepts of color, and particularly for the color terminology. Portius believes, of course, that colors consist of a mixture of white and black in different proportions. He distinguishes between the matter and the form of colors. The matter is the body on the surface of which color is perceived; the "form" is light, that is, the specific brightness of their hues.[150] There are an infinite number of "intermediary colors," since there are infinite possibilities of blending light and darkness. Portius betrays a fine sensibility in the perception of values and disposes them according to their specific brightness. Beside his distinction between the different shades of one color, Portius at least makes reference to an arrangement of primary colors in a continuous row, again according to the particular degree of luminosity. "Yellow shines more than purple; and red shines brighter than violet blue or than glittering violet."[151] Although Portius does not give a comprehensive color scale, he is aware of the principle of a consistent arrangement.

The most important and most elaborate exposition of a color scale in the sixteenth century is by Cardano. This versatile scholar dealt with colors in several of his books and conceived of them as of a means to investigate nature. In his short *De gemmis et coloribus* as well as in his comprehensive work *De rerum varietate,* Cardano presents a detailed color scale. He begins with the traditional number of colors—seven: "white, yellow, red, green, wine color, and black."[152] White and black occupy a special position in this list; as in Aristotle, they are primordial colors that cannot be produced by mixtures. The other five are "intermediate colors" and consist of mixtures of white and black in different proportions. A serial order prevails in the list, since the ratio in which light and darkness are blended determines the exact position of each color. Thus, red is placed in the center of the scale, at an equal distance from both extremes, because it contains an equal amount of white and black. The place of a color is indicated either by defining its position in the whole scale, that is to say, between white and back, or by determining its immediate neighboring colors. It is significant that in both cases the word "between" is employed to describe the exact place of each color. "Red is therefore between dark green [*viridis*] and grass green [*herbaceus*]; scarlet [*puniceus*] is intermediate between white and black. . . . True purple is between green and black." [153]

In *De gemmis et coloribus* Cardano actually gives several color scales. There are some discrepancies among these scales, and there are inconsistencies in the number of colors as well as in their names. However, this fact does not affect the serial order that prevails in the various scales. Cardano expresses his awareness of the serial order in his attempt to define the brightness of each color by means of numbers, that is, by means of indicating the quality of light contained in each color: "we assume that white contains a hundred parts of light, scarlet fifty, black nothing." [154] White, red, and black are the crucial points of the scale—its beginning, middle, and end. But Cardano goes on to describe the specific degree of luminosity of each of the other colors. Yellow contains sixty-five to seventy-eight parts of light, green sixty-two, grass green forty, red (apparently purple is here meant) thirty, blue twenty-five, and *fuscus* only twenty.[155] Thus, each shade has its noninterchangeable place in the list, and the list itself is a full color scale. The criterion for disposing the colors is clearly their degree of brightness.

When we now return from the consideration of philosophy and natural science to the art theory of the Cinquecento, we cannot help but feel disappointed. In spite of the elaborate treatment of color problems, color scale was formulated only once in the theory of that century. It is true that some vague allusions to the gradation of colors may be found in several art treatises of the period,[156] but only in Lomazzo's *Trattato* is a scale elaborated. Even in this most comprehensive work of Renaissance theory of art the criterion for disposing the colors along the scale is not as clearly established as in other fields of learning. On the other hand, however, Lomazzo enriches the subject of the color scale by endowing it with a new artistic meaning.

The third chapter of the "Book of Color" in the *Trattato* contains a list of colors.

There are seven species, or kinds, of colors. Two are the extremes and, so to speak, the parents of all the others; and the five middle ones are

pale [*pallido*], red, purple, yellow, green. As to the origin and
generation of colors, frigidity is the mother of white ... heat is the
father of black, and it is born from a small quantity of white and
much warmth. ... Red is made of mixture of white and black. Violet,
or pale, is made of much white and little red. Saffron [*croceo*], which is
yellow, is made of much red and little white, purple of much red and
little black, green of little black and much red. That is sufficient at the
beginning for establishing the origins of colors.[157]

Lomazzo does not explicitly mention a scale but further examination
reveals that a serial order prevails in this list. The extreme colors are white
and black, orienting the whole list in the traditional direction from light to
darkness. By making white and black the limits of a color list, the
minimum condition for conveying the idea of an inner order is established.
If these two colors are not included (as in the Italian version of Alberti's
book), or if they are not placed at the extremes (as with Cennini), the other
colors lose all sequence and cannot be said to form even the loosest unit.

More important, however, is the other traditional concept, namely, that
the five "intermediate" colors are produced by mixtures of white and black
in different proportions. Lomazzo indicates the exact proportion in which
white and black mingle in each color, and according to which the colors can
be arranged in a continuous sequence. This sequence is not based upon a
vague allusion to a sequence ranging from light to darkness; on the
contrary, here each color has its definite place. Thus, pale and yellow are
between red and black. But even in this limited space of half the scale (i.e.,
from white to red and from red to black), the places of the colors are not
interchangeable. Pale is placed between white and yellow, yellow between
pale and red; purple lies between red and green, green between purple and
black. Such an arrangement is a scale.

Lomazzo's scale is not based on practical foundations and is not derived
from workshop experiences. It is interesting to notice in this context that
his observations on the origins of different colors are in sharp contradiction
to workshop experience. During his activity as a painter before he lost his
sight, Lomazzo could not have failed to remark that a mixture of black and
white on the palette produces not red but gray. If he, nevertheless, observes
that red is a mixture of white and black, he derives this concept not from
the practice of the painter but from the Aristotelian tradition in philosophy

and natural science. His statement thus concerns the "essence" of colors rather than their use; the mixture to which he refers is ontological rather than technical. A comparison of the theoretical foundations of Leonardo's and Lomazzo's color scales reveals the great gap that separates them. In the intervening century the theory of art had changed from a practical doctrine, which formulated workshop experiences based on observations of nature, into a speculative science.

Thus far we have noted that Lomazzo suggests a color scale based on the nature or "essence" of colors, which is their composition of light and darkness. However, the color scale is dealt with in the *Trattato* in still another connection, namely, in the investigation of the aesthetic appearance of colors. This appearance is characterized by Lomazzo in the traditional terms of a system of "friendship" and "hostility" between colors. It is true that these terms have two different meanings, referring to the material nature of colors as well as to their aesthetic appearance. As far as the material nature is concerned, the theoreticians assumed that hostile colors do not mix well while friendly colors lend themselves to good mixtures. Thus, the proportions of white and black in each color form active relations between the shades. The aesthetic appearance of colors is dealt with in terms of harmony. Friendly colors stand beside each other in beauty and harmony, while hostile colors create dissonances. It is this last aspect that concerns us here.

In *Istorie,* Lomazzo points out, many figures are represented wearing garments of different colors. In the arrangement of these garments the painter should create a "certain harmony that is sweet to the eyes and he should avoid dissonances." [158] Dissonance will result when we see a lively green next to a fiery red. The juxtaposition of contrasting shades, recommended by Alberti as the most feasible method of disposing of colors, is now perceived as a dissonance. To the painter of the late sixteenth century true harmony consists of gradual, gentle transitions. The idea of gentle transition as an aesthetic value and as a formal artistic device appeared, as we know, as early as the end of the fifteenth century in Leonardo's concept of *sfumato.* By *sfumato* Leonardo means mainly the gradual and gentle transition from light to darkness without markedly stressing the transition from one color to another.[159] Lomazzo, however, does not mean the transition from a brighter to a darker tone of the same color but rather the transition from one primary color to another. How should the painter arrange the colors in order to achieve that "soft, sweet transition"? Here Lomazzo returns to the color scale, submitting it now to a more exact definition.

> ... according to the doctrine already expounded ... the colors are, as Aristotle says, not more than seven; two extremes, that is, white and black, and five middle ones [*mezzani*] and in their center red which is composed of equal parts of white and black; and between white and red there is yellow that inclines to red, and pale that inclines to white; between red and black there is purple which inclines to red and green that inclines to black.[160]

Except for a few details this scale is not new. Similar arrangements of colors are found in Cardano's *De gemmis et coloribus* and in a former passage of Lomazzo's *Trattato*. There is, however, one peculiar aspect in the above passage that should be emphasized, namely, the reference to the "inclination" of colors. This inclination indicates the friendship and hostility which prevails among colors. The painter who wants to achieve the "sweet harmonies" should be acquainted with these friendships and hostilities. It is significant that the emotional relations between the shades actually reflect the relations of the color scale. A color is friendly to one that stands next to it in the scale while it is hostile to a color separated from it by other shades.

> Thus one sees that red is an enemy of pale which is removed from it by white, and [an enemy] of green which is equally removed from it by black, and it [i.e., red] is a friend of yellow and purple; likewise white and black being extremes cannot stand next to each other, since the one is too light and the other too dark. And this is the first root and adherence to their suitability [of the colors] and constant avoidance of extremes makes for that beauty that we seek in pictures.[161]

Thus, Lomazzo's aesthetic color scale takes us back to the practice of the painter from which Leonardo's color list originated. But the theory of art assimilated some of the metaphysical and scientific thought of the century that separated these two formulations. This speculative thought, given an artistic formulation in the aesthetics of the color scale, gave a new meaning to the painter's activity. In Lomazzo's color scale, humanistic heritage merges with workshop experience and constitutes a new aesthetic ideal.

V. Styles of Light and Color

Perhaps the most significant part of Lomazzo's theory, resulting from the impact of the new sources and trends, is his view that there are different styles of light and color in painting. This concept, suggested in some scattered passages of the *Trattato,* is concisely formulated in two short chapters of *Idea,* where Lomazzo speaks of different modes of coloring and "different styles of illumination" *(diverse maniere d'allumare).*[162] In his descriptions of the coloring and illumination in the works of the various painters, he conceives of these *maniere* as being of distinguishable types, each of them having certain well-defined properties and displaying specific and constantly recurring features. These *maniere,* then, are really regarded as styles.

As we know, in the *Idea* Lomazzo sets forth the doctrine that there are seven "governors" of the art of painting (the seven pillars of his allegorical "Temple of Painting"), represented by the seven artists whom he most admired (Michelangelo, Gaudenzio Ferrari, Polidoro, Leonardo, Raphael, Mantegna, and Titian). Each of these is the accomplished master of one particular art of the "art of painting" (proportions, emotions, color, light, perspective, form, composition), but at the same time each of them also has a particular style in all the other parts. Lomazzo's views of the specific characters of light and color in the works of the seven artists may be summed up as follows:

Michelangelo's light is "terrible"; in his coloring he has served the "fury and depth of design." Gaudenzio's light is "large and regular," and he has established the hitherto unknown mode of expressing the soul's longing to perceive God; in his application of colors, Gaudenzio evinced variety and grace. Polidoro's light is "sharp, violent and martial"; his coloring is characterized by similar metaphors, although the description of his color is less articulate than that of his light. Leonardo's light, which is superior to that of any other painter, is described as "divine"; a term by which Lomazzo apparently means a soft, well-balanced illumination that unites the extremes of bright and dark and fills the picture with a harmonious atmosphere. In his coloring Leonardo varied lights and shadows, covering his paintings with "veils over veils"; but he also had a "noble fury of coloring." Raphael's light is "graceful, amorous, and sweet"; his style is characterized as "regular in the diffusion of colors" and his figures have beauty and relief. Mantegna's light is "quick and minute" but gracefully tempered by reflections; he colored his paintings with "diligence and sharpness of genius." Titian, finally, painted a "terrible and sharp light"; in his coloring he was graceful, particularly significant in the representation of textures and landscapes.[163]

We are, of course, not concerned with the question whether these descriptions and characterizations of the styles of the seven painters do indeed agree with our own impressions (as they sometimes obviously do not). It is evident that Lomazzo borrowed conventional descriptive terms and phrases from the literature of different fields and that he applied them rather haphazardly to the styles of the seven masters (a fact that may explain certain differences, and sometimes even contradictions, between the characterization of the light and the coloring of the same painter).[164] These details need not detain us here. What is significant in our context is the fact that the existence of different styles of light and color is acknowledged without connecting them to a scale of values. In principle, at least, Lomazzo would seem to agree that all these different styles are equally good; the difference in character is not a difference in aesthetic value.[165] The revolutionary meaning of this idea becomes evident when we compare it with the views and opinions held in previous periods.

Artists and authors of the fifteenth and early sixteenth centuries certainly knew that in the representation of light and color there is a wide range of possibilities. Light and color can differ according to the themes or objects represented, or according to the natural conditions which the painter represents. There must always have been some perception that a certain painter tended to a certain type of light and preferred a certain range of colors. Such observations, however, remained inarticulate and did not lead to detailed comparisons. In other words, the apprehension of individual differences among painters did not develop into comprehensive concepts. The idea of different *styles* of light and color could therefore not occur.

Within the basic structure of fifteenth- and early-sixteenth-century theory of art, an explicit recognition and comprehensive description of the plurality of light and color styles were hardly possible. Given the prior assumption that art is a "science," artists and authors of art theoretical treatises apparently believed that there is only one "correct" or "true" way of representing light and of applying colors. The different applications of illumination and coloring were perceived as differences in value and were therefore properly described by terms like "better" or "worse." It is significant that the question whether there are different styles of light and color and, if so, whether they can be equally good, never arose in the Quattrocento and in the early Cinquecento. This fact alone points toward the implicit assumption that there is but one "true" manner of representing light and applying color. Our inference can, I think, be substantiated in some detail by a careful analysis of certain practical precepts given to painters. Where the authors speak of different categories of light (as we have seen in the chapter on Leonardo), they mainly mean light in nature or in the artist's workshop. In both cases, "light" is not the product of the artist's activity but a condition and means of visibility. The very importance assigned to the conditions of light in nature or in the workshop tends to reduce the possibility of an essential transformation of light and color in the artist's work as the result of his character and personality. Moreover, in the few passages where different types of light and color in painter's works is mentioned (mainly in Venetian literature), one type is usually more appreciated than another.[166] Even here, then, the recognition of different types of light and color implies a value judgment.

Seen against this background, the full scope of Lomazzo's departure from the traditional approach can be appreciated. By accepting a plurality of styles unconnected with a scale of values, Lomazzo is indeed presaging some important artistic and critical developments of later periods. Conceding a plurality of styles which are all equally good was bound to lead to an overturning of the established norms in the theory of art.

It is, however, obvious that Lomazzo derived these "modern" ideas from an unmodern, traditional source, namely, from the astrological typology of human beings as "children of the planets." It has been observed in recent research that Lomazzo's description of the particular qualities of the seven artists largely corresponds to the characteristic features of the seven planets.[167] For some of the seven artists Lomazzo himself explicitly stated the connection with specific planets, although he did not do so in respect to light and color. In a broader sense, he advised painters to acquaint themselves with "their" planets in order not to work against their natures.[168] In his analysis of the seven styles of light and color he does not directly refer to the nature of the seven planets, but in describing these styles he frequently uses terms that were traditional planetary adjectives, like the "terrible" nature of Michelangelo's light (Michelangelo is elsewhere in the *Idea* described as "Saturnine"), or the proud and "Martial" character of Polidoro's light and color. Considering all this, it seems fairly certain that his concept of the seven styles of light and color is derived from, and reflects, the traditional views of the seven planets.

Needless to say, astrological typology itself does not specifically refer to art. It is a system of classifying celestial "influence" and of explaining the character of people, but not of artifacts. Art theory did not find ready formulations in the literature of astrology that could easily be transplanted into the context of art and fit the needs of teaching a system of painting.

The reception and assimilation of astrological typology by the theory of art was, therefore, not simply a taking over of ready found formulas; it was a rather complex process of change that sometimes amounted to a radical transformation of the traditional astrological images and notions. But in that process some of the basic concepts of the traditional theory of art itself were overturned. Some of these changes were explicit at the time; others were only implied, and their impact became evident centuries later.

An interesting detail related to the theme of this study attests to the scope of the transformations undergone by astrological imagery when applied to art. As we have seen, Lomazzo's typology, and particularly his description of the *maniere d'allumare,* are influenced by Agrippa's *De occulta philosophia.* In this context it is interesting to notice that Agrippa of Nettesheim related only colors to planets but did not ascribe such associations to types of light. Differences of light would probably have evoked in him the image of emanation, that is, of a gradual descent from the highest to the lowest level of being. He did not, and probably could not, conceive of differences of light as variations of equal value.[169] This, however, is precisely what Lomazzo did. The careful reader of the *Idea* notices that Lomazzo's formulation is rather vague in his characterization of the coloring of the seven masters, but it is definite and precise in the description of their styles of light. In the description of the seven light styles the astrological symbolic imagery, originally referring only to colors, is transplanted to the realm of light. Lomazzo's motives for such a transplantation can be understood. Light is a principal problem for the painter. When the theory of art, in its intrinsic development, reached a point where it could acknowledge a plurality of light styles reflecting a plurality of types of artists, it borrowed the best-known typology available, that is, the typology of colors in astrology. This is, I think, a significant case of adapting an astrological pattern to the specific conditions and exigencies of art and its theory. Such an adaptation, however, involves changes, both in the transference of characteristic properties from color to light, and from natural, or supernatural, phenomena to the style of artists and works of art.

This detail indicates a problem of a broader significance. The influence of astrology on the theory of art led to several general consequences. One is the establishment of a closer connection between the artist and the stylistic properties of his work. In the late sixteenth century the artist was not considered, as was typical for the earlier periods of the Renaissance, as the "maker" of the work who shapes it according to normative, but therefore anonymous, "rules"; his more specific type and "nature" are now believed to be projected on to the work of art. Ideas of this kind had, of course, already appeared in earlier stages of Renaissance culture, but it was only in Lomazzo's literary work that they crystallized into a doctrine of style.

Not less important is another aspect of his doctrine, namely, the fact that the styles are largely defined and described according to criteria of expression. These criteria, defined in stereotypical formulas such as "terrible"; "violent"; "graceful, amorous, and sweet"; and "quick and minute" invariably refer to qualities of character and of emotions. Their application to painting necessarily emphasizes the expressive qualities of art. What I have previously said of Lomazzo's doctrine of color may also be applied to his concepts of style: his categories of style are obviously derived from traditional astrological models; but they have been, so to speak, translated into a language of emotions, and therefore have explicitly expressive connotations.

These broad tendencies are, of course, not restricted to light and color; they encompass all the "parts" of painting and can be discerned in the doctrines of proportion and *moto,* body structure, perspective, and iconography. A discussion of these further aspects is beyond the scope of this study. It is important, however, that light and color take part in this process and fulfill a significant function in the system of styles. It is probably no exaggeration to say that they become specific bearers of expression and that in the discussion of *lume* and *colore* the new tendencies are more precisely formulated than in the analysis of the other "parts" of painting. This may be one of the motives for Lomazzo's granting to light and color particular significance, as we have observed at the beginning of this chapter.

Notes

1. There has been some discussion on the question of whether the Leonardo tradition in Milan actually crystallized in an Academy. See L. Olschki, *Die Literatur der Technik und der angewandten Wissenschaften vom Mittelalter bis zur Renaissance* (Geschichte der neusprachlichen wissenschaftlichen Literatur, I) (Heidelberg, 1919), pp. 239-251, and N. Pevsner, *Academies of Art: Past and Present* (Oxford, 1940), pp. 25 ff. For the persistence of the Leonardo tradition in Lombardy, cf. below, note 37.

2. A good survey of Milanese painting in the late sixteenth century is given by Dell'Acqua, Gian Alberto, "La pittura milanese della meta del XVI secolo al 1630," *Storia di Milano,* X (1957), 678 ff. Cf. also E. Arslan, *Le pitture del Duomo del Milano* (Milan, 1947), *passim.*

3. Cf. E. Panofsky, *The Iconography of Correggio's Camera di San Paolo (Studies of the Warburg Institute,* vol. XXVI) (London, 1961), pp. 30 ff.

4. On Agrippa and his influence on sixteenth-century scholars in Italy see F. A. Yates, *Giordano Bruno and the Hermetic Tradition* (Chicago, 1964), passim, esp. pp. 130-143. Cf. also D. P. Walker, *Spiritual and Demonic Magic from Ficino to Campanella* (London, 1958), pp. 90-96, and Lynn Thorndike, *A History of Magic and Experimental Science,* V, pp. 127-138. For Agrippa's influence on Lomazzo, cf. below, pp. 146 ff., 168 ff.

5. Lomazzo, *Trattato,* III, p. 272: "... e di molte altre cose che si possono in gran parte studiare per gli autori citati nella genealogia dei Dei degli antichi, e nella

sposizione dell' immaginare loro che v'ha fatto Vincenzo Cartari. ..." For bibliographical details of Lomazzo's writings see note 15.

6. Lomazzo, *Trattato,* II, p. 384.

7. Cf. the well-known works of C. Dejob, *De l'influence du Concile de Trente sur la littérature et les beaux arts chez les peuples catholiques* (Paris, 1884); E. Mâle, *L'art religieux de la fin du* XVIe *siècle, du* XVIIe *siècle et du* XVIIIe *siècle* (Paris, 1951); R. Wittkower, *Art and Architecture in Italy 1600-1750* (Baltimore, 1958), with a good bibliography. As an example I should like to quote Gilio's description of the tortured Christ who should be "afflitto, sanguinoso, pieno di sputi, depelato, piagato, differmato, livido e brutto, di maniera che non avesce forma d'uomo" (P. Barocchi, *Trattati d'arte del Cinquecento,* II [Bari, 1961], p. 40). Those artists who portray the suffering Christ as "beautiful and delicate" do so only in order to "show the force of their art" (p. 39). For a formulation similar to Gilio's see Antonio Possevino, *Tractatio de possi et pictura* (Lyon, 1595), as quoted by Wittkower, op. cit., p. 2.

8. See Francesco Bocchi, *Eccellenza del San Giorgio di Donatello,* reprinted in P. Barrochi, *Trattati d'arte del Cinquecento,* III, pp. 127-194. The passage quoted on p. 142. Bocchi's treatise, apparently the first book devoted to a single work of art, appeared in 1584, but it was composed as early as 1571. For his views on expression see my study, "Der Ausdruck in der italienischen Kunsttheorie der Renaissance," *Zeitschrift für Asthetik und Kunstwissenschaft,* XII (1967), 33-69.

9. See Bottari Ticozzi, *Raccolta di lettere,* V, pp. 68-73; the sentence quoted may be found on p. 69. The letter was reprinted in the volume of Lomazzo's poetry which appeared in Milan in 1587.

10. Bottari Ticozzi, *Raccolta di lettere,* VI, pp. 60-78, the passage quoted on p. 70. It should, however, be said that Giovanni Battista Paggi (1554-1627), a well-known Genovese painter and writer on art, mentions, as well as the religious value of painting, other, more secular reasons which were common currency in Renaissance humanistic circles. For Paggi see Thieme-Becker, *Künstlerlexikon,* XXVI, p. 141, and especially Schlosser, *Le letteratura artistica* (1964), pp. 397 ff.

11. See above, the first two sections of the chapter on Venetian theory of art.

12. Carlo Borromeo, *Instructiones Fabricae et Supellectilis Ecclesiasticae* (Milan, 1577), reprinted in P. Barocchi, *Trattati d'arte,* III, pp. 3-113. Cf. A. Blunt, *Artistic Theory in Italy: 1450-1600* (Oxford, 1940), p. 127; R. Wittkower, *Art and Architecture in Italy, 1600-1750,* p. 74.

13. Gregorio Comanini, *Il Figgino ovvero il fine della pittura* (Milan, 1591), reprinted in Barocchi, *Trattati d'arte,* III, pp. 239-379. Comanini, about whose life

we know very little, was bishop in Mantua. The book is written in the form of a dialogue which takes place in the house, and with the participation, of the Milanese painter Ambrogio Figino (1548?-1608) who was a pupil of Lomazzo (cf. *Trattato,* II, p. 383). For Figino see R. P. Arslan, "Disegni di Ambrogio Figino," *Critica d'arte* VIII, 48 (1961), 32-55; J. H. Turnure, "The Late Style of Ambrogio Figino," *Art Bulletin,* XLVII (1965), 35-55. Comanini's book made a certain impression on the learned circles of his time. T. Tasso wrote a sonnet in praise of it which is mentioned by Lomazzo *(Idea,* chap. 38). See also E. Spina-Barelli, "Il Figino ovvero il fine della pittura," *Arte Lombarda,* IV (1959), 123-125. For the topic of light and color, however, Comanini's book is not important.

14. Lomazzo's biography is still to be written. The main source is his autobiography in verse, published in his *Rime* (Milan, 1587), pp. 529 ff. See also C. Casati's careful study, based on research in archives, *Leone Leoni d'Arezzo, scultore e Giov. Paolo Lomazzo milanese* (Milan, 1884); and, for interesting new material, see E. Battisti, *Rinascimento e Barocco,* (Turin, 1960), pp. 238-254. G. M. Ackerman, in an unpublished thesis on "The Structure of Lomazzo's Treatise on Painting" (Bryn Mawr, 1964), pp. 9-18, has summarized what is known of "Lomazzo's Life and Milieu." The main data for Lomazzo's life (1538-1600) are his training in the workshop of G. B. della Serva, a student of Gaudenzio Ferrari (to whom Lomazzo erected a literary monument in his *Idea),* and his extensive travels in Italy and probably in the Netherlands (he is recorded at least in Antwerp) before he lost his sight at the age of thirty-three.

15. Two of Lomazzo's works, on which the following section is based, are the *Trattato dell'Arte della Pittura Scultura ed Architettura* (Milan, 1584) (the original edition bearing the more appropriate title, *Trattato dell'Arte della Pittura, diviso in VII libri, nai quali si contiene tutta la Teoria e la Pratica di essa Pittura).* I shall quote the edition of Rome, 1844 (in three volumes), indicating volume and page. The other work important for our purpose is his *Idea del Tempio della Pittura* (Milan, 1590). Other works by Lomazzo as well as studies of different aspects of his theory will be quoted in the following discussion. Here I should like to mention the important studies which are largely based on Lomazzo's work: Rensselaer W. Lee, *Ut Pictura Poesis: The Humanistic Theory of Painting,* appeared originally in *Art Bulletin,* XXII (1940), 197-269, and subsequently in book form (New York, 1967); and K. Birch-Hirschfeld's older study, *Die Lehre von der Malerei im Cinquecento* (Rome, 1912). For bibliographical details see Schlosser, *La letteratura artistica,* p. 402.

16. See, e.g., the last page of the *Trattato,* III, pp. 299 ff., where he says that all the seven "parts" are specific for the art of painting but demonstrates his assertion by adding "like the lights and the colors."

17. *Trattato,* II, pp. 102 f. "Uno è che io non sono dell' opinione di quelli filosofi peripatetici, che dicono non esservi alcun colore, quando non vi è lume e chiarezza che allumi i colori. Anzi dico liberalmente, che i raggi, o lume del sole, o di qualsivoglia altra luce, non generano, o producono i colori, perchè inanzi che vi concorra la luce, stanno già attualmente prodotti nel soggetto." See also *Trattato,* I, p. 392, where he says that light itself has no color but has the ability to reveal the colors where they are ("manifesta i colori dove sono"); cf. also *Trattato,* I, p. 414. (the bodies show their color by virtue of light) and II, p. 109 (light does not change the color of the bodies).

18. *Trattato,* I, p. 364. A painting which is "dissegnata, motuata, e colorita senze lumi" cannot be understood without being illumined—a clear indication, I think, that Lomazzo conceived of the coloring and the illuminating of a painting as of two distinct phases in the production of a picture.

19. *Trattato,* I, pp. 361-365.

20. *Trattato,* I, p. 364, and *Idea,* chap. 22. Since Alberti this had been, of course, a commonplace in art theory and can be regarded as a hallmark of Renaissance criticism of painting.

21. *Trattato,* I, p. 362. "Onde veggiamo che essendo sparsi tutti i lumi perfetti e proportionati sopra un corpe mal disegnato, e senza muscoli, porge un maggior diletto in riguardanti, eccitando in loro un desiderio di vedere. . . ." The metaphor of light evoking desire was current in Neoplatonic thought of the Renaissance. Cf., e.g., Ficino's *Convivium,* V, 11.

22. *Trattato,* I, p. 363. Here Lomazzo emphasizes the theoretical aspect as opposed to the purely empirical. Armenini, who was influenced by Lomazzo, speaks in a similar context of *giuditio* and *arte, giuditio* being an irrational gift and *arte* the theoretical system of rules. See *De veri precetti della pittura,* p. 83.

23. *Trattato,* I, p. 365.

24. *Trattato,* I, p. 363. In the other Lombard treatises on painting Correggio is not mentioned at all. In Venice, however, his colorism seems to have made a deep impression. Dolce, in his *"L'Aretino"* (ed. Barocchi, I, p. 199), says: "Ma fu [i.e., Giuliano Romano] vinto di colorito e di più gentil maniera da Antonio da Correggio, leggiadrissimo maestro, di cui in Parma si veggono pitture di tanta bellezza, che par che non si possa disiderar meglio." Vasari did not mention these particular paintings by Correggio. Lomazzo seems to have seen them as his formulation suggests (". . . due quadri di mano di Antonio Correggio, che si ritrovano in questa città presso il cavalier Leone Aretino"); in his evaluation he may have been influenced by Venetian taste. Armenini praises Correggio for his bold

foreshortenings, especially in the ceiling frescoes in Parma *(De veri precetti,* p. 155), but he says nothing of his light and color.

25. *Trattato,* I, p. 374. For Vasari's description of Correggio's *Nativity* see below, note 44.

26. Birch-Hirschfeld, *Die Lehre von der Malerei in Cinquecento,* p. 53.

27. In the sonnet on Titian *(Rime* [Milan, 1587], p. 94) he says: "Unico e questo al mondo hor frà pittori Nel dar spirito e color à le pitture"; of Tintoretto (p. 101): "Con si gran furia e si viuaci moti/ Pingi le tue figure in diuersi atti/ Con tai lumi riflessi e mischie e tinte/ Ch'al ver paion dipinte"; of Veronese's paintings he says: "I colori viuaci, i fieri scorti/ Gl'affetti espressi ..." (p. 102).

28. On Lomazzo as a painter cf. Dell'Acqua (see note 2), pp. 688-695, and A. Venturi, *Storia dell'arte italiana,* IX, *La Pittura del Cinquecento* (Milan, 1934), pp. 503-513. See also (more for the local background and especially for light and color in Milanese painting of the late sixteenth century) R. Longhi, "Quesiti Caravaggeschi," *Pinacoteca* (1928-1929), 351 ff., reprinted in R. Longhi, *'Me pinxit' e quesiti Caravaggeschi* (Florence, 1968), pp. 81-143.

29. *Trattato,* I, pp. 365 ff.

30. *Trattato,* I, p. 371.

31. In the long description of light quoted above which is copied from Agrippa of Nettesheim's *De occulta philosophia* (see below, note 40) Lomazzo inserts the phrase "come dice Marsilio Ficino sopra Platone" *(Trattato,* I, p. 366), which does not occur in Agrippa's text and suggests Ficino as the source.

32. Cf. Erwin Panofsky, "Artist, Scientist, Genius: Notes on the 'Renaissance-Dämmerung,'" *The Renaissance* (New York and Evanston, 1962), pp. 121-182, with extensive bibliography. Panofsky does not discuss optics in this context.

33. For the editions of *De coloribus* see E. Franceschini, "Sulle versioni Latini medievali del Περι Χρωματων," *Autour d'Aristote: Recueil d'etudes de Philosophie ancienne et medievale,* offert a A. Marsion (Louvain, 1955), pp. 451-469.

34. For the influence of Vitelo's *Perspectiva* in the sixteenth century cf. C. Baeumker, *Witelo: Ein Philosoph und Naturforscher des XII Jahrhunderts (Beiträge zur Geschichte und Philosophie des Mittelalters),* III, 2, p. 606. For the translation and study of Neckham's treatise on perspective see above, p. 49.

35. For the editions of Gregorius Reisch's *Margarita philosophica* see J. Wilbenforce, *A List of Editions of the "Margarita Philosophica 1503-1599"* (New York, 1884). The more important editions appeared in 1503, two in 1504, two in 1508, 1512, 1515, 1517, 1535, 1583, 1599. In the Italian translation I used (Venice,

1600) the chapter on light is on pp. 590 ff. (Trattato secondo del libro X, cap. vii). And see also pp. 1129 ff.

36. Lomazzo mentions Alberti in *Trattato,* II, p. 141. Apart from specific questions Lomazzo relies on Alberti by the very fact that he writes a systematic theory of art, partly based on *regole* and science.

37. Lomazzo's acquaintance with Leonardo's manuscripts has been studied by C. Pedretti, *Studi Vinciani* (Geneva, 1957). For the persistence of Leonardo's theories in the late sixteenth century in Lombardy, cf. Erwin Panofsky, *The Codex Huygens and Leonardo da Vinci's Art Theory* (London, 1940).

38. I have found no explicit mention of Venetian authors in Lomazzo's writings. Lomazzo was, however, well read, and it seems unlikely that he was not acquainted with treatises on art which appeared during his life time. Some passages in the *Trattato* suggest an acquaintance with Venetian treatises on painting. When mentioning Alberti (see note 36) he stresses the "veil" and couples him with Dürer, a combination which we have found in Pino. He also speaks of the *alchimia dei pittori veneziani* in *Trattato,* I, p. 326.

39. "Lume adunque è qualità senza corpo," *Trattato,* I, p. 371. Cf. Ficino, *Convivium,* V, 4. The characterization of light as "bodiless" is, of course, widely diffused and therefore Lomazzo could have derived it from different sources. The whole passage in the *Trattato,* however, is closely related to the chapter of Ficino quoted. For Lomazzo's "borrowings" from Ficino, see E. Panofsky, *Idea,* pp. 55, 122-130, and R. Lee, *Ut pictura poesis,* pp. 13, 26.

40. *De occulta philosophia,* I, chap. 49: "lumen etiam qualitas multum formalis, & simplex actus intelligentiae, & imago: primo a divina mente in omnia diffusa, sed in ipso deo patre, qui est pater luminum, est prima vera lux: deinde in filio illiu illustrans splendor & exuberans: in spiritu sancto ardens fulgor, superans omnem intelligentiam etiam, ut inquit Dionysius, seraphinorum. In angelis itaque diffusa fit splendens intelligentia; profusumque gaudium super omnis ratioais terminos, diversis tamen gradibus secundum suscipientis intelligentiae naturam suscepta: descendit deinceps in coelestia, ubi fir copia uitae & efficax propagatio, etiam visibilis splendor." R. Klein, "Les sept gouverneurs de l'art selon Lomazzo," *Arte Lombarda,* IV, 2, pp. 277 ff., noticed that Lomazzo's color description is taken over from Agrippa. Agrippa's description of light is given at the beginning of the same chapter. A similar, although more abbreviated, description of the hierarchy of light is also given by Ficino, *Convivium,* V, 4. For other influences of Agrippa on Lomazzo see, for example, the former's advice that the scholar find "his planet" in order to work according to his possibilities as prescribed by the stars *(De occulta*

philosophia, III, chap. 21), and Lomazzo's similar advice to the painter. "Essendo adunque di tanto momento che 'l pittore e qualunque altro artefice conosca il suo genio, e, dove più l'inclini l'attitudine e disposizion sua d'operar più facilmente e felicemente per uno modo che per un' altro. . . ." *Idea,* chap. 2, passim, esp. at the end of the chapter. "Inclination" is, of course, an astrological term.

41. See above, notes 5 and 6.

42. Lomazzo praises Dürer's "invenzioni mirabili . . . che tutte significano il suo concetto sotto velami d'animali, come nella porta dell'onore di Massimiliano Imperatore." *Idea,* chap. 31.

43. A good example is Alciati's emblem "In colores." Cf. *Emblemata d'Andrea Alciati* (Lyon, 1551), pp. 128-129.

44. Vasari's description *(Le vite,* ed. Milanesi, IV, p. 117) reads: ". . . une Natività di Cristo, ove partendosi da quello uno splendore, fa lume a'pastori e interno alle figure che lo contemplano; e fra molte considerazioni avute in questo suggetto, vie e una femina che volende fisamente guardare verso Cristo, e por non potere gli occhi mortali sofferire la luce della sua divinita, che con i raggi par che percuota quella figure, si mette la mano dinanzi agli occhi, tante bene espressa, che e una maraviglia. Evvi un coro di Angeli sopra la capanna che cantano, che son tanto ben fatti, che per siano piuttosto piovuti dal cielo, che fatti dalla mano d'un pittore." Lomazzo's description *(Trattato,* I, p. 374) is contained in the discussion of the "second primary light" and reads: ". . . una luce divina, si come rappresenta una tavola di Antonio da Correggio, ch'egli dipinse alla sua città, la quale è tra le opere di pittura una delle singolari che siano al mondo. E questa luce ha da essere dimostrata in modo chi risplenda ne' corpi tanto più, quanto più eglino gli sono vicini. Tale doveva essere la luce dell' angelo cha apparve a Cristo nell' orto, il cui lume divino abbagliare, e restringer doveva tutti gli altri, ancora che non fosse stato notte. . . ."

45. The paintings are the *Martyrdom of St. Lawrence* (Venice, Church of the Jesuits), mentioned by Lomazzo in *Trattato,* I, p. 376, and by Vasari in *Le vite,* VII, p. 453; and the *Trinity* (see Lomazzo, I, p. 374, and Vasari, VII, p. 451).

46. See Ackerman (cf. above, note 14), passim.

47. *Trattato,* I, p. 372, and *Idea,* chap. 22.

48. *Idea,* chap. 29. The term "natural light" obviously shows that this is the common, usual type of light.

49. *Trattato,* I, p. 373. The first primary light is essentially identical with Leonardo's specific light. Leonardo in his *Treatise* (ed. McMahon, 760) describes the illumination of an object inside a room as having the same qualities (sharp

differences between light and shadow) that Lomazzo would ascribe to the "first primary light."

50. The reference to the illumination of the ancient idols in *Idea,* chap. 29. Lomazzo may have had in mind the Pantheon which he describes *(Trattato,* I, p. 411) as "dedicato a tutti gli Dei, che in cima pigliando il lume dal cielo, con dolce scorrere al basso comparte alle statue per le cappelle dilettevol lume, facendogli risaltare le membra con ordine soavissimo."

51. *Trattato,* I, p. 409.

52. Cf. Armenini, *De veri precetti,* pp. 81 ff. It must be admitted that Armenini was influenced by Lomazzo, and therefore the origin of his passage may well be Lomazzo's *Trattato.* However, the very fact that Armenini took over this observation would indicate that it appealed to the late-sixteenth-century workshop whose attitude Armenini often expresses.

53. *Trattato,* I, p. 408. A similar precept was proposed by Alberti, *Della pittura,* ed. Mallè (Florence, 1950), pp. 99 ff. For a related precept which is equally far removed from actual visual experience that the most vivid colors be given to the "noble and principal figures" in a composition, see *Idea,* chap. 28. See also the precept that angels should not receive the "divine light" from the sides but should radiate it from the center of their figures *(Trattato,* I, p. 398).

54. *Idea,* chap. 29. "Onde fanno che le figure pigliano lume falso e contrario, mentre che essi si persuadono di dar tali lumi con ragione, e così si ritrovano poi al tutto confusi." In this chapter Lomazzo also speaks of "lume falsamente distribuito."

55. *Trattato,* I, pp. 373 ff. In *Idea,* chap. 29, Lomazzo omits the term "first, second, third," but divides the primary light (here called *lume principale)* into "celestial, divine and artificial" light. "Celestial," contrary to "divine," has no metaphysical or symbolic meaning but denotes light that comes from the sky, i.e., sunlight. In the same chapter he simply says "celesto ovvero natural lume."

56. In the late sixteenth century these particular paintings seem to have been regarded as a climax in the representation of mysterious light expressing or symbolizing divine radiance. Vasari describes Raphael's *Transfiguration* in terms which emphasize the effect on the beholder who looks at a divine appearance. The disciple "ha a terra il capo. e chi con fare ombra agli occhi con li mani si difende dai raggi e dalla immensa luce dello splendore di Cristo" *(Le vite,* IV, p. 372). Vasari describes the effect of the divine light in Correggio's *Nativity* in similar terms (see above, note 44). Sorte (ed. Barocchi, p. 294), in describing the dazzling and at the

same time diffuse light which he calls "divina luce," also mentions the scene of the Transfiguration but does not refer to Raphael's picture.

55. *Trattato,* I, p. 375.

58. *Trattato,* I, pp. 374 ff. The biblical descriptions of all the scenes mentioned by Lomazzo indicate a dazzling, glaring light. Besides the Transfiguration the principal scenes are: God's appearance to Moses on Mount Horeb (Exodus 3:2) and on Mount Sinai (Exodus 19:16 ff.–in Lomazzo's formulation, "dove esso Mose era da tutti fuggito per il soverchio splendore che aveva contratto"); Moses' shining face when he spoke to Aaron (Exodus 34:30–this scene was also mentioned by Sorte, p. 294, in this particular context); the Column of Fire, and God's glory over the Tabernacle (Exodus 40:34 ff.). It is characteristic that in the description of the last-mentioned scene Lomazzo adds to the biblical text the words "the radiance of Whom [God] nobody could endure."

59. Sorte, pp. 294 ff.

60. Sorte, p. 295. Giulio Campo worked at that time in Milan. The *Campi cremonesi* are mentioned, among other well-known artists, by Lomazzo in *Trattato,* III, p. 297.

61. Cf. Alberti, *Della Pittura,* ed. Mallè (Florence, 1950), p. 64.

62. *Trattato,* I, p. 376. "Questo lume distribuisce le forze sue i suoi raggi e dilatazioni, ora piu da una parte, ora da un' altra, secondo che la fiamma avvampa."

63. *Trattato,* I, p. 377.

64. The list of themes, mainly sacrifices and other scenes requiring the representation of open fires, is given in *Trattato,* I, pp. 377 ff. The sentence quoted appears on p. 378.

65. For those trends see R. Longhi, "Quesiti Caravaggeschi," *Pinacoteca,* I (1928), 17-33, 258-320. And see particularly pp. 281 ff. for a discussion of light.

66. *Trattato,* I, pp. 379-381, and a brief summary, consisting of only several lines, in *Idea,* chap. 22.

67. *Trattato,* I, p. 372. The *fisiologici* are, of course, not his single source; earlier (p. 371) he also mentions Aristotle, St. Thomas Aquinas, and Vitelo.

68. For the term *ricepzione dei lumi* see Alberti, ed. Spencer, pp. 68, 81-85.

69. "Quanto alla prima [i.e., disposizione], se le superficie sono concave ed angulari si richiedono i lumi aspri ed acuti, se sono rotonde soavi, se piane dilatati, se eminenti fieri." *Idea,* chap. 22.

70. In *Trattato,* I, p. 381, Lomazzo uses the term *composizione;* in *Idea,* chap. 22, he says *qualità delle materie.* The term *qualità* with this particular meaning is also used in *Trattato,* I, p. 385.

71. *Trattato,* I, p. 383, and in many other places. See, for example, *Trattato,* II, p. 107, where Lomazzo says that in depicting the "choleric man" the color should be adapted to his "composition."

72. *Trattato,* I, p. 382. "E pero essendo, e trovandosi lore in tutte le cose di ciascuno dei tre ordini, vedesi che in queste cose inferiori eglino sono grossi e fecciosi; nelle celeste sono più puri e mondi; ma nelle sopra celesti sono, come dicono i platonici, pieni di vita, e totalmente perfetti e beati." But at the end of the same chapter of the "Book of Lights" (xii), Lomazzo introduces a division into five levels: God, the angels, the heavens, our world *(a noi)* and hell *(inferno).* The hierarchic arrangement of materials and phenomena from God down to Lucifer occurs also in other parts of the *Trattato.*

73. *Trattato,* I, 384. And cf. Sorte's descriptions which is clad in the form of a criticism of contemporary painters: "... che facciano grandamente errore i pittori che lo [i.e., God] dipingono con colori fissi rinforzati di ombre fine al nero ... le cose divine ... sono sempre accompagnate da un grandissimo splendore ..." (p. 294). An additional indication for Lomazzo's possible acquaintance with Sorte's *Osservazioni nella pittura* can be found in his description of Tintoretto's style. Sorte, stressing Tintoretto's temperament, which is expressed in the creative act, says: "... come ne' gesti, nella faccia, nel mover degli occhi e nelle parole è pronto e presto ... l'ombre, le mezze tente, i rilievi e le carni benissimo imitate, e con così fatta gagliarda prattica, velocità e prestezza, ch'è una meraviglia venerlo operare" (pp. 299 ff.). Lomazzo, who did not know Tintoretto, describes his style in *Rime,* p. 101, in similar terms:

Con si gran furia e si viuaci moti
Pingi le tue figure in diuersi atti,
Con tai lumi riflessi e mischie e tinte
Ch'al ver paion dipinte.

74. *Trattato,* I, p. 385. The attribution of sharp lights to the fire of hell may be derived both from Platonic philosophy (the lower regions being more material than the higher ones and, therefore, "receiving" more light) and from the observation of paintings.

75. Those views are set forth, in a rather confused fashion, in chaps. 14-17 of the "Book of Light" *(Trattato,* I, pp. 386-399). The phrase "sicura regola degli effetti causati del lume" occurs in a discussion of *composizione (Trattato,* I, p. 387).

76. *Trattato,* I, pp. 387 f. It is interesting to note that Alberti (ed. Spencer, p. 94; ed. Janitschek, p. 155) advised the painter to draw after "a mediocre sculpture [rather] than excellent painting." While this is said against the medieval practice according to which the apprentice copies the works of his master (see Cennini, pp. 14-15), it shows that drawing after a sculpture was an idea and practice acceptable to Alberti. Leonardo rejected this idea for the reason that "he who can go to the fountain does not go to the water jar" (Richter, 490; see also 484-485). Lomazzo was opposed to this practice for a completely different reason, which today we would call the appreciation of texture. Both the Leonardo tradition and especially the influence of Venetian theory of art would seem to account for Lomazzo's position.

77. ". . . ed appresso della carne, dando più lustrezza a quelli parti che più sono propinque alle ossa, come sono i nodi della dita, le spalle, le ginocchia, e simili apparimenti, che dipoi riescono più soavi le parti piu carnose: e questa è la vera strada che a loro imitazione si deve tenere." *Trattato,* I, p. 391. As we know, this advice became a basic element in the tradition of Academies of Art from the seventeenth century onward.

78. *Trattato,* I, p. 392.

79. *Trattato,* I, pp. 395 f.

80. "e nel fuoco infernale, vogliono i demoni, e le anime tormentate nelle fiamme spesse e gravi aver luce acutissima della maggior chiarezza. . . . E queste regole si hanno da osservare in tutti i fuochi. . . ." *Trattato,* I, p. 398.

81. *Trattato,* I, pp. 402 ff.

82. See F. Boll, *Die Lebensalter* (1913), reprinted in the volume of his essays *Sternkunde des Altertums* (Leipzig, 1950), pp. 156-224, esp. pp. 183-190.

83. See, for instance, Alberti, ed. Spencer, p. 92; ed. Janitschek, p. 149. In the representation of the different ages Leonardo placed his main emphasis on the difference in gestures (ed. McMahon, 252-255, 385, pp. 106, 146). Dolce, in a very general way, says: "Il simile è convenevole che si osservi in una donna, distinguendo sesso da sesso, et età da età, e dando a ciascuno convenientemente le parti sue" (p. 177). Pino (ed. Barocchi, p. 117) also mentions "young and old" claiming that the coloring of the flesh should be appropriate to the age. None of

these authors, however, divides the life span of man into seven ages (nor into any other well-established group of "ages"), nor does he connect them with the planets.

84. "Onde il colorir si può dir la radice della Pittura e quello che gli de la perfezione. . . ." *Idea,* chap. 21.

85. ". . . che senza esso [i.e., color] la pittura non si puo adempire, ne ricevero la sua perfezione; perciocchè ogli è quello che esprime disegnate con la forza degli altri generi." *Trattato,* I, pp. 323 f.

86. Denis Mahon, *Studies in Seicento Art and Theory* (London, 1947), pp. 93 ff.

87. Giovanni Pietro Bellori, *Le vite de' Pittori, Scultori ed Architteti moderni* (Rome, 1672), pp. 203 ff.

88. It seems that Leonardo's influence was not characteristic of the whole region of Lombardy but was limited to Lomazzo. A treatise on painting, composed in the late sixteenth century by an artist who was closely connected with the Leonardo tradition, has only a short passage on color and light (cf. E. Panofsky, *The Codex Huyghens and Leonardo da Vinci's Art Theory* [*Studies of the Warburg Institute,* vol. XIII] [London, 1940], pp. 60-62), whereas it discusses the other aspects at great length. While the influence of Leonardo's style of light and color on Venetian painting is recorded in Renaissance literature (see Vasari, *Le vite,* ed. Milanesi, IV, p. 92, "Aveva venduto Giorgiono alcune cose di mano di Leonardo molto fumeggiate e cacciate, come si e detto, terribilmento di scuro: e questa maniera gli piacque tanto, che, mentre visse, sempre ando dietro e quella, e nel colorito a olio la imito grandamente"), no mention of such an influence is made in Lombard theory of art before, or except for Lomazzo.

89. "Colore, come dice Aristotile, è la estremità della cosa giudicata e visibile in corpe terminato, ovvero è qualità visibile terminata nell' estremità del corpo opaco, la quale innanzi che sia allumata e visibile in potenza, e per beneficio del lume si vede in atto." *Trattato,* I, p. 325.

90. For Aristotle's color concepts see the still basic work of Prantl, *Aristoteles über die Farben,* 1849.

91. Aristotle's views on the subject of color were restated and elaborated in the Renaissance editions of, and commentaries to, the pseudo-Aristotelian *De coloribus* (for the editions see above, note 33). As examples of the paraphrasing of the Aristotle's views, I should like to quote the introduction to *De coloribus libellvs, a Simone Portius,* pp. 5-21, that gives an interesting survey of the history of the concepts of light and color in antiquity, especially in Aristotle; for a briefer statement of Aristotle's concepts see *Margarita philosophica,* p. 592.

92. See, e.g., R. Borghini, *Il Riposo* (Florence, 1730), p. 180 (original edition, p. 227).

93. *Trattato delle perfette proporzioni,* ed. Barocchi, *Trattati d'arte del Cinquecento,* I, pp. 243 ff. ("Ciascuna delle pietre, tra l'altre cose, hanno in sé questa qualità di composti: cioè colore e durezze . . ."), p. 248 ("Tutte le varietà de colori dell' erbe cioè di più chiare e meno chiaro verdezze, procedano della qualità del composto degli umori. E da questo viene che l'un' erba è dall' altra riconosciuta. . . .").

94. Cf. *De gemmis et coloribus* in *Hieronymi Cardani Mediolanenada . . . operum* (Lyon, 1563), II, pp. 552 ff.; see also *De rerum varietate, Opera,* III. pp. 43 ff., 267, and *De subtilitate, Opera,* III, p. 447.

95. *Idea,* chap. 21. See passages like "Fra gli elementi dimostra il colore . . . e nella terra [colors show] le differenze delle pietre, come dei grisoliti, diamanti, eraldi, giacinti, e carbonchi. . . . I drappi ancora si conoscono diversi per li colori. . . . Ne meno per il colore si distinguono l'un dall'altro gli stromenti e di qual materia sian formati."

96. Cf. Pino, ed. Barocchi, pp. 117, 102.

97. See the long and detailed discussion, based on the parallelism between humoural types and planets, in *Trattato,* II, pp. 103-105, 123-125. The color of the choleric man is composed of two parts of red, one part of yellow, and three parts of "fair" *(chiaro)* color; the color of the sanguinic type consists of one part of red, two parts of fair, and three parts of fair (p. 105); the phlegmatic's complexion is portrayed by a mixture of one part of pink, three parts of bright dull gray *(bigio chiaro),* and three parts of white; the melancholic's skin, finally, is composed of one part of dull gray, two parts of dark yellow, and three parts of fair color. Red, the traditional color of life, is the key hue in this list. The choleric, the most lively of the four humoural types, has two parts of red, the sanguine only one, the phlegmatic only pink (i.e., a pale, diluted red); and the melancholic, the least lively type, has no red at all. It is significant that Lomazzo discusses the mixture of the four types in this sequence of a descending scale of red.

98. Klibansky, Saxl, and Panofsky, *Saturn and Melancholy* (London, 1964), esp. pp. 112 ff., 369 ff.

99. The belief that the color complexion is a symptom of the humoural constitution of a person was, of course, widespread in the different types of medical literature. For an interesting example see the physiognomic studies of the fifteenth-century friar and writer John of Hayn *(Ioannis ab Indagine introductiones in . . . Physiognomiam, Complexiones Hominum . . .* [1630], pp. 166 ff.), where the color of

the skin is considered as a criterion for the identification of the temperament and explained scientifically.

100. *Trattato,* II, p. 102.

101. In Lomazzo's text the two aspects are not neatly divided, but one can easily distinguish between them by asking what particular problems are being discussed. However, Lomazzo himself alludes to the two aspects in some formulations. Thus he says that there is a friendship and hostility among colors "cosi per materia come par apparenza" *(Trattato,* I, p. 323). The term *materia* here probably means the compatibility of certain colors to be blended with others, while *apparenza* refers, I believe, to the aesthetic appearance.

102. *Trattato,* I, p. 327.

103. *Trattato,* I, p. 331.

104. *Trattato,* I, p. 329.

105. *Trattato,* I, p. 329. "E che cio sia vero troviamo per esperienza. . . ."

106. *Idea,* chap. 21; *Trattato,* I, pp. 327 ff. The six media are: oil painting, fresco, tempera, scraffito, "the new manner" of pastelle (in which Leonardo excelled as can be seen in the heads of Christ and the Apostles—*Trattato,* p. 328), and watercolor, which he considers as applicable only in book illumination. Sometimes *(Idea,* beginning of chap. 21) there seems to be some confusion between purely technical media (like oil painting or fresco) and some rather stylistic types of representation, like "chiaro e scuro, ombrando e lineando solamente," which seems to refer to some kind of grisaille.

107. See above, section VI of the chapter on the School of Venice.

108. *Trattato,* I, pp. 336 ff. As Lomazzo visited the Netherlands, he also might have known Flemish paintings that could not be seen in Italy.

109. *Trattato,* I, pp. 334 ff.

110. "Imperocché i colori più vivi appartengono ai panni delle figure nobili e principali. . . ." *Idea,* chap. 28.

111. *Trattato,* I, pp. 336, 400: ". . . i lumi sono acuti e lustri come sopra i meloni, e sopra la punta del naso, e della fronte."

112. *Trattato,* I, pp. 338 ff. The case of changeant colors provides an interesting example of the fact that the theory of art is not a faithful reflection of actual artistic practices. Changeant colors were, of course, well known not only in textile production but also in art. At least since the fourteenth century Italian painters had

often represented the wings of angels in a clear and consistent attempt to produce a changeant effect (perhaps influenced by the observation of the wings of birds). In art theory, however, the *colori cangianti* were virtually disregarded until the late sixteenth century.

113. *Trattato,* I, pp. 326 ff. (the "alchemy of Venetian painters"); p. 337 (Flemish painters). From these traditions Lomazzo could, of course, also have inherited his high regard for oil painting.

114. "E quivi sono forzato ancora detestare quella corrottissima ragion di colorire secondo i colori, ch'è tanto andata avanti ch'omai tutta l'Italia e le Germanie ne sono impiastrate, sìche per parlare alla schietta, a questi tempi i pittori più sono solleciti dei colori che del disegno, della vaghezza che della forza dell'arte. . . ." *Idea,* chap. 28.

115. *Trattato,* II, p. 104.

116. *Trattato,* I, pp. 321 f.

117. See my study, "Der Ausdruck in der italienischen Kunsttheorie der Renaissance" (cf. above, note 8).

118. "Perchè tutti i colori hanno una certa qualità diversa fra di loro, causano diversi effetti a chiunque li guarda. . . . Ora per cominciare troviamo che i colori neri, lucidi, terrei, plumbei, ed oscuri generano per gli occhi nell' animo del riguardante la qualita loro, le quale non è altro che tristezza, tardità, pensiero, melancolia e simile. I colori neri, verdi, di color di saffiro, alquanto rossi, ed oscuri, di color d'oro mischio con l'argento, cioè flavo, rendono soavità, e giocondità. I colori rossi, ardenti, focosi, o flammei, violacei, purpurei, e di color di ferro ardente, e di sangue, causano spirito, acutezza nel guardare, e quasi inducono fierezza ed ardire, svegliando la mente per l'occhio non altrimenti che il fuoco. I colori d'oro, gialli, e purpurei chiari, e più lucidi fanno l'uomo intento nel guardare, e rendono grazia e dolcezza. I colori rosati, verdi chiari, ad alquanto gialli rendono piacevolezza, allegrezza, diletto, e soavità. Il color bianco genera una certa semplice attenzione quasi più melancolica che altrimenti." *Trattato,* I, pp. 342 ff. (chap. ii of the Book of Color"). The chapter is called *Degli effetti che causano i colori.*

119. Black, for instance, on the one hand generates sadness and melancholy, but on the other it renders softness and playfulness. On the question as to whether this is the same black, see above p. 170. Some purples induce fierceness; others render softness and playfulness. The very term *alquanto gialli* is a characteristic indication of the fact that the same basic color may have perhaps indifferent shades, different meanings.

120. See Alberti, ed. Spencer, pp. 95 ff.; ed. Janitschek, pp. 145 ff. For Leonardo, cf. his *Treatise on Painting,* ed. McMahon, 250 (p. 105), 403 (p. 151). For a possible influence of ancient rhetorics on Leonardo's observations cf. Rensselaer Lee, *Ut pictura poesis,* p. 25.

121. Blushing and growing pale, the most obvious cases of a natural change in color as an expression of an emotional experience, do not seem to have been noticed or discussed in Renaissance theory of art.

122. *Trattato,* I, pp. 344-356 (chaps. 12-18 of the "Book of Color").

123. R. Borghini, *Il Riposo,* pp. 183 ff. (first edition, pp. 230 ff.).

124. *De occulta philosophia,* I, chap. 49. This has been noticed by R. Klein, "La forme et l'intelligible," *Archivio di Filosofia* (1958), 103 ff. Cf. also Klein's article quoted in note 40 of this chapter.

125. *Il Mostruosissimo Mostro, di Giovanni de'Rinaldi* (Brescia, n.d.), fol. 2v: "Pertanto douendo io scriuere queste cose non a filosofi & huomini d'alto sapere, ma a semplici amanti, quali volontieri leggono cosi fatte inuentioni, ho donuto scriuere con purita di dire, adornato solo quanto basta a dilettare loro. . . ."

126. *Anthoni Thylesi Consentini Libellvs de coloribvs. . .* (n.d.; 1529?). The opening sentences of the little treatise read as follows: "Dicam aliquid de Coloribus in hoc libello: non quidem unde conficiantur, aut quae fit eorum natura: necq enim Pictoribus haec traduntur, aut Philosophis, sed tantum Philologis, qui Latini sermonis elegantiam studiose inquirunt."

127. Ibid., chap. 3. "Differt in hoc a colore nigro: ut omnis ater est niger, sic non omnis niger est alter: horrendus est hic, tristis, uisu inuicundus, lugentibus, accommodatus, ille contra non nunquam lepidus ac uenustus: ut humani oculi sunt complures, quos nemo Atros diceret, sed nigros, tamen nihil maiori cum uoluptate spectamus."

128. See Ariosto, *L'Orlando furioso,* V, 47 (the symbolism of white); VI, 13 (the combination of black and yellowish green); VIII, 85 and IX, 2 (the symbolism of black); XVII, 12 (symbolism and expression); XXXII, 47 (wilted foliage). Many more examples could be found in this poem. An interesting discussion of Ariosto's color symbolism in connection with customs at the court of Ferrara is given by G. Bertoni, *"L'Orlando Furioso" e la Rinascenza a Ferrara* (Modena, 1919), pp. 221-227. Some suggestive remarks on color symbolism in the late Middle Ages may be found in J. Huizinga, *Der Herbst des Mittelalters* (Stuttgart, 1938), pp. 170, 407 ff. For medieval color symbolism see also W. Wackernagel, "Die Farben–und Blumensprache des Mittelalters," *Abhandlungen zur deutschen Altertumskunde und*

Kunstgeschichte (Leipzig, 1872), pp. 143-240 (dealing with German literature), and J. Braun, "Zur Entwicklung des liturgischen Farbenkanons," *Zeitschrift für christliche Kunst,* XV (1902), cols. 82-88, 111-119, 143-152, 171-176.

129. See above, the chapter on the School of Venice, section III.

130. Pino, ed. Barocchi, pp. 116, 122.

131. Dolce, pp. 184 f., Pino, ed. Barocchi, p. 117.

132. For Aristotle's color theory cf. P. Kucharski, "Sur la théorie des couleurs et des saveurs dans le *de sensu* Aristotélicien," *Revue des études grecques,* LXVII (1954), 335 ff.

133. Cf. for example. E. Wiedemann, "Avicennas Lehre vom Regenbogen nach seinem Werk as Schifa," *Meteorologische Zeitschrift* (1913), Heft XI, pp. 533 ff., and the observations of Roger Bacon as quoted by A. G. Crombie, *Robert Grosseteste and the Origins of Experimental Science* (Oxford, 1953), pp. 156 f.

134. Cf. Meyer Schapiro "On the Aesthetic Attitude in Romanesque Art," *Art and Thought* (London, 1948), pp. 130 ff.

135. Cennini, *Il Libro dell' arte,* chap. 36.

136. "Missam faciamus illam philosophorum disceptationem qua primi ortus colorum investigantur. Nam quid iuvat pictorem novisse quonam pacto ex rari et densi aut ex calidi et sicci frigidi humidique permixtione color extet. Neque tamen eos philosophantes aspernor qui de coloribus ita disputant ut species colorum esse numero septem statuant album atque nigrum duo colorum extrema. Unum quidem inter medium. Tum inter quodque extremum atque ipsum medium binos quod alter plus altero de extremo sapiat quasi de limite ambigentes collocant. Pictorem sane novisse sat est qui sint colores et quibus in pictura modis hisdem utendum sit. Nolim a peritioribus redargui qui dum philosophos sectantur duos tantum esse in rerum natura integros colores asserunt album et nigrum caeteros autem omnes ex duorum permixtione istorum oriri. Ego quidem ut pictor de coloribus ita sentio. Permixtionibus colorum alios oriri colores pene infinitos." Quoted from Spencer's edition, p. 49, and (the Latin text), p. 104, note 22.

137. Alberti, ed. Janitschek, p. 67.

138. See ed. Janitschek, pp. 227 f.

139. Alberti, ed. Janitschek, p. 139.

140. Alberti, ed. Janitschek, p. 65. For Pliny's concept of four basic colors cf. *Natural History,* XXXV, xxxii, 50 ("quattuor coloribus solis immortalia ella fecere"). Cf. W. Seibt, *Helldunkel, I, Von den Griechen bis Correggio* (Frankfurt,

1885), pp. 9 ff. A further classical source for the assumption of only four basic colors is the passage of Aristotle's *Meteorologica* (372a), quoted above, although the fourth color, yellow, does not seem to be as basic a shade as the other three.

141. Alberti, ed. Janitschek, p. 139.

142. Alberti, ed. Janitschek, p. 137.

143. J. P. Richter, *The Literary Works of Leonardo da Vinci* (Oxford, 1939), 280 (I, p. 227). Cf. also Leonardo's *Treatise on Painting*.

144. *Treatise on Painting,* ed. McMahon, 176; ed. Ludwig, 254. For a different list consisting of eight principal hues see ed. McMahon, 178; ed. Ludwig, 213. For the concept that white is not a color see also ed. McMahon, 204; ed. Ludwig, 247.

145. *Marsili Ficini Florentini proemium in librum de lumine ad Magnanimum Petrum Medicum* (Basel, 1519), chap. 2, fol. 106v.

146. Ficino, *Opera,* I (Basel, 1561), pp. 825-826. See also A. Chastel, *Marsile Ficin et l'art* (Genève-Lille, 1954), p. 103.

147. Cf. S. Jayne, *John Colet and Marsilio Ficino* (Oxford, 1963), p. 122; cf. also pp. 112 ff. (color lists of John Colet). I owe acquaintance with these texts to the kindness of Mr. J. B. Trapp of the Warburg Institute in London.

148. See above, note 39.

149. *Proemium in librum de lumine . . .,* chap. 12, fol. 105v. Here Ficino gives a color scale slightly different from the one quoted above.

150. *De coloribus libellus a Simone Portio* (Florence, 1548), p. 15. Light as a "form of color" is a common concept in the Middle Ages. Cf. A. Crombie, *Grosseteste,* pp. 243 ff.

151. Portio, op. cit., pp. 77, 79.

152. *De gemmis et coloribus in Hieronymi Cardani Mediolanensis . . . operum,* II (Lyon, 1563), p. 552.

153. Ibid., p. 556.

154. Ibid.

155. The exact shade of *fuscus* was apparently not clear in the sixteenth century; it oscillated between black and brown. Cardano, II, p. 552, described it as a kind of black ("Nigri quattuor sunt species: ater, niger, fuscus, et lividus"), while Alciati states that *fuscus* is what "nos vernacula lingua Brunim vocamus." Cf. *D'Andreae Alciati Mediolanensis . . . operum,* Iv (Basel, 1582), p. 318.

156. Sorte, *Osservazioni*, p. 295, alludes to the hierarchy of angels which should be expressed by a hierarchy of lights.

157. *Trattato*, I, p. 325.

158. "Abbiamo da considerare che nelle istorie dove s'introducono infinite figure vestite, nel compartire i colori si ha da rappresentare una certa armonia soave agli occhi, si che non si vi scorga alcuna dissonanza. . . ." *Trattato*, II, p. 114. Note that this theoretical statement is made in connection with an important "practical" problem confronting the painter in his work, the distribution of colors in the garments of figures. It is also worth noting that in the theory of art this specific context was often the place where views of color harmony and relationship among colors were discussed. See above, pp. 31, 106.

159. See above, pp. 73 ff.

160. "Ora dico che secondo la dottrina già data, quando trattai che cosa fosse colore, essi colori, come dice Aristotile, non sono più che sette, due estremi che sono il bianco ed il nero, e cinque mezzani, nel mezzo dei quali è il rosso composto di pari potenza del bianco e del nero; e fra il rosso ed il bianco vi è il giallo, che tende al rosso, ed il pallido che tende al bianco; fra il rosso e il nero vi è la porpora che tende al rosso, ed il verde che tende al nero." *Trattato*, II, pp. 114 ff. For further connotations of the seven colors see also R. Klein, "Les sept gouverneurs de l'art selon Lomazzo," *Arte Lombarda*, IV, pp. 277 ff.

161. "Sicche [following on the quotation in note 160] si vede che il rosso è nimico al pallido siccome lontano da lui per il bianco, ed al verde siccome parimenti lontano da lui per il nero, ed è amico del giallo è della porpora; similmente il bianco ed il nero, siccome estremi, non vi possono stare appresso, per essere l'uno troppo chiaro, e l'altro troppo oscure. E questa è la prima radice, e convenienza loro, la qual seguendo, e fuggendo sempre gli estremi, ne risulta quella vaghezza che si ricerca nelle pitture." *Trattato*, II, p. 115.

162. *Idea*, chaps. 13 (styles of color) and 14 (styles of light). In this particular context the term *maniera* is used in chapter 14.

163. A concise description of the styles is to be found in chaps. 13 and 14 of *Idea*.

164. There is, e.g., an obvious inconsistency between the characterization of Titian's color and the description of his light. Lomazzo emphasizes softness as the most characteristic feature of Titian's coloring: "E spezialmente esso Tiziano ha colorito con vaghissima maniera i monti, i piani. . . . E nelle carni ha avuto tanta venustà e grazia con quelle sue mischie e tinte, che paiono vere e vive, e

principalmente le grassezze e le tenerezze che naturalmente in lui si vedono ..."
(Idea, chap. 13). But in his description of light he stresses different qualities.
"Tiziano ultimamento ha usato un terribile ed acuto lume, e di qui è ch'egli solo
con la sua furia e grandezze ha ottenuto la palma sopra gli altri nel fare le cose di
rilievo ..." *(Idea,* chap. 14).

Lomazzo's description of Titian's color perhaps shows some influence of
Venetian treatises on painting. Thus, Lomazzo's assertion that "among all the
others Titian shines like the sun among tiny stars, not only among Italians but also
among all the painters of the world, in figures as well as in landscapes ..." recalls
Pino's statement (ed. Barocchi, p. 134) that he saw "wonderful landscapes by the
hand of Titian which are much more graceful than those of the Flemish
[painters]." Similarly, Lomazzo in his sonnet on Titian *(Rime,* p. 94), says:

> Vnico è questo al mondo hor frà pittori
> Nel dar spirito e color à le pitture.
> E nel pinger paesi auanza ogn'vno.

165. This is implied in the assumption that all the seven artists are the pillars of
the allegorical Temple of Painting. But Lomazzo is sometimes more explicit. See,
for instance, the opening sentence of chap. 13 of the *Idea,* which reads: "In the
third part of painting, which is on color, one perceives no less diversity among
these great men [i.e., the seven masters] than that which we have noticed in
proportion, and in this diversity, none of them is lacking in excellence."

166. See, for instance, Pino, ed. Barocchi, p. 118, and Leonardo, *Treatise,* ed.
McMahon, 134.

167. See R. Klein, "La forme et l'intelligible," *Archivio di Filosofia* (1958), 103-
121. The article by E. Spina Barelli, "Il Lomazzo o il ruolo della personalità
psichologiche nella estetica dall'ultimo manierismo lombardo," *Arte Lombarda,* III
(1958), 119-124, does not contribute to our discussion.

168. At the end of chap. 2 of *Idea* Lomazzo says that the painter should "conosca
il suo genio, e dove più l'inclini l'attitudine e disposizion sua d'operar piu
facilmente e felicemente per un modo che per un'altro. ..." (Earlier in the same
chapter Lomazzo speaks of the "disposizione, il genio e la inclinazione" of the
artist—all astrological terms.) For a further connection between the astrological type
of the artist and his inclination to represent certain kinds of figures, see *Trattato,* II,
p. 165.

169. In *De occulta philosophia,* I, chap. 49, Agrippa of Nettesheim did indeed give a description of light, patterned after the model of emanation, which Lomazzo copied in his *Trattato* (see above, notes 29, 40). In this chapter, which also contains Agrippa's descriptions of colors and their astrological meaning, light is not considered as a series of types, different in character but equal in value; on the contrary, here the gradations of light are obviously conceived as gradation of aesthetic value.

CONCLUSION

IN THIS BOOK I have tried to analyze the main stages and ramifications of views on light and color in Renaissance art theory. We may now briefly return to some of the general questions asked in the introduction: Can we justifiably speak of a history of these ideas in the Renaissance? What were the principles that determined changes, and what were the sources from which the authors drew? The present study, I hope, has shown the complexity both of the attitudes themselves and of their sources. Obviously, no simple answers can be given to these questions, and the whole phenomenon cannot be neatly summarized.

Reviewing the sequence of art theoretical schools and of individual writers and the different aspects of light and color emphasized by them, however, one cannot doubt, I believe, that the Renaissance concepts of *lume* and *colore* do indeed have a history. One notes, first, that the problem of light and color persisted and fascinated the minds of various authors. In all the treatises devoted to painting, light and color play a significant part and, following Alberti, are usually considered as one of the "parts" of the "art of painting." The persistence of the problem itself provides a continuity, though perhaps an intermittent continuity, that enables us to speak of a history. But a history of the concepts of light and color in Renaissance theory of art is not based only on the fact that authors in the fifteenth and sixteenth centuries, and in the different regions of Italy, kept asking what light and colors are, and how they should be applied; often, more direct links can be found. We have seen that well-established workshop precepts were transmitted from one generation to another and from one school to another. The literary formulations of earlier generations were carefully studied by later artists and writers, who built upon what they inherited. Sometimes we also found a direct influence of one school or local tradition on another. The concepts of light and color in Renaissance theory of art show, then, a certain coherence, both in sequence of time and in dispersion over different cultural regions.

Obviously, diversity and changes are more prominent in our history than continuity. Even the taking over of earlier views and formulations was a process of selection and of reinterpretation. Further, local schools of thought saw new aspects and discovered new dimensions of the problem. The shifts in emphasis and the accumulation of aspects amount, I believe, to a gradual transformation of the whole Renaissance attitude to light and color; the "functional" approach which prevailed in fifteenth-century Florence was gradually replaced by a deeper appreciation of the aesthetic values and expressive force of light and color. By comparing the views held in early-fifteenth-century Florence (Alberti) with those prevailing in mid-sixteenth-century Venice and in late-sixteenth-century Milan (Lomazzo), one can measure both the unfolding of the problem as a whole and the depth of the transformation which these concepts underwent.

The complexity and diversity of the sources from which our authors drew are comparable with, and perhaps even surpass, those of the views they expressed. Clearly the concepts discussed in this book were shaped by many factors, but three groups of sources seem to have been of particular significance. One of them was the persisting workshop tradition which, usually conservative, had an inherent tendency toward simplification, a propensity for transforming complex ideas and themes into workshop precepts. Such workshop precepts were probably less intimately connected with a specific school, region, or even stage of development than the other types of sources, and therefore they constitute an important element in the unity of Renaissance views on the subject.

New tendencies of style emerging in actual painting constitute another important source. The different character and scope of the discussion of light and color in the art theory of Florence, Venice, and Milan can, in part, be explained by the impact of the different tendencies of Florentine, Venetian, and Lombard painting. But the effect of painting on the theory of art does not only explain the general character of the discussion; it also largely accounts for the emergence of new concepts, or categories of light, new functions assigned to color, and the observation of new aspects in both nature (e.g., texture) and paintings (e.g., brushstrokes). The frequent discussion of contemporary artists and paintings not only reflects the art of the time, but it also had a considerable influence on the character of art theory itself. While the workshop tradition naturally tended toward conservatism, the influence of painting had the effect of continuous renewal.

The last major group of sources, of wide scope and variegated character, consists of broad cultural, nonvisual traditions. We have tried to show that for the concepts of light and color in Renaissance art theory these scientific, literary, and symbolic traditions are not merely a "background" but play an active part in the formation of views and attitudes. The heritage of ancient and medieval optics fulfilled a vital function in the formation of Alberti's and Leonardo's views on light and color; the literary style, and the scale of aesthetic values prevailing in Venice molded the attitude of Venetian art theory; astrological traditions were an essential part of Lomazzo's doctrines. It is from an interpenetration of such disparate traditions and activities that Italian Renaissance theory of art emerged and developed, and its history is mirrored in the history of its concepts of light and color.

BIBLIOGRAPHY

THE FOLLOWING BIBLIOGRAPHY – so far as I know, the first of its kind – makes no claim on systematic coverage, let alone completeness. It is hoped, however, that even a first, tentative list of Renaissance sources on light and color might have a stimulating effect on further research.

I have included in the list some classical and medieval works which had had a direct significant influence on Renaissance thought on light and color.

SOURCES

Agrippa of Nettesheim. *De occulta philosophia libri tres.* Antuerpiae, 1531. Especially part I, chap. 49, on astrological color symbolism.

Alberti, Leon Battista. *Della pittura.* Edizione critica a cura di Luigi Mallé. Firenze, 1950. English ed. translated by J. R. Spencer. Yale, 1966. German ed. by H. Janitschek. Vienna, 1877.

Alciati, Andrea. *Opera omnia in quatuor tomos.* ... Basileae, 1582. Cols. 317-319: explanation of origin and meaning of colors. Col. 1142, *Emblemata,* cf. emblem "In colores."

Alhazen. See Hasan Ibn Hasan.

Der Anonimo Moreliano (Marcanton Michiel's Notizia d'opere del disegno). Text und Ubersetzung von Thdr. Frimmel. In: *Quellenschriften für Kunstgeschichte und Kunsttechnik.* ... Neue Folge. Bd. I. Vienna, 1888.

Aretino, Pietro. *Il Filosofo.* Vinegiz, 1546. See esp. V, 4. Il primo (-sesto) Libro de le lettere di M. Pietro Aretino. 6 vols. Paris, 1609. Many descriptions of colors in nature and in painting.

Ariosto, Lodovico. *Orlando Furioso,* secondo l'edizione del 1532 con le varianti delle edizioni del 1516 e del 1521, a cura di Santerro Debenedetti de Cesare Segrè. Bologna, 1960. (Collezione di opere inedite e rare, vol. 122.) Contains many observations on astrological color symbolism, on colors of dresses, etc.

Aristotle. *De anima.* With translation, introduction, and notes by R. D. Micke. Cambridge, 1907. Greek and English.

– – –. *De coloribus libellus,* a Simone Portio. . . . latinitate donatus, & commentarijs illustratus: unà cum eiusdem praefatione, etc. Florentiae, 1548. Greek and Latin.

– – –. *Meteorologica.* With an English translation by Henry D. P. Lee. London, 1952. Greek and English.

Armenini. *De veri precetti della pittura . . . libri tre.* Ravenna, 1586. Reflects ideas and usages of the late Cinquecento workshop.

Baldinucci, Filippo. *Opera,* vol. III. Milano, 1809. Occasional definitions of color terms.

Bellori, Gio. Pietro. *Le vite de pittori, scultori et architteti moderni.* Roma, 1672.

Biondo, Michel Angelo. *Della nobilissima Pittura, et della sua arte.* Vinegia, 1549.

Bisagno, Francesco D. *Trattato della pittura, Fondato nell' autorità di molti Eccellenti in questa Professione.* Esp. pp. 43 (chaps. 6-7); 88-125 (chaps. 12-13); 211-216 (chap. 34, on meaning of colors in relation to planets); 223-233 (chap. 36, on value and power of coloring). Influenced by Lomazzo.

Bocchi, Francesco. *Eccelenza della statua del San Giorgio di Donatello . . . .* Fiorenza, 1584. Reprinted in P. Barocchi, *Trattati d'arte del Cinquecento,* vol. 3.

Borghini, Raffaello. *Il Riposo . . .* in cui della pittura, e della scultura si fanella, de' più illustri pittori, e scultori, e delle più famoso opere loro si fa mentione; e le cose principali appartenenti a dette arti s'insegnano. Fiorenza, 1584. Occasional descriptions of colors, particularly interesting for distinction of tones and values.

Borromeo, Carlo. *Instructionum fabricae et supellectilia ecclesiasticae.* Mediolani, 1577. Reprinted in P. Barocchi, *Trattati d'arte . . . ,* Vol. 3.

Boschini, Marco. *Le ricche minere della pittura Veneziana. . . .* Seconda impressione (of "Le minere della pittura") con nove aggiunta. Venezia, 1674. An important source for the study of sixteenth- and seventeenth-century color techniques. Of particular importance is the introduction, *Breve instruzzioni.*

Bruno, Saint, of Asti, Bishop of Segni. De sacramentis ecclesiae. In: *Migne, P. L.,* 165, col. 1105.

Cardano, Girolamo. *Hieronymi Cardani . . . opera omnia . . .* 10 vols. Lugduni, 1663. "De gemmis et coloribus," *Opera . . . ,* vol. 2, pp. 552 ff.: gives a color scale based on measurable quantities. "De rerum varietate Libri XVII," *Opera . . . ,* vol. 3, book III, chap. 14 (on composition of colors); book XIII, chap. 67. "De subtilitate Libri XXI," *Opera . . . ,* vol. III, book XVII (pp. 610, 626) – observations of color in nature.

Castiglione, Baldassare, Count. *Il libro del Cortegiano.* Venetia, 1528.

Cennini, Cennino. *Il libro dell'arte.* Ed. by Daniel V. Thompson, Jr. (The *Craftsman's Handbook,* translated by D. V. Thompson, Jr. 2 vols. New Haven, London, 1932-1933.) Italian and English.

Cicero, Marcus Tullius. *De finibus bonorum et malorum.* With an English translation by H. Rackham. London, 1951. (Loeb Classical Library.) III, VI.

– – –. *De natura deorum.* Edited by Arthur Peaso. Cambridge, 1955. I, 30.

– – –. *De oratore . . .,* 2 vols. London, 1942. (Loeb Classical Library.) I, 30.

The Codex Huyghens and Leonardo da Vinci's Art Theory. A reprint of selected folios with an introduction by Erwin Panofsky. London, 1940. *(Studies of the Warburg Institute,* vol. 13.) Lombardic theory of art.

Comanini, Gregorio. *Il Figgino overo del fine della pittura.* Mantova, 1591. Reprinted in P. Barocchi, *Trattati d'arte . . . ,* Vol. III. Not important for the study of light and color.

Dante, Alighieri. *Il convivio . . .* commentato da G. Busuelli e G. Vandelli, con introduzione di Michele Barbi. 2d ed. Firenze, 1964. Esp. IV, 20.

– – –. *The Inferno.* London, 1946. Italian and English. Esp. V, 89, 90.

Danti, Vincenzo. *Il primo libro del trattato delle perfetti proporzioni di tutti le cose. . . .* Edizione seconda dopo la rarissima de "Giunti" del 1567. Perugia, 1830. Reprinted in P. Barocchi, *Trattati d'arte . . . ,* Vol. I. Color as a cognitive criterion in stones, vegetation, etc.

Deschamps, Eustache, *Oeuvres complètes.* Edited by De Queux de Saint Hilaire et G. Raynaud. 11 vols. Paris, 1878-1903 (sec. des anciens textes français). V, VIII, p. 201, no. 1489.

Dolce, Lodovico. *Dialogo della Pittura. . . . intitolato l'Aretino.* Nel quale si ragiona della dignità di essa Pittura, e di tutte le parti necessarie, che a perfetto pittore si acconvengene. Con esempi di pittori antichi e moderni: e nel fine si fa mentione . . . della virtù e delle opere del Titiano. Vinegia, 1557. Reprinted in P. Barocchi, *Trattati d'arte . . . ,* 1. English translation by Mark W. Roskill, *Dolce's "Aretino" and Venetian Art Theory of the Cinquecento.* New York, 1968. The principal statement of Venetian theory of art.

– – –. *Dialogo di M. Lodovico Dolce nel quale si ragiona della qualità, diversità e proprietà de i colori.* Venice, 1565. One of the most detailed discussions of secular color symbolism in the sixteenth century. As a rule, painting is not given much attention in this book.

Doni, Antonio Francesco. *Disegno. . . .* Venetia, 1549.

Draelius. De coloribus et artibus Romanorum. In: Merrifield, M. P., *Original Treatises Dating from the XIIth to XVIIIth Centuries on the Arts of Painting . . . ,* Vol. 1. London, 1849. Latin and English.

Du Cange, Charles du Fresne, Sieur. *Glossarium mediae et infimae latinitatis....* 10 vols. Miert, 1883-1887.

Dupuy du Grèz, Bernard. *Traité sur la peinture pour en apprendre la théorie & se perfectionner dans la pratique.* Toulouse, 1699. French theory of art, reflecting a deep influence of Italian *trattati* of the late Cinquecento.

Ficino, Marsilio. *Fol. iv Marcilli Ficini prohemium in librum de sole ad magnanimum Petrum Medicem., Fol. 17v. Marsilii Ficini Florentini prohemium in librum de lumine,* etc. Florentie, 1493. Contains a color scale.

– – –. *Marsilio Ficino's Commentary on Plato's Symposium.* (Commentarium ... in convivium Platonis de amore.) The text and a translation, with an introduction, by Sears Reynolds Jayne. Columbia, 1944. *(University of Missouri Studies,* vol. XIX, no. 1.)

Giraldus Cambrensis. Topographia Hibernica. In: Lehmann-Brockhaus, O., *Lateinische Schriftquellen zur Kunst in England, Wales und Schottland vom Jahre 901 bis zum Jahre 1307,* vol. III, p. 217, no. 5940. Munich, 1955-1960.

Hasan Ibn Hasa, called Alhazen. *Opticae Thesaurus,* Alhazani Arabis libri septem nune primum editi. Eiusdem libri de orepusculis et Mubium assensionibus (Gerardo Cremonenae interprete). Item Vitellenis Thuringepeloni libri X. Omnea instaurati, figuris illustrati & aueti, adiectis otiem in Alhazenum comentariis a F. Risnero. 2 parts. Basileae, 1572.

Hippiatrica. *Veterinariae medicinae libri due,* à Jeanne Ruellio. ... Ed. by Simon Grynaeus. Basiliae, 1537. The Hippiatrica commonly attributed to Constantine Porphyrogenitus.

Honorius Augustodunensis. Sacramentarium. In: *Migne, P. L.,* 172, cols. 762-763. Cap. 29: De vestibus presbyteri.

Hugh de Avalon, Saint, Bishop of Lincoln. *Metrical Life of St. Hugh, Bishop of Lincoln.* Now first printed from ms. copies in the British Museum and Bodleian libraries. Edited, with introduction and notes, by J. F. Dimock. Lincoln, 1860. Latin. Reprinted in O. Lehmann-Brockhaus, *Lateinische Schriftquellen ...,* vol. II, pp. 27 ff., no. 2372.

Innocentii III Papae, De sacro altaris mysterio libri sex. In: *Migne, P. L.,* 217, cols. 799-802. Lib. I, cap. LXV.

Jean de Hayn, Chartreux. *Joannis ab Jndagine Introductiones apotelesmaticae in physiognomiam.* ... Argenterati, 1630. Esp. book VI (pp. 164 ff.) on color complexion of different temperaments.

Leonardo da Vinci. *The Literary Works of Leonardo da Vinci.* Compiled from the original manuscripts by Jean Paul Richter. 2d ed., revised by Jean Paul Richter and Irma A. Richter. 2 vols. London, 1939.

– – –. *The Notebooks of Leonardo da Vinci.* Arranged, rendered into English, and introduced by Eduard MacCurdy. New York, 1939.

– – –. *Treatise on Painting "Codex Urbinas latinus 1270,"* by Leonardo da Vinci. Translated and annotated by A. Philip McMahon. With an introduction by Ludwig H. Heidenreich. 2 vols. Princeton, N.J., 1956. Translation and Facsimile.

Lomazzo, G. P. *Idea del Tempio della Pittura.* Milan, 1590. See esp. chaps. 13, 14, 21, 22, 28, 29, 30.

– – –. *Rime* . . . divise in sette libri . . . con la vita del auttore descritta da lui stosso in rime s'iolto, Milano, 1587. Esp. pp. 92 ff., 558 ff.

– – –. *Trattato dell'Arte della Pittura, Scultura ed Architectura.* 3 vols. Rome, 1844. Milan edition, 1584. The major work of late-sixteenth-century theory of art. For our subject, cf. particularly book III and book IV.

Lucretius Carus, Titus. Lucretius: *De rerum natura.* With an English translation by W. H. D. Rouso. 3d ed., rev. London, 1966. (The Loeb Classical Library, 181.)

Marullus, Michael Tarchanista. *Hymni et epigrammata Marulli.* Florentiae, 1497. Poetry of a Byzantine refugee. Contains a *Lalda* of the Sun.

Mersenne, Marin. *Harmonicarum libri (12)* . . . . 2 parts. Lutetiae Parisiorum, 1635. Observations on color symbolism. Comparisons of colors and musical harmonies.

Morato, Fulvio Pellegrino. *Del significato de colori.* Vinegia, 1535. Secular color symbolism.

Moreliano, Anonimo. See Der Anonimo Moreliano.

Occolti, Coronato. *Trattato de' Colori* . . . con l'aggiunta del significato di alcuni doni. . . . Parma, 1568. Secular color symbolism.

Ordo Romanus XIII, vel Ceremoniale Romanum. Editum jussu Gregorii X. In: *Migne, P. L.,* 78, col. 1116, 18 ff.

Ordo Romanus XIV, v. Ordinarium S.R.E. auctore, ut videtur, Jacopo Caietano cardinale. In: *Migne, P. L.,* 78, cols. 1154-1171, cap. 49-54.

Ovidius Haso, Publius. *Altfranzösische Übersetzung der Remedia Amoris des Ovid.* . . . Hrsg. von G. Koerting. Leipzig, 1871. Preface, p. xxiii.

– – –. *Metamorphoses.* With an English translation by Frank Justus Miller. 2 vols. London, 1946. (Loeb classical library.) VI, 60-66, on changeant cloth.

Patrizi, Francesco. *De Regno et Regis Institutione Libri IX* . . . , Paris, 1567. Neoplatonic metaphysics of light.

Pausanias. *Description of Greece.* With an English translation by W. H. S. Jones. London, 1918-1935. (Loeb Classical Library.) II, xxvii, 3.

Peckham, John. *Prespectiva communis Johannis archiepiscopi cantuariensis.* Mediolani, ca. 1480. Scientific optics.

Piles, Roger ds. *Dialogue sur le coloris.* Paris, 1699.

Pino, Paolo. *Dialogo di pittura.* Ed. critica con intred. et note a cura di Ridolfo ed Anna Palluchini. Venezia, 1940. Reprinted in P. Barocchi, *Trattati d'arte . . . ,* 1. First treatise of Venetian theory of painting.

Plato. *The Timaeus.* Edited, with introduction and notes, by R. D. Archer-Hind. London, 1888.

Plinius Secundus, C. *Natural History.* With an English translation by H. Rackham. 10 vols. London, 1938-1963. (Loeb Classical Library.)

Pomponius Gauricus. *De sculptura.* Florence, 1504. Edition used: Edition annotée et traduction par A. Chastel et R. Klein. Genève-Paris, 1969. Especially chap. 3, section "De colore," pp. 160-162, discussing mainly complexion.

Possevino, Antonio. *Tractatio de poesi et pictura ethnica, humana et fabulosa collata cum vera, honesta et sacra.* Lugduni, 1594. Discussion of common topics. A book much read in the period.

Rabelais, François. *Gargantua et Pantagruel.* Texte transcrit et annoté par Henri Clouzot. 3 vols. Paris, 1925. Book I, chaps. 9, 10, on color symbolism, especially in the color of dresses.

Raccolta di lettere sulla pittura, scultura, ed architettura scritte da'più celebri personaggi dei secoli XV, XVI, e XVII, publicata da M. Gio Bottari, e continuata fino ai nostri giorni da Stefano Ticozzi. 8 vols. Milano, 1822-1825.

Reisch, Gregor. *Margarita filosofica. . . .* Tradotta della lingua latina nell'italiana da Giovan Paolo Gallucei. Venezia, 1600. An encyclopedia popular in the sixteenth century. Contains a section on optics and colors.

Rinaldi, Giovanni de. *Il monstruosissimo mostre . . .* diviso in due trattati, nel primo de'quali si ragiona del significato de colori, nel secundo si tratta dell' herbe, & flori. Ferrara, 1584. Interesting source of secular color symbolism of the sixteenth century.

Sansovino, Francesco. *Delle cose notabili che sono in Venetia, libri due. . . .* Venetia, 1562.

Sorte, Christoforo. *Osservazioni nella pittura.* Venetia, 1580. An important treatise of Venetian art theory of the late sixteenth century.

Telesius, Bernardinus. *De colorum generatione opusculum.* Neapoli, 1570. Scientific discussion of the origin of colors.

Tertullianus, Quintus Septimius Florens. *Apology, De spectaculis.* With an English translation by T. R. Glover. Cambridge, Mass., 1960. (Loeb classical library.) Apologeticum, XXI, 12-13. De spectaculis, IX.

–––. *De paenitentia. De pudicitia.* Texte latin, traduction française, introduction et index, par Pierre de Dabrielle. Paris, 1906. (Textes et documents pour l'étude historique du christianisme, III.) De pudicitia, XX.

–––. *De pallio liber;* cum notis Franciscii Junij. Lugduni Bataverum, 1595.

–––. *Q. Septimi Florentis Tertulliani De Corona.* Sur la couronne (par) Tertullien. Edition, introduction, et commentaire de Jacques Fontaine. Paris, 1966. De corona, XV.

Theophilus. Called also Rugerus. *The Various Arts.* Translated from the Latin, with introduction and notes, by C. R. Bodwell. London, 1961. English and Latin.

Thylesius, Antonius. *Libellus de coloribus, ubi multa leguntur praeteralierum opinionem.* Venetiis, 1528. Discussion of Latin color terms.

Varchi, Benedetto. *Due Lezzioni* . . . nella prima delle quali si dichiara un sonetto di Michelagnelo Buonarotti; nella seconda, si disputa, qual si piu nobile, la Scoltura e la Pittura, con una lettera d'esso Michelagnolo, e piu altri . . . pittori, et scultori sepra la questione sepradetta. Fiorenza, 1549. Reprinted in P. Barocchi, *Trattati d'Arte* . . . , 1.

Varro, Marcus Terentius. *De re rustica.* London, 1967. (Loeb classical library.) II, 5.

Vasari, Giorgio. *Le vite de'più eccelenti pittori, scultori ed architettori* . . . Con nuovo annotazioni e commenti di Caetano Milanesi. 9 vols. Firenze, 1878-1885.

–––. *Le vite,* nell'edizione del MDL, a cura di Corrado Ricci. 4 vols. Milano-Roma, 1927.

Witelo [13th cent.]. *Vitellionis mathematici doctissimi, id est de natura, ratione, & preiectione radiorum visus, luminum, colorum atque formarum, quam vulge perspectivum vocant, libri X* . . . , Horimbergae, 1535.

Zarlino, Gioseffo. *Institutioni harmoniche.* Venice, 1558. A central work of music theory in the sixteenth century. Comparisons of colors and musical tones. Color symbolism.

–––. *Supplimenti musicali del rev. m. Gioseffe Zarlino.* Venetia, 1588. A central work of sixteenth-century music theory; contains many comparisons of tones and colors (esp. to explain the expressive value of tones).

Zuccari, Federigo. *L'Idea de'pittori, scultori et architetti, divisa in due libri.* Torino, 1607.

STUDIES

Ackerman, G. M. "The Structure of Lomazzo's Treatise on Painting." Bryn Mawr, 1964. An unpublished thesis.

Agostini, A. *Le prospettive e le ombre nelle opere di Leonardo da Vinci.* Pisa, 1954.

Arslan, E. *Le pitture del Duomo del Milano.* Milan, 1947.

Arslan, R. P. "Disegni di Ambrogio Figino." *Critica d'arte,* VIII 48 (1961), 32-55.

Baeumker, C. *Witelo: Ein Philosoph und Naturforscher des XIII. Jahrhunderts.*

Münster, 1908. (Beiträge zur Geschichte und Philosophie des Mittelalters, Bd. III, Heft 2.)

Baldwin, Ch. S. *Renaissance Literary Theory and Practice.* Gloucester, Mass., 1959.

Barasch, M. "Der Ausdruck in der italienischen Kunsttheorie der Renaissance." *Zeitschrift für Asthetik und Kunstwissenschaft,* XII (1967), 33-69.

– – –. "Christoforo Sorte as a critic of art." *Arte lombarda,* X (1965), 253 ff.

– – –. "Quelques remarques sur l'esthétique chez Theophile le Moine." *Revue d'esthétique,* XIII (1960), 257-272.

Battisti, E. *Rinascimento e Barocco.* Turin, 1960.

Bayer, R. *Léonard de Vinci: La grace.* Paris, 1933.

Behn, I. *Leone Battista Alberti als Kunstphilosoph.* Strasbourg, 1911.

Bertoni, G. *L'Orlando furioso e la Rinascenza a Ferrara.* Modena, 1919.

Birch-Hirschfeld, K. *Die Lehre von der Malerei im Cinquecento.* Rome, 1912.

Blunt, A. *Artistic Theory in Italy, 1450-1600.* Oxford, 1940.

Boll, F. J. *Die Lebensalter.* Leipzig, 1913.

Braun, J. "Zur Entwicklung des liturgischen Farbenkanons." *Zeitschrift für christliche Kunst,* XV (1902), cols. 82-88, 111-119, 143-152, 171-176.

Bruyne, E. de. *Etudes d'esthétique medievale.* Brugge, 1946.

Bultmann, R. "Zur Geschichte der Lichtsymbolik im Altertum." *Philologus,* XCVII (1948), 1-56.

Casati, C. *Leone Leoni d'Arezzo, scultore e Giov. Paolo Lomazzo milanese.* Milan, 1884.

Chastel, A. *Art et humanisme à Florence au temps de Laurent le Magnifique.* Paris, 1961.

– – –. "Léonard et la culture." In: *Léonard de Vinci et l'experience scientifique au XVIe siècle.* (Colloques internationaux du Centre National de la Recherche Scientifique.) Paris, 1953. Pp. 251-263.

– – –. *Marsile Ficin et l'art.* Génève, 1954.

Cicogna, E. A. "Memorie intorno la vita e gli scritti di Messer Lodovico Dolce." *Memorie dell I.R. Istituto Veneto,* XI (1862), 93-113.

Clark, K. "Leon Battista Alberti on Painting." *Proceedings of the British Academy,* XXX (1940).

– – –. *Leonardo da Vinci.* Cambridge, 1939.

Crombie, A. C. *Robert Grosseteste and the Origins of Experimental Science.* Oxford, 1953.

Cumont, F. *Lux perpetua.* Paris, 1949.

D'Adda, G. *Leonardo da Vinci e la sua libreria.* Milano, 1873.

Dejob, C. *De l'influence du Concile de Trente sur la littérature et les beaux arts chez les peuples catholiques.* Paris, 1884.

Dell'Acqua, G. A. "La pittura a Milano della metà del XVI secolo al 1630." *Storia di Milano,* X (1957), 678 ff.

Duhem, Pierre. *Etudes sur Léonard de Vinci. Série 1-2.* Paris, 1955.

Eranos Jahrbuch, X (1943).

Franceschini, E. "Sulle versioni latini medievali del Περι Χρωματων" in: *Autour d'Aristote: recueil d'études de philosophie ancienne et médiévale offert à A. Marison.* Louvain, 1955.

Fumagalli, G., ed. *Leonardo, omo sanza lettere.* Florence, 1943.

Garin, E. "La cultura fiorentina nel età di Leonardo." *Belfagor* (1952), 272-289.

– – –. *Medioevo e Rinascimento.* Bari, 1954.

Gengaro, L. M. *Orientamenti della critica d'arte nel Rinascimento Cinquecentesco.* Milan, 1941.

Gessner, S. *Werke,* hrsg. von Ad. Frey. Berlin, 1884. (Deutsche National Literatur, hrsg. von Joseph Kürschner, Bd. 41, Abt. 1.)

Gilbert, C. E. "Antique Frameworks for Renaissance Art Theory: Alberti and Pino." *Marsyas,* III (1943-1945), 87-106.

Gombrich, E. H. "Controversial methods and methods of controversy." *Burlington magazine,* no. 105 (1963), 90-93.

– – –. "Light, Form and Texture in XVth Century Painting." *Journal of the Royal Society of Arts,* CXII (1964), 826-849.

– – –. "Renaissance Artistic Theory and the Development of Landscape Painting." *Gazette des beaux arts,* no. 41 (1953), 335-360.

Hetzer, Th. *Tizian: Geschichte seiner Farbe.* Frankfurt, 1948.

Heuck, E. *Die Farbe in der französischen Kunsttheorie des XVII. Jahrhunderts.* Strasbourg, 1929.

Heydenreich, L. H. *Leonardo da Vinci.* London, 1954.

Huizinga, J. *Der Herbst des Mittelalters.* Munich, 1924.

Jahrbuch für Antike und Christentum. I (1929), pp. 271-290; VI (1940), pp. 1-56.

Jayne, S. *John Colet and Marsilio Ficino.* Oxford, 1963.

Johnson, M. "Pourquoi Léonard de Vinci cherchait-il les manuscrits scientifiques d'Archimède et comment les trouva-t-il?" In: *Léonard de Vinci et l'expérience scientifique au XVIe siècle.* (Colloques internationaux du Centre National de la Recherche Scientifique.) Paris, 1953. Pp. 23-29.

Keele, K. D. *Leonardo da Vinci on the Movement of the Heart and the Blood.* London, 1952.

Klein, R. "La forme et l'intelligible." *Archivio di filosofia* (1958), 103-121.

– – –. "Giudizio et gusto dans la théorie de l'art au Cinquecento." *Rinascimento.* 2d ser., I (1961), 105-116.

–––. "Les sept gouverneurs de l'art selon Lomazzo." *Arte lombarda,* IV (1959), 277 ff.

Klibansky, R. "Copernic et Nicolas de Cues." In: *Léonard de Vinci et l'expérience scientifique au XVIe siècle.* (Colloques internationaux du Centre National de la Recherche Scientifique.) Paris, 1953. P. 227.

Klibansky, R., Saxl, F., and Panofsky, E. *Saturn and Melancholy; Studies in the History of Natural philosophy, Religion and Art.* London, 1964.

Kucharski, P. "Sur la théorie des couleurs et des saveurs dans le *De sensu* Aristotelicien." *Revue des études grecques,* LXVII (1954), 335 ff.

Kurz, O. "Time the painter." *Burlington magazine,* no. 105 (1963), 94-97.

Lee, R. W. *Ut Pictura Poesis: The Humanistic Theory of Painting.* New York, 1967.

Léonard de Vinci et l'expérience scientifique au XVIe siècle. Paris, 4-7 juillet 1952. Paris, 1953. (Colloques internationaux du Centre National de la Recherche Scientifique.)

Longhi, R. "Quesiti Caravaggeschi." *Pinacotheca,* I (1928-1929), 17-33, 258-320.

Mahon, D. *Studies in Seicento Art and Theory.* London, 1947.

Mâle, E. *L'art religieux de la fin du XVIe siècle, du XVIIIe siècle et du XVIIIe siècle .* Paris, 1957.

Meiss, M. *Giovanni Bellini's St. Francis in the Frick Collection.* Princeton, 1964.

–––. "Light as Form and Symbol in Some Fifteenth-Century Paintings." *Art Bulletin,* XXVII (1945), 175-181.

Michel, M. P. *La pensée de L. B. Alberti.* Paris, 1930.

Monk, S. "A Grace Beyond the Reach of Art." *Journal of the History of Ideas,* V (1944), 131 ff.

Mueller-Walde, P. *Leonardo da Vinci. Lebensskizze und Forschungen über sein Verhältnis zur Florentiner Kunst und zu Rafael.* München, 1889.

Olschki, L. *Die Literatur der Technik und der angewandten Wissenschaften vom Mittelalter bis zur Renaissance.* Heidelberg, 1919.

Ortolani, S. "Le origini della critica d'arte a Venezia." *L'arte,* XXIV (1923), 3 ff.

Pallucchini, R. *La critica d'arte a Venezia nel Cinquecento.* Venice, 1943.

Panofsky, E. "Artist, Scientist, Genius: Notes on the Renaissance-Dämmerung." In: *The Renaissance: Six Essays.* New York, 1962. Pp. 123-182.

–––. *Early Netherlandish Painting.* Cambridge, Mass., 1953.

–––. *The Iconography of Correggio's Camera di San Paolo.* London, 1961. *(Studies of the Warburg Institute,* vol. XXVI.)

–––. *Idea* Leipzig, 1924.

–––. "The Ideological Antecedents of the Rolls-Royce Radiator." *Proceedings of the American Philosophical Society,* CVII (1963), 273 ff.

–––. "Die Perspektive als Symbolische Form." *Vorträge der Bibliothek Warburg* (1924-1925).

–––. *Renaissance and Renascences in Western Art.* Stockholm, 1960.

–––. *Studies in Iconology: Humanistic Themes in the Art of the Renaissance.* New York, 1962.

Pedretti, C. *Studi Vinciani.* Gènéve, 1957.

Perosa, A. "Studi sulla formazione di raccolte di poesie del Marullo." *Rinascimento,* I (1950), 125-156.

Pevsner, N. *Academies of Art, Past and Present.* Cambridge, 1940.

Pittaluga, M. "Eugene Fromentin e le origini della moderna critica d'arte." *L'arte,* XX (1917), 240-258.

Pope, A. *An Introduction to the Language of Drawing and Painting.* Cambridge, Mass., 1929-1931.

Randall, J. H., Jr. *The School of Padua and the Emergence of Modern Science.* Padova, 1961.

Robb, N. *Neoplatonism of the Italian Renaissance.* London, 1935.

Ronchi, V. *Histoire de la lumière.* Paris, 1956.

–––. "Leonardo e l'ottica." In: *Leonardo: saggi e richerche,* ed. Marazza. n.d. Pp. 161-185.

–––. "L'optique de Leonard de Vinci." In: *Léonard de Vinci et l'expérience scientifique au XVIe siècle.* (Colloques internationaux du Centre National de la Recherche Scientifique.) Paris, 1953. Pp. 115-120.

Roskill, M. W. *Dolce's "Aretino" and Venetian Art-Theory of the Cinquecento.* New York, 1968.

Ruhemann, H. "Leonardo's Use of Sfumato." *British Journal of Aesthetics,* I (1960-1961), 231 ff.

Rumpf, A. "Classical and Post-Classical Greek Painting." *Journal of Hellenic Studies,* LXVII (1947), 10-21.

Santillana, G. de. "Léonard et ceux qu'il n'a pas lus." In: *Léonard de Vinci et l'expérience scientifique au XVIe siècle.* (Colloques internationaux du Centre National de la Recherche Scientifique.) Paris, 1953. Pp. 43-59.

Sarton, G. "Léonard de Vinci, ingénieur et savant." Ibid., pp. 11-22.

Schapiro, M. "On the Aesthetic Attitude in Romanesque Art." In: *Art and Thought.* London, 1941. Pp. 130 ff.

Schlosser, J. von. *La letteratura artistica.* 3^a ed. italiana aggiornata da O. Kurz. Vienna, 1964.

–––. "Lorenzo Ghibertis Denkwürdigkeiten . . .," *Kunstgeschichtliches Jahrbuch d. K. K. Zentral-Kommission für Erforschung und Erhaltung der Kunst . . . ,* IV (1910), 135 ff.

Schöne, W. *Uber das Licht in der Malerei.* Berlin, 1954.

Schulz, J. "Cristoforo Sorte and the Ducal Palace in Venice." *Mitteilungen des Kunsthistorischen Instituts in Florenz,* X (1962), 193 ff.

Séailles, G. *Léonard de Vinci: l'artiste et le savant.* Paris, 1919.

Seibt, W. *Studien zur Kunst- und Kulturgeschichte. Bd. III; Helldunkel 1. Von den Griechen bis zu Correggio.* Frankfurt, 1885.

Seidlitz, W. von *Leonardo da Vinci, der Wendepunkt der Renaissance.* Berlin, 1909. 2 Bd.

Semmerau, J. *Pietro Aretino: ein Bild aus der Renaissance.* Vienna, 1925.

Shearman, J. *Andrea del Sarto.* Oxford, 1965. 2 vols.

–––. "Leonardo's Colour and Chiaroscuro." *Zeitschrift für Kunstgeschichte,* XXV (1962), 13-47.

Siebenhühner, H. *Uber den Kolorismus der Frührenaissance, Vornehmlich dargestellt an dem Trattato della pittura des L. B. Alberti.* Diss. Leipzig, 1935.

Solmi, E. *Le fonti dei manoscritti di Leonardo da Vinci.* Turin, 1908.

Spina Barelli, E. "Il Figino ovvero il fine della pittura." *Arte lombarda,* IV (1959), 123-125.

–––. "Il Lomazzo o il ruolo della personalità psicologicha nella estetica dell'ultimo manierismo lombardo." *Arte lombarda,* III (1958), 119-124.

Thiis, J. *Leonardo da Vinci. The Florentine Years of Leonardo and Verrocchio.* London, 1913.

Thorndike, L. *A History of Magic and Experimental Science.* New York, 1941. Vols. 5-6.

Tintori, M. and Meiss, M. *The Painting of the Life of St. Francis in Assisi.* New York, 1962.

Tiraboschi, G. *Storia della letteratura italiana.* 2a ed. Modena, 1787-1794.

Toffanin, G. *Il Cinquecento.* 3d ed. Milan, 1945.

Trabalza, C. *Storia della grammatica italiana.* Milan, 1908.

Turnure, J. H. "The Late Style of Ambrogio Figino." *Art Bulletin,* XLVII (1965), 35-55.

Valentiner, W. R. "Leonardo as Verrocchio's Coworker." *Art Bulletin,* XII (1930), 43-89.

Venturi, A. *La pittura del Cinquecento.* Milan, 1934.

–––. *Storia dell'arte italiana.* Vol. IX. Milano, 1901.

Venturi, L. "Pierre Arétin, Paul Pino, Louis Dolce ou la critique d'art à Venise au XVIe siècle." *Gazette des beaux-arts,* IX (1924), 39 ff.

Voss, H. *Die Malerei der Spätrenaissance in Florenz und Rom.* Berlin, 1920.

Vossler, K. "Pietro Aretinos künstlerisches Bekenntnis." *Neue Heidelberger Jahrbücher,* X (1900), 38 ff.

Wackernagel, W. "Die Farben- und Blumensprache des Mittelalters." *Abhandlungen zur deutschen Altertumskunde und Kunstgeschichte* (1872), pp. 143-240.

Walker, D. P. *Spiritual and Demonic Magic from Ficino to Campanella.* London, 1958.

Walter, J. *Die Geschichte der Aesthetik im Altertum.* Leipzig, 1893.

Weinberg, B. *A History of Literary Criticism in the Italian Renaissance.* Chicago, 1961.

Werner, O. *Zur Physik Leonardo da Vincis.* Erlangen, 1910.

Wiedemann, E. "Avicennas Lehre vom Regenbogen nach seinem Werk as Schiza," *Meteorologische Zeitschrift* (1913), Heft XI, pp. 533 ff.

Wilbenforce, J. *A List of Editions of the Margarita Philosophica 1503-1599.* New York, 1884.

Wittkower, R. *Art and Architecture in Italy 1600-1750.* Baltimore, 1958.

Yates, F. A. *The French Academies of the Sixteenth Century.* London, 1947. (Studies of the Warburg Institute, XV.)

–––. *Giordano Bruno and the Hermetic Tradition.* Chicago, 1964.

INDEX

Name Index

Agrippa of Nettesheim, 137, 146ff., 155, 168ff., 187ff., 194
Agucci, criticism of Caravaggio, 159
Alberti, L.B., 11ff.
  and medieval optics, 13
  and the artistic workshop, 10ff., 19ff.
  color theory, 14ff., 26ff.
  combination of colors, 31
  "friendship of colors," 176
  four colors (Pliny), 29
  on gold, 15, 21
  on light, 13ff.
  functional concept of light, 16, 30
  light and color, 30
  Lomazzo, his influence on, 145
  On Painting, structure of, 12
  on *rilieuo,* 113
  on textures, 21
Aquinas, St. Thomas, xviii, n.2
Archimedes, 49

Aretino, Pietro, 95, 100
Ariosto, 170
Aristotle,
  De coloribus, 23, 27, 28, 145, 161
  Meteorologica, 172ff.
  De sensu, 172ff.
Armenini, 110

Baldinucci, F., 89
Bellini, Giovanni, 101
Bembo, Pietro, 95
Benedetto dell'Abbaco, 49
Biondo, 91
Bocchi, F., 138
Borghini, R., 109, 168
Borinski, K., 34
Borromeo, Carlo, 138ff.
Boschini, Marco, 100, 102, 104, 115
Bronzino, 105
Bultmann, R., xix, n.5

Campo, Bernardino, 164
Cardano, G., xv, 161
　on color scale, 179ff.
Cartari, 137, 146
Castiglione, B., xv, 95
Cellini, B., 105
Cennini, C., 1-11
　blending of pigments, 68
　corpse, color of, 7
　color, 6ff.
　colors, natural, 7
　exempla, 7
　gold, 8
　humanistic learning, 3
　illumination, 4ff.
　Libro, 1ff.
　light, aesthetic value of, 5
　light, diffuse, 59
　light, functional, 4
　on materials, 26
　medieval traditions·in, 1ff.
　mountains, representation of, 3
　seven color scheme, 174
　shades, 9ff.
　smoke, 5, 73
　texture, 8ff., 21, 112
　tones, three, 10
Chastel, A., 82
Comanini, Gregorio, 139
Correggio, 142, 147, 149, 196

Danti, Vincenzio, 161
Dolce, L., 91ff., 104
Doni, *Disegno,* 91
Duhem, P., 76ff.

Edgerton, S., 36, 38
Eyck, Jan van, representation of textures, 22

Ficino, on color scale, 177ff.
　and Lomazzo, 146
　on splendor, 23

Galen, 49
Gaudenzio, in Lomazzo, 184
Giorgione, 45, 101, 104, 119
Gilbert, C., 38
Giotto, 17
Gombrich, E.H., 24, 36, 40, 41
Grèz, Dupuy de, 89, 129 n.59

Heraclius, *De coloribus,* 10

Leonardo da Vinci, 44-89
　color scale, 176
　light and color as central problems, 44
　light, types of, 58ff.
　impressionistic tendencies, 66
　and Lomazzo, 184
　and medieval optics, 45
　omo senza lettere, 49ff.
　optics, interest in, 45
　sfumato, 75
　sources of, 48ff.
　texture, 113
Lomazzo, Gian Paolo, 100, 135-212
　and Agrippa of Nettesheim, 168ff.
　and Alberti, 145
　color, 159-171
　light, 143-158
　Idea, 184ff.
　Rime, 142ff.
　Trattato, 141
　Venetian influences, 145ff.

Mantegna, in Lomazzo, 185
Marullo, M., 50, 79ff.
Masaccio, 17

Meiss, M., 34, 40, 41
Mersenne, Père Marin, 108
Michelangelo, psychological type, 95
  in Lomazzo, 184
Morato, Fulvio Pellegrino, 109

Nesi, G.F., 49

Panofsky, E., xix, 34, 36, 136ff.
Peckham, *Perspectiva,* 49ff., 79ff.
Pierino del Vaga, 163
Pino, P., 91ff.
  and Alberti, 93ff.
  Dialogue on Painting, 91ff.
  oil painting, invented in Italy, 117
  his system, 95-102
Plato, *Timaeus,* 23
Pliny, colors, 175ff.
  tone, 107
  splendor, 22
Polidoro, in Lomazzo, 184
Polygnotus, 29
Portius, S., commentary on *De coloribus,*
  179

Raphael, S., in Lomazzo, 185
  his *Transfiguration,* 149
Reisch, *Margarita philosophica,* 23, 45
Rinaldi, Giovanni, 169ff.

Shearman, J., 85, 103
Schlosser, J., v., *passim*
Schöne, W., 39
Sorte, C., 91, 98, 106ff., 111, 116, 119,
  120ff., 150, 155
Suger, Abbot, 23

Theophilus, *Schedula diversarium artium,*
  10
Thylesius, 170
Tintoretto, Lomazzo's poem about him,
  198
Titian, 104, 115, 149, 151
  in Lomazzo, 185
Toscanelli, Paolo, 49

Varchi, Benedetto, 105
Vasari, G., 44ff., 109, 113ff., 117ff.,
  146ff.
Valeriano, Pierio, 137, 146
Verrocchio, A., 48ff.
Vitello, *Perspectiva,* 145

Zarlino, Gioseffe, 108, 130
Zeuxis, 18
Zubov, V., 38

Subject Index

"Accidental colors," 68ff.
Astrological symbolism, 187
Astrological imagery, 157ff.
Artificial, light (Lomazzo), 151ff.
Ater, 170

Black as darkness (Alberti), 175

cesio (grey), 121
chiaroscuro, 51
circumscrittione, 96

Color:
  "accidental colors," 68ff.
  aesthetic arrangement of, 31

bellezza of, 103
property of bodies, 160ff.
colori naturali, 7
contrasting, 70
"cool" colors, 172
of dead figures, 7
definition of, x
of elements, 28
expression of, 119-121, 165ff., 167
four color scheme, 6
functional conception of, xiii
modified by light, 46
in Lombardic workshops, 163ff.
"middle colors," 183
"natural colors" (Cennini), 6
oil colors, 117-119
oil colors suitable for tonal effects, 118
ordine del colore, 172
"picture color" and "object color," xiii
pure colors, status of, 105
"real colors" (Leonardo), 69
scale of colors, 171-184
seven color scheme, 6, 28
shades of colors, 9
styles of colors, 184-189
as surface quality, xii
symbolism of, 109, 121
"true colors" (Alberti), 27
"warm" colors, 172
Complexion, in medicine, 162
composizione dei colori, 154, 172
Counter Reformation, 135ff.
"Creative nature" (Leonardo), 46

Darkness, in Leonardo, 52
Differentiation of light and color (Alberti), 30

disegno, 95ff.
elements, colors of, 28, 156
Emblematics, 137ff., 146
Expression, appreciated in Venice, 119

Facilità, 98
Fayum, mummy portraits, 22
filosofi peripatetici, 140
Four color scheme, 28
Fresco, 117ff.
Friendship of colors, 32, 128
  Alberti, 176
  Lomazzo, 182ff.
fuscus, 180
giudizio, 96
  as sureness of hand, 98

Gold, 8, 15

Invisible god, 121
Impressionistic tendencies in Leonardo, 69
istoria, 12
Illumination, 4ff.
Interpretation in seeing, x
isfumata, 119

Lalda del Sole, 56
Light:
  aesthetic value of, 5
  "compound" light, 52
  definition of, ix, 143
  functional conception, xiii, 16
  Lokalfarbe, xii, 10, 32, 103
  luce and *lume,* 53, 55, 64
  lume divino, 149ff., 152ff.
  lume naturale, 148ff.
  lustro, 22, 71ff., 164
  means of representation, xii
  metaphysics (Neoplatonic) of, 143ff.

in Milanese theory of art, 140-158
"primary" and "secondary," 148
reflected light (Alberti), 20
reflected light is colored, 20, 64
reflected light (Leonardo), 62ff.
refracted light (Lomazzo), 153
restrained light, aesthetic value of, 25
"specific light," 60ff.
struggle between light and darkness
     (Leonardo), 54
styles of light, 184-189
transparent light, 66ff.
types of light (Leonardo), 58ff.
"universal light," 58
Lombard art, 136

macole, xiii
maniere d'allumare, 184
meze tente, 100
"mezzo," 50ff.
minutezze, 25, 110
moto, 188
Mountains, how to represent, 3
Music theory in Venice, 107ff.

Neoplatonism and Leonardo, 49
"Negro drawn in white chalk," x
"nigro," 170

Oil colors, 117-119
suitable for tonal effects, 118
Oil painting, appreciated by Lomazzo,
     164
ordine dei colori, 172

proprietà, 96ff.
in relation with textures, 114
prontezza, 96ff.
prospettiva di colore, 52
Pure colors, low status of, 105

Rainbow, model for color scale, 173ff.
receptione de lume, 13, 15
"regola," 93
Relief, illusion of, purpose of painting,
     46
result of light and shade, 18

Scale of colors, 171-184
scienza della pittura, xi, xv, 90
sfumato, 47, 70, 73ff., 100, 104, 182
and aerial perspective, 75
in Cennini, 5, 10
defined by modern restorers, 73ff.
expression of soft mood, 75
Shadows:
"adhering" (Leonardo), 53
cast, according to source of light, 19
cast, new theme, 20
compound, 52
as crystallization of *"mezzo,"* 52
long, produced by fire, 19
separate, 53
significance of (in Leonardo), 47ff.
transparent, 44, 53
types of, 53, 81
"smoky contour," 75
Splendor, 22ff.
Styles of color, 184-189
Styles of light, 184-189
Sun, Neoplatonic hymn to, 49ff.
Symbolism of color, 109, 121, 167ff.

terribilità, 95
Texture, 112
in Cennini, 8ff.
pictorial representation of, 21ff.
in Venetian art theory, 111ff.
Theory of art:
defined, xiv
specific position of, xviff.

and science, xv
sources of, xv
in Renaissance workshop, xvi

Venetian theory of art, 90ff.
Venetian, its characteristics, 92ff.
Venetian, prefers dialogue form, 93
Venetian, and Florence, 92, 93ff.
Volume, illusion of, major value in
    painting, 17ff.
tinte, 115
Tonality and pure colors, 103
"Tone," 102ff.

terms for, 104
three tones (Cennini), 10
"Value," 102ff.
varietà, 24
Variety of styles, 185ff.

White, 22
  as pure light (Alberti), 175
Workshop, accumulation of experience
    in, xvi
  window in, 99
"Warm" color, 172